NAVIGATING CHALLENGES IN QUALITATIVE EDUCATIONAL RESEARCH

How do education researchers navigate the qualitative research process? How do they manage and negotiate myriad decision points at which things can take an unexpected—and sometimes problematic—turn? Whilst these questions are relevant for any research process, the specific issues qualitative researchers face can have impactful repercussions that, if managed adeptly, can lead to successful and even new research opportunities.

Navigating Challenges in Qualitative Educational Research includes narratives that provide real world experiences and accounts of how researchers navigated problematic situations, as well as their considerations in doing so. These contributions give students and researchers a chance to understand the possibilities of research challenges and better prepare for these eventualities and how to deal with them.

Providing educative windows into the challenges and missteps even seasoned researchers face along the way, this book is an invaluable resource for graduate students and early career qualitative researchers, particularly those who are interested in education.

Todd Ruecker is Associate Professor of Rhetoric and Composition at the University of Nevada, Reno, USA.

Vanessa Svihla is Associate Professor with appointments in Organization, Information & Learning Sciences and Chemical & Biological Engineering at the University of New Mexico, USA.

NAVIGATING CHALLENGES IN QUALITATIVE EDUCATIONAL RESEARCH

Research, Interrupted

Edited by Todd Ruecker and Vanessa Svihla

Routledge
Taylor & Francis Group

LONDON AND NEW YORK

First published 2020
by Routledge
2 Park Square, Milton Park, Abingdon, Oxon OX14 4RN

and by Routledge
52 Vanderbilt Avenue, New York, NY 10017

Routledge is an imprint of the Taylor & Francis Group, an informa business

© 2020 selection and editorial matter, Todd Ruecker and Vanessa Svihla; individual chapters, the contributors

British Library Cataloguing in Publication Data
A catalogue record for this book is available from the British Library

Library of Congress Cataloging-in-Publication Data
Names: Ruecker, Todd Christopher, author. | Svilha, Vanessa, editor.
Title: Navigating challenges in qualitative educational research : research, interrupted / edited by Todd Ruecker and Vanessa Svilha.
Description: Abingdon, Oxon ; New York, NY : Routledge, 2019. | Includes bibliographical references.
Identifiers: LCCN 2019008469| ISBN 9780367173609 (hardback) | ISBN 9780367173623 (pbk.) | ISBN 9780429056352 (ebook)
Subjects: LCSH: Education–Research–Methodology. | Qualitative research.
Classification: LCC LB1028 .N3365 2019 | DDC 370.21–dc23
LC record available at https://lccn.loc.gov/2019008469

ISBN: 978-0-367-17360-9 (hbk)
ISBN: 978-0-367-17362-3 (pbk)
ISBN: 978-0-429-05635-2 (ebk)

Typeset in Bembo
by Taylor & Francis Books

We dedicate this collection to the researchers who persevere in the face of interruptions in their work and who emerge more reflective as a result, and to the mentors, advisors, and senior scholars who protect and support students and early career researchers, enabling them to tackle ambitious and socially just research.

CONTENTS

List of illustrations   x

List of contributors   xi

1 Introduction: sanitized research descriptions and messy realities:
   A story of contrasts   1
   Todd Ruecker and Vanessa Svihla

PART 1
Getting started: navigating bureaucracies and
recruiting participants   **13**

2 The wheels of bureaucracy go round and round   15
   Kendi M. Ho

3 Research methods for reaching urban students from groups
   underrepresented in STEM disciplines   26
   Steven McGee, Randi McGee-Tekula, Lucia Dettori,
   Andrew M. Rasmussen and Ronald I. Greenberg

4 Chasing the team: Participant recruitment strategies for
   qualitative research into student-athlete writers   39
   J. Michael Rifenburg

5 Navigating administrator–researcher roles: Developing recruitment strategies for conducting programmatic assessment with diverse undergraduate and graduate writers 51
Tanita Saenkhum and Joseph Anthony Wilson

Part 1 discussion questions and activities 62

PART 2
Relationships across contexts: geographical, cultural, political, institutional **65**

6 The predicaments of "being there": Conflict and emotional labor 67
Romeo García

7 Researchers or service providers?: A case of renegotiating expectations in a research–practice partnership 80
Victor R. Lee, Mimi Recker and Aubrey Rogowski

8 Representation and emotion: Researching in the rural US in a politically polarized time 95
Todd Ruecker

9 Criss-cross applesauce, "Where are you from?" and other intellectual challenges 109
Ilene R. Berson, Michael J. Berson, Aaron Osafo-Acquah and Joyce Esi Bronteng

Part 2 discussion questions and activities 122

PART 3
Interruptions during data collection: making it work **125**

10 Thinking backward and forward: Everyday interruptions in school-based research 127
Maggie Dahn

11 Two steps forward, one step back: Obstacles and progress in conducting research in elementary classrooms 140
Sharon L. Smith, Loren Jones and Luciana C. de Oliveira

12 On pursuing quixotic goals: What are worthwhile interruptions to research? 151
Michael Tan

Part 3 discussion questions and activities 163

PART 4
The disruptive forces of scholarly peer review   **165**

13 Excessive peer review and the death of an academic article   167
    Grant Eckstein

14 From broader impacts to intellectual merit: An interruption in
    interdisciplinary publishing   180
    Vanessa Svihla

15 "There are notable linguistic problems": Publishing as a
    non-native speaker of English   193
    Aliya Kuzhabekova

    Part 4 discussion questions and activities   206

    Afterword: What interruptions can tell us about the nature of
    qualitative educational research   210
    Amanda K. Kibler

Index   *216*

ILLUSTRATIONS

Figures

7.1 Reflection instrument designed to help reestablish focus, elicit perceptions, and reduce asymmetries in the RPP, including one librarian's handwritten responses   89

7.2 K'Nex construction sets—an approachable form of assembly-oriented making that was popular with the librarians (left); and paper circuit holiday cards—a new maker experience for one librarian that instilled personal pride (right)   92

10.1 List of administrative interruptions   131

Table

3.1 Demographic information about Taste of Computing study participants relative to all Taste of Computing students and all Chicago Public Schools high school students   31

CONTRIBUTORS

Ilene R. Berson is a Professor of Early Childhood at the University of South Florida. She conducts participatory research and uses visual methodologies to study young children's civic engagement in educational settings. Her research explores the intersection of technology and the pedagogy of inquiry in the early years with a focus on children's affordances of digital innovations.

Michael J. Berson is a Professor of Social Science Education in the Department of Teaching and Learning at the University of South Florida and a Senior Fellow in the Florida Joint Center for Citizenship. His areas of inquiry include pedagogy of the Holocaust, visual research methods in education, digital citizenship, and promotion of critical visual literacy with primary sources.

Joyce Esi Bronteng is a bilingual and literacy Lecturer at the University of Cape Coast, Ghana. Her research focuses on bilingual and literacy studies involving Ghanaian young learners, parents, and teachers. She has co-published textbooks for public Basic Schools in Ghana as well as articles on enhancing early literacy acquisition in linguistically diverse classrooms.

Maggie Dahn is a doctoral candidate in the Urban Schooling Division of UCLA's Graduate School of Education & Information Studies and 2018 NAEd/Spencer Dissertation Fellow. Her research focuses on how students learn in and through the arts, the development of voice and identity through art making, and instructional design that bridges theory and practice to reimagine learning experiences.

Luciana C. de Oliveira, Ph.D., is Professor and Chair in the Department of Teaching and Learning at the University of Miami. Her research focuses on issues related to teaching emergent to advanced bilinguals at the K-12 level and teacher preparation. She is President (2018–2019) of the TESOL International Association.

Lucia Dettori is an Associate Dean in the College of Computing and Digital Media at DePaul University and Interim Director of the Office of Computer Science in the Chicago Public Schools. Her research interests include computer science education with an emphasis on broadening participation, medical image processing, and scientific computing.

Grant Eckstein is an Assistant Professor of Linguistics at Brigham Young University. He studies second language reading and writing development, assessment, pedagogy, and curriculum design. He has published in journals such as *TESOL Quarterly, Research in the Teaching of English*, and the *Journal of Second Language Writing*. He is currently co-editor of the *Journal of Response to Writing*.

Romeo García is Assistant Professor of Writing and Rhetoric, University of Utah. His research on rhetorical theory, cultural rhetorics, and critical theory emerges from work with Mexican American students. García has published in the *Writing Center Journal* and *Community Literacy Journal*. He is co-editor of *Rhetorics Elsewhere and Otherwise*, published by Studies in Writing and Rhetoric.

Ronald I. Greenberg is a Professor of Computer Science at Loyola University, Chicago. He has engaged in many computer science education and outreach efforts as well as research on algorithms.

Kendi M. Ho is a Second Language Studies doctoral candidate and CELTA Course Trainer at the University of Hawai'i at Mānoa. Her research interests include language assessment for program development and evaluation, workforce development for adult immigrants, and health communication in elder care. She has presented at AAAL, TESOL, and Cross Cultural Healthcare conferences.

Loren Jones, Ph.D., is an Assistant Clinical Professor in the Department of Teaching and Learning, Policy and Leadership in the College of Education at the University of Maryland, College Park. She is bilingual in English and Spanish, and her research focuses on best practices for literacy and language instruction to support linguistically and culturally diverse students in K-12 settings.

Amanda Kibler is an Associate Professor in the College of Education at Oregon State University. She uses qualitative and mixed-methods approaches to investigate the language and literacy development of multilingual children and adolescents from immigrant backgrounds. Her work can be found in the *American Educational Research Journal, Applied Linguistics, Journal of Second Language Writing*, and *TESOL Quarterly*, among others.

Aliya Kuzhabekova is an Associate Professor of Higher Education Leadership, Nazarbayev University, Kazakhstan. Her research focuses on internationalization of higher education and research capacity building in post-Soviet contexts, including how Kazakhstani academics deal with pressure to publish in international journals and how Kazakhstani journals react to the increasing pressure to acquire an international impact factor.

Victor R. Lee is an Associate Professor of Instructional Technology and Learning Sciences, Utah State University. His research interests include the quantified self movement as a means for people to learn with their own data and the opportunities for learning associated with the maker movement. He examines issues of conceptual change, libraries, health education, and unplugged computing education.

Steven McGee is President of the Learning Partnership and co-founder of the Chicago Alliance for Equity in Computer Science. He leads large-scale implementation research studies in urban settings. His current research interests include engaging students in authentic STEM experiences that promote both learning and interest and the development of school capacity to support and sustain authentic STEM in the classroom.

Randi McGee-Tekula is Vice President of the Learning Partnership. She conducts case study research on teaching practices in STEM classrooms. Her research interests include teacher change, measurement of teaching practices, and equity in STEM teaching.

Aaron Osafo-Acquah is a Senior Lecturer in Educational Psychology at the University of Cape Coast in Ghana. His research interests include early childhood education and basic education pupil performance in Ghana.

Andrew M. Rasmussen is the CS4All Project Coordinator at Chicago Public Schools. His research interests include computer science education and ultrafast electron transfer; his current work involves bringing a computer science mindset to the world of public school administration.

Mimi Recker is a Professor in the Department of Instructional Technology and Learning Sciences, Utah State University. Her research investigates ways to aid teachers to use open educational resources more effectively to support their teaching practice. Her research involves developing new teacher tools, using learning analytics, and studying teacher professional development. She studies computational thinking and maker-oriented digital learning tools.

J. Michael Rifenburg, Associate Professor of English at the University of North Georgia, serves as Director of First-Year Composition and Senior Faculty Fellow for Scholarly Writing with UNG's Center for Teaching, Learning, and Leadership. He authored *The Embodied Playbook: Writing Practices of Student-Athletes* (Utah State University Press, 2018) and co-edited *Contemporary Perspectives on Cognition and Writing* (WAC Clearinghouse, 2017).

Aubrey Rogowski is a doctoral candidate in the Department of Instructional Technology and Learning Sciences at Utah State University. After spending several years as an elementary school teacher, she returned to academia to study how teachers can meaningfully integrate technology and STEM-rich maker activities to help students learn.

Todd Ruecker is Associate Professor of Rhetoric and Composition and Director of Core Writing at the University of Nevada, Reno. His work explores the increasing diversity of educational institutions and advocates for institutional and policy changes to support student and teacher success. His work has appeared in various journals and he has published several books.

Tanita Saenkhum is Associate Professor and Director of ESL at the University of Tennessee, Knoxville. Her book *Decisions, Agency, and Advising* (USUP, 2016), considers the role of students' agency in the placement of multilingual writers in US college composition programs. Her scholarship has also appeared in the *Journal of Second Language Writing, WPA: Writing Program Administration*, and several edited collections.

Sharon L. Smith is a doctoral candidate specializing in literacy and language learning for multilingual students in the Department of Teaching and Learning at the University of Miami. She holds degrees in Elementary Education and Spanish, and her research focuses on best practices for literacy and language instruction to support emerging bilingual learners in the elementary school context.

Vanessa Svihla is an Associate Professor at the University of New Mexico with appointments in learning sciences and engineering. A recipient of the National Academy of Education/Spencer Foundation postdoctoral fellowship and the National Science Foundation CAREER award, her research focuses on how learners can be supported to gain agency over their learning and designing through problem framing.

Michael Tan is a research scientist at the National Institute of Education, Singapore. His current research interests are in the careful adaptation of makerspace principles for the teaching and learning of science. His current project involves teachers nurturing their students into transgressive individuals and communities for the betterment of humanity.

Joseph Anthony Wilson is a doctoral student at the University of Washington, where his research areas include L2 writing program administration, genre and discourse studies, and transfer. He formerly served as Assistant Director of ESL at the University of Tennessee, Knoxville, and as a Fulbright English Teaching Assistant in Kazakhstan through a grant from the United States Department of State.

1

INTRODUCTION: SANITIZED RESEARCH DESCRIPTIONS AND MESSY REALITIES

A story of contrasts

Todd Ruecker and Vanessa Svihla

Introduction

Read the literature, develop research questions or hypotheses, design a study to answer them, collect data, analyze data, write up the results. The research process discussed in many articles, methodology textbooks, and methodology courses often comes across as linear and tidy. For instance, Johnson & Christensen (2016) said little about the nuances and challenges of participant recruitment and instead discussed the importance of sampling in a way that overlooks the agency and humanity of research participants: "Once these inclusion boundaries are set, the researcher knows whom he or she wishes to study and can then attempt to locate and observe the sample" (p. 273). They urged researchers to pick a sample that can be used to answer research questions while "meeting cost and other constraints," noting that "Trade-offs will always be present" (p. 273). To be fair, broad survey textbooks like Johnson & Christensen's (2016) have to cover a lot of material in a short amount of time. Methods books focused specifically on qualitative or ethnographic research tend to cover issues such as rapport (Marshall & Rossman, 2016) and how open and honest one can be with participants (Hammersley & Atkinson, 2007). Yet, even with this advice, understanding what this looks and feels like in practice can be unclear. Paris & Winn (2013) drew attention to researcher emotionality, writing that methodology courses "ignore the obvious; some of the dehumanizing processes, conditions, and experiences that our participants/students/friends have encountered will remind us of our own lived experiences. No one tells emerging scholars that, yes, sometimes 'we cry'" (p. 1). Unfortunately, broad methods courses may not always include books and topics like these and early researchers may feel deficient when they fail to meet the neat plans described in their textbooks and the articles they read.

As a number of scholars have noted (e.g., Cook, 2009; Lerum, 2001; Mellor, 2001; Thomas, 1998), challenges and disruptions underlying the research process tend to be left out of depictions of the research process for various reasons: our fields' preoccupation with objectivity in research; space limitations in a typical journal article; and perhaps the fear of looking naive as a researcher. These issues may often be connected back to what Lerum (2001) referred to as "academic armor," the "linguistic, physical, and ideological" moves that academics make to "protect their expert positions and jurisdictions" (p. 470). Lerum (2001) argued that academic researchers "have clearly marked their turf as the intellectual, the detached, the objective, and hence, because of the cultural privileging of these qualities, the superior realm" (p. 471). The dominance of this "academic armor" is evident in the experience that inspired this collection, which Ruecker details in Chapter 8. Here, he emotionally raises concerns about how immigrants were treated in a school where he was conducting research, resulting in him being disinvited from future visits. As he unsuccessfully tried to publish an article detailing this in two different venues, he faced a mix of enthusiasm and skepticism, ultimately resulting in rejections without a chance to revise. Reviewer comments at one venue noted appreciation for a provocative discussion on the real challenges faced by researchers while rejecting it, in part because of a sense of bias towards participants and its focus on one experience. In response, Ruecker toned down some of the comments revealing his true feelings about the situation and submitted it elsewhere. There, one reviewer was generally enthusiastic, noting that we needed to do more of this type of reflection and discussion of the challenges we face as researchers. The other reviewer strongly advised not to publish this piece in part because it would make Ruecker look emotionally and politically naive and hurt his reputation as an early career scholar—the risk of dropping his "academic armor" was deemed too great.

As is evident from our work on this collection, we share concerns that these reviewers' comments are symptomatic of a research culture in which discussions of interruptions and researcher emotionality are suppressed—or at least not shared in ways that support growth and learning—even though our discussions with others indicate they are quite common. As early career researchers and while working with graduate students developing their research abilities, we have been concerned that the sanitized realities so common in methodology descriptions may lead emergent researchers to question themselves and their work when something does not go as neatly as planned. This led us to craft a call for proposals, which posed questions such as the following:

- What are some challenges you have faced in recruiting participants?
- Have you put yourself at risk physically, mentally, financially or otherwise, in conducting your research?
- In what ways have language or cultural differences created tensions in or otherwise interrupted your work?
- What are some of the ethical dilemmas you've faced while researching and how did they impact your work?

Our drive in working on this collection stemmed from a desire to hear stories of interruption at various stages of research processes, as we believed these stories needed to be heard and that both new and established researchers would learn through reading how other researchers navigated challenges.

Challenge and mess in research: what we know

By and large, the clean portrayals of methodological processes presented in published research have gone unquestioned. There have been a few exceptions to this trend in the various fields we inhabit—education, learning sciences, applied linguistics, engineering education, and writing studies—and we review some of these here. For instance, action researchers, perhaps because of their increased focus on researcher positionality, have been more open than others about some of the methodological challenges they have faced, and we found several examples in the journal *Educational Action Research*. We argue that positivist traditions have, in some cases covertly and in others overtly, structured expectations about the research process, and this has encouraged researchers to avoid transparency in reporting on their work. We share consequences of this, including misleading novice researchers about the research process, rendering some findings suspect, and limiting the potential of our work.

Thomas (1998) provided one early critique of the positivist tradition, in which faults in research approaches and designs are typically masked or suppressed, leading to an approach in which "fertility is sacrificed to orderliness" (p. 143). He problematized the idea that the researcher is expected to consistently make order out of chaos, in his words a modern day Midas who is expected to turn everything into theory: "In the modern circumstances of the education academic this predisposition provides a predilection to make shape and theory out of chaos. And having once constructed the shape we of course have to start being analytic and rational about it" (p. 146). Researchers in the field of writing studies—a field that has an established tradition of questioning the objectivity of traditional research modes—have openly discussed such challenges. Describing her ethnographic dissertation project, Cook (1998) explained how "ethnography can seem spectacularly out of control" (p. 107).

Some qualitative researchers have reported challenges getting study approval from institutional review boards (IRBs), as—in their regulatory role—these bodies tend to encourage researchers to coerce their studies into traditional positivist designs (Babb, Birk, & Carfagna, 2017; Patel, 2015). While all IRBs are guided by federal mandates, it is relevant to note that they make determinations based on the opinions of local reviewers and administrators; when such boards are primarily staffed by those from positivist traditions, their guidance and decisions can diminish study design. For instance, Lunsford & Lunsford's (2008) national study of error and feedback in writing classes—a replication of an earlier study (Connors & Lunsford, 1988)—included a reflection titled "A new study of student writing: those IRB blues." The authors discussed how the process of soliciting research approvals had changed dramatically in the intervening 20 years. In the first study, the protocol "easily gained approval from their home institution IRBs—and that approval covered all requirements" (Lunsford & Lunsford, p. 787), allowing them to study classrooms at many other institutions. In the second study, the authors' IRB required them to seek approval from *all* institutions where their participants were enrolled, a process that extended what had been three months in the first study to eighteen months in the second, while also reducing the number of participating institutions. Furthermore, whereas in the first study they were able to use entire, intact classrooms, in the second they were typically restricted from using data unless students consented, resulting in a much smaller dataset. They described this process in some detail:

> To our surprise, instead of exempting or expediting local approval in light of the Stanford and UCSB approvals, many officials then asked us to go through their own full review process. Thus began the tedious, the time-consuming, the mind-numbing task of filling out dozens upon dozens of IRB forms, each with slightly different emphases and questions, and then waiting, sometimes for months, for a response.
>
> *(Lunsford & Lunsford, p. 787)*

What is notable about this instance is how institutional requirements, while well intentioned, dramatically reduced the number of participants in the study.

Researchers who work outside the positivist paradigm may also face rejection at the hands of journal editors and other gatekeepers. Work that does not fit into particular molds of what reviewers see as new, rigorous, and objective can be deemed unsuitable for publication and that work may never be published. We are not disputing the value of the peer review process but note that it can present additional challenges to researchers whose work does not fit in particular molds. And, as Svihla explains in Chapter 14, these challenges can be time consuming, but also discouraging to the point of abandoning an initial commitment of sharing findings with the people most positioned to act upon them. As Ruecker (2017) explained elsewhere and Svihla discusses in Chapter 14, publishing challenges can be especially acute for interdisciplinary researchers, as many in education are. For instance, Ruecker reported that applied linguistics reviewers would critique his writing style as too subjective, delaying the publication process as he strove for a more impersonal, objective, and *sanitized* voice.

These sanitized representations of the research process provide an impoverished view of research for novice researchers. For instance, Strauss (1995) revealed how his research led him into multiple periods of despair and self-doubt about his ability as a teacher, writing at one point in his journal: "Maybe I'm just not a very good teacher. Maybe teaching is, knowing what the children are learning and responding to that knowledge. Maybe there's nothing else to it, and I'm not very good at it" (p. 33). Another action researcher, Cook (2009), described feelings of doubt in light of the published descriptions of research: "We saw a gap between our more convoluted practice and published models of neat research. This led to doubts as to whether we were doing 'proper research' or whether we were doing 'research properly'" (p. 278). A different Cook (1998) wrote that only after completing her ethnographic dissertation did she feel comfortable talking about some of the challenges she faced, including feeling "deviant" throughout the process. These comments highlight the sense of risk that novice researchers encounter when things don't go quite as planned.

McKinley & Rose (2017) noted that sanitized versions of research are "depriving researchers of valuable insights from which we can grow and allow novice and experienced researchers alike the chance to learn from our pitfalls, mistakes, and follies" (p. 14). Their edited volume invited applied linguistics researchers to shift their focus away from the findings of an already published study and more closely examine the methodological implications of their work. By not being more transparent about the realities of our research, we make it harder for newer researchers to learn the trade, particularly as they might struggle with feelings of self-doubt as they are unsure how to proceed when facing challenges.

Researchers who are experienced with the complexities of doing longer term, larger scale, or more critical research have also raised concerns about the limitations posed by typical final form representation. In light of her experiences with mess in research, Cook (2009) argued that it is not necessarily a sign of sloppy, poorly done research but in fact "an indicator of serious critique taking place" (p. 285). Upon recognizing that the research process as reported in journal articles is not always the whole story, some researchers react with suspicion about published findings. Writing about the "messiness" of action research, Mellor (2001) explained how he initially came to research with the impression that it was a neat, linear process involving three steps: "collect data, analyze data, write up" (p. 467). He described how he came to be "suspicious of 'hygienic' accounts" and that "messy method" was the norm: "if we are honest, we all work this way" (pp. 474–475). In talking with other researchers, Mellor found that, while some said their work aligned to the neat approaches described in journal articles (whether they were honest or not is another question), others admitted to messiness in their own research process. Cook (2009) argued that hiding this mess from view in published research makes "it difficult for future researchers to understand how outcomes were achieved and how they might build on those outcomes" (p. 289). In that sense, detailing researcher challenges and interruptions can be vital if other researchers are to replicate the process and really understand how the researcher came to the conclusions they did.

An increasing number of researchers in education and related disciplines have challenged the traditional research paradigm in recent decades, recognizing that rigid paradigms fail to serve researchers well in a complex world. In the oft-cited book *After Method*, sociologist John Law (2004) made an argument somewhat similar to Cook's (2009): "hegemonic and dominatory pretensions" (p. 4) within the traditional, restrictive culture of research methods limit researchers in their quest to capture a complex, messy reality. He wrote, "if we want to think about the messes of reality at all then we're going to have to teach ourselves to think, to practise, to relate, and to know in new ways" (p. 2). Part of this new way of thinking and practicing involves room for emotionality in research as well as an understanding that the researcher plays an integral role in shaping a reality that we can never have a complete, firm grip on. Prior (2017) exposed the emotional side of analyzing participant narratives, writing: "I was not just exposed to emotionality by vicariously 'reliving' participants' narratives through repeated data analysis; I was also (re)exposed to emotionality by reliving the intensity of the interviews and the fieldwork" (p. 176). The emotional aspect of researching is often avoided and even discouraged under the guise of objectivity. Prior's (2017) suggestions of self-care and taking breaks from data are welcome. Appleby (2017) discussed how to deal with controversial findings in which participants express racist views or detail illegal activities or emotionally charged experiences. He suggested thinking through issues that might arise in advance, so one can think of how to respond or not. For instance, should one be silent or speak out if interviewees express ideas that are objectionable to the researcher? As Ruecker details in Chapter 8, speaking out carries risks that can interrupt the research, especially if relations with participants are not fully established.

Law (2004) argued that we need to dismiss our notion of "hygiene" (p. 9) in research because our obsession with clean, neat research methods limits researchers' abilities to uncover new findings in their work. It can also limit researchers from tackling ambitious and challenging critical work. For instance, Kubota (2017) explained that she has generally avoided studying those less powerful than herself, such as migrants, because of the discomfort and risks of ignoring the institutions and policies that oppress less powerful groups. Cook (1998) detailed the challenges she faced when reluctantly trying to recruit students as a white outsider at an HBCU, noting that in her original writing she relegated this challenge to a brief footnote. She described the process of calling and leaving messages for participants; she did no further follow up with students at the HBCU, telling herself they were too busy with their work and school commitments to participate in her study. The present collection builds on these past concerns, illustrating some of the challenges researchers have faced and providing a vivid and vicarious account of how they navigated them.

Researching in a messy world: new paradigms

As mentioned earlier, ethnographic researchers have a longer tradition of recognizing the diversity of our world and the ways that research changes based on the context in which one is working and their relationships with participants. Hammersley & Atkinson (2007) devoted extensive discussion to issues such as how researchers present themselves to a particular community through their dress and what they choose to share. They acknowledged that some aspects of a person (e.g., their gender or their race/ethnicity) cannot be hidden and will shape the research context, yet noted that a researcher "often has to suppress or play down personal beliefs, commitments, and political sympathies" (p. 72), even going so far as silently to tolerate situations that they might find "distasteful or shocking" (p. 72), while noting that a researcher can never fully suppress their own biases and convictions.

In contrast, in *Humanizing Research*, Paris & Winn (2013) aimed to embrace the tension that comes with being concerned about social justice while also being educational researchers. Their collection included chapters that detailed "humanizing approaches as those that involve the building of relationships of care and dignity and dialogical consciousness raising for both researchers and participants" through "reciprocity and respect" (p. xvi). They rejected "the kind of research that does not take as a starting point the humanity and dignity of all people" (p. 251). For instance, Irizarry & Brown (2014) argued for the importance of participatory action research with youth in schools while detailing how their project was shut down by administration a semester early, noting that "the highly political nature of urban schools makes [participatory action research] and other approaches to humanizing research simultaneously difficult and necessary" (p. 77).

Patel (2015) similarly argued that education research has traditionally been a colonizing enterprise, positioning particular populations in need of interventions and salvation by more privileged researchers. She critiqued Western colonizing frameworks that have shaped research processes, making a strong case that research is "a fundamentally relational, cultural, and political practice" (p. 62) and that research should not just focus on answering questions but, rather, should be accountable to the contexts and participants involved.

To pursue such work, we again take advice from *After Method*, in which Law (2004) suggested that we "need to teach ourselves to know some of the realities of the world using methods unusual to or unknown in social science" (p. 2). While he resisted imposing "a new orthodoxy" (p. 154) for how this should look, he suggested we reimagine our methods by considering metaphors such as "localities," "multiplicities," and "interferences" (p. 156). These metaphors resonate particularly well with the depictions of interrupted research shared in this collection.

The present collection

We approached this collection with an aim to draw out honest stories of how research was interrupted and how researchers navigated and made sense of their experiences. In evaluating proposals, we looked for diversity in different senses: racial/ethnic, institutional, geographic, and disciplinary. We were turned off by proposals that focused too much on the author's successes. We received a number of proposals sharing this trait, perhaps because the authors had been conditioned by an increasingly competitive research environment in education where researchers are discouraged from dropping their "academic armor" and admitting and discussing failings.

We would be remiss not to mention the proposals we did *not* receive for this collection. In our editorial discussions, we considered the potential for unintended consequences should we publish a transparent account written by someone very early in their career. For instance, we had one advisor who said she forwarded the call to a student with an "incredible story" but was unsure if she would submit (she did not). A new assistant professor queried us about the potential of a chapter focused on his research being threatened when his dissertation advisor refused to sign off on the continuing review of his IRB proposal; he recognized the personal and professional risks of writing about this experience and ultimately decided not to submit. We heard from another graduate student who wanted to write about how political constraints in his home country, where speech is often restricted, impacted what he could say or do in his research; after further discussion, he came to the realization that he would not feel comfortable writing openly and honestly about these challenges due to the potential for professional repercussions. Across each of these non-submissions, we see a theme of risk, which further clarified the need for a volume of this nature.

We organized the collection into four sections following this introductory chapter. Our organization traces the research process, from planning through publication. In Part 1, the chapters share stories related to navigating the research approval process and recruiting study participants. Many submissions, including chapters in other parts, reported recruitment issues. It is unsurprising, then, that these issues stemmed from many sources, such as cross-cultural challenges and misunderstandings, power dynamics, and distrust. The chapters in Part 2 report on interruptions due to relationships of various kinds, including with participants as well as with other researchers. These narratives provide a vivid account of the potential complexity and emotionality of qualitative research and the challenges of building relationships across contexts. In Part 3, the chapters detail interruptions— due to mundane, bureaucratic, or major issues—during data collection that lead researchers to abandon or redesign their projects. Finally, the chapters in Part 4 report on challenges faced in the publication and dissemination process, such as prejudices against particular research methodologies or non-standard varieties of English. These are followed by an Afterword that responds to and reflects on the ideas discussed throughout the preceding chapters. We detail each part below.

Part 1, "Getting started: navigating bureaucracies and recruiting participants," begins with Chapter 2, by Kendi M. Ho, who describes challenges of navigating the Department of Education (DOE) in the state where her research was conducted. She explores a year-long process of applying for a data-sharing agreement with the DOE, only to secure approval just as she was informed of the program being shuttered. In sharing these experiences, Ho explores how researchers need to be ready to adapt their projects based on contextual changes that the researcher has no control over. Chapter 3, by Steven McGee, Randi McGee-Tekula, Lucia Dettori, Andrew M. Rasmussen, and Ronald I. Greenberg, is based on research in Chicago Public Schools and explores the ethics of "do no harm." They describe the challenges, especially selection bias, that arise when teachers have a distrust of outsiders in part due to distrust of the district as a whole. They offer strategies they have used to overcome these biases, such as offering a pizza party if 90 percent of the students in a class return a consent form, even if the form indicates nonparticipation. In Chapter 4, J. Michael Rifenburg takes us to the university level as he describes challenges he faced in recruiting student athletes. He explores how athletes are often buried in levels of institutional protection and discusses the importance of gatekeepers and key informants in facilitating the recruitment process. Chapter 5, by Tanita Saenkhum and Joseph Anthony Wilson, continues this post-secondary focus by exploring the power dynamics they encountered as program administrators seeking to interview students about university assessment practices and placement techniques. They focus particularly on second language speakers of English, which contributed to challenges, as some students were reluctant to participate because they feared their English speaking abilities were not sufficient, or agreed to participate but misunderstood the purpose of the interview as an assessment of their skills.

The chapters in Part 2, "Relationships across contexts: geographical, cultural, political, institutional," explore the opportunities and challenges inherent in maintaining relationships with participants after the recruitment process, as well as the challenges encountered in cross-cultural relations between researchers. Chapter 6 continues the focus on recruitment challenges while transitioning to broader concerns of relationship building across contexts. Here, Romeo García describes his return to the region where he grew up and his awakening upon discovering that he was no longer the insider he imagined himself to be. He describes how he traded in his rental car for a lower model, dressed more casually, and worked to adopt the dialect of the region while grappling with the emotionality of political realities beyond his control that impacted participants: economic pressures, being arrested, and the threat of deportation.

In Chapter 7, Victor R. Lee, Mimi Recker, and Aubrey Rogowski explain how district restructuring meant that the people with whom the researchers had initially partnered were different from the ones they ended up working with when the project started. During this shift, the researchers learned that the librarians (and others in their schools and the district) had come to see the university as a service provider of programs and resources; consequently, their role as researchers was obscured and hindered. They explain how they worked to readjust their role and relationship with the district and participants. In Chapter 8, Todd Ruecker explores his experience of being disinvited from future visits to a research site after he sent an email decrying racist behaviors against the immigrant students his work focused on. He explores issues such as the way researchers represent themselves to participants as well as the impact of emotionality on researchers and their relationships to their projects and participants. He ends by reflecting on navigating the tension between preserving one's project and standing up for personal values. In Chapter 9, Ilene R. Berson, Michael J. Berson, Aaron Osafo-Acquah, and Joyce Esi Bronteng explore cross-cultural challenges faced while engaging in a comparative multi-case study of civic education in kindergarten classrooms serving low-income students in the US and Ghana. They focus especially on their relationships with one another, noting how the US and Ghanaian researchers had to negotiate their different understandings, from the design of interview protocols to the analysis of data.

Part 3, "Interruptions during data collection: making it work," delves into the various interruptions that can happen during the data collection process and how researchers have adapted, sometimes resulting in completely different studies. In Chapter 10, Maggie Dahn explores the everyday interruptions in school-based research that range from unplanned fire drills to the deportation of a student's family. In arguing that interruptions are the norm in educational research, Dahn encourages researchers to let go of the urge to control everything and instead embrace some ambiguity as a means to improve their work. In Chapter 11, Sharon L. Smith, Loren Jones, and Luciana C. de Oliveira continue this focus on everyday interruptions, ranging from their focal teacher switching grades just before the school year started to the impact of a natural disaster in the form of Hurricane Irma. Harkening back to the discussion on bureaucracies in Part 1, they explore the challenges they faced navigating the IRB process as they sought to adapt their project to account for these changes. Chapter 12, by Michael Tan, is based on case study research in Singapore and explores the challenges he faced, first trying to find purpose as his research plans changed, then making sense of drastic changes in his case study teacher's approach. He soon learned that the teacher's contract was not being renewed by the school, a factor that abruptly changed his teaching.

Part 4, "The disruptive forces of scholarly peer review," includes three chapters focused on interruptions while attempting to disseminate work. In Chapter 13, Grant Eckstein describes his attempt to publish in a top-tier journal and his resilience during six agonizing revise-and-resubmit requests; he ultimately decided to drop the attempt before the paper was rejected. Eckstein describes how the insights he gained through this process helped him navigate future publication experiences as well as develop his own thought processes when he became the founding co-editor of a journal. In Chapter 14, Vanessa Svihla details challenges she faced when the aims of her research shifted and revealed practical implications. She felt strongly that her work should be published in a journal that would be read by scientists who could actually implement her findings, but after three journals rejected the work as not methodological, she resolved to publish it in a more welcoming—if less likely to have worldly impact—journal. Chapter 15, by Aliya Kuzhabekova, focuses on the challenges that non-native speakers of English face when publishing in English, something they are increasingly pressured to do at universities around the world. She describes a time in which an edited collection editor heavily edited her English and took credit in the chapter acknowledgements without seeking her permission, as well as financial and other challenges posed by seeking editors for work to ensure it meets the "standards" of international journal editors.

The collection closes with an Afterword by Amanda K. Kibler. Guided by her extensive qualitative research in diverse settings, Kibler draws out lessons from the preceding chapters. She critically considers the chapters to reveal structural concerns and opportunities related to the kinds of experiences new qualitative researchers might benefit from as well as institutional barriers that could be improved. Finally, she articulates the significance of the collection by elucidating some of the insights from such transparency.

References

Appleby, R. (2017). Dealing with controversial findings. In J. McKinley & H. Rose (Eds.) *Doing research in applied linguistics: Realities, dilemmas, and solutions* (pp. 203–213). New York: Routledge.

Babb, S., Birk, L., & Carfagna, L. (2017). Standard bearers: Qualitative sociologists' experiences with IRB regulation. *American Sociologist*, 48(1), 86–102.

Cohen, L., Manion, L., & Morrison, K. (2011). *Research methods in education*, 7th edition. New York: Routledge.

Connors, R. J., & Lunsford, A. A. (1988). Frequency of formal errors in current college writing, or Ma and Pa Kettle do research. *College Composition and Communication*, 39(4), 395–409.

Cook, D. (1998). Secrets and ethics in ethnographic writing. In S. Fontaine & S. Hunter (Eds.) *Foregrounding ethical awareness in composition and English studies* (pp. 105–120). Portsmouth, NH: Boynton/Cook.

Cook, T. (2009). The purpose of mess in action research: Building rigour though a messy turn. *Educational Action Research*, 17(2), 277–291.

Hammersley, M., & Atkinson, P. (2007). *Ethnography: Principles in practice*. New York: Routledge.

Heath, S. B., Street, B. V., & Mills, M. (2008). *On ethnography: Approaches to language and literacy research*. New York: Teachers College Press.

Irizarry, J. G., & Brown, T. M. (2014). Humanizing research in dehumanizing spaces: The challenges and opportunities of conducting participatory action research with youth in schools. In D. Paris & M. T. Winn (Eds.) *Humanizing research: Decolonizing qualitative inquiry with youth and communities* (pp. 63–80). London: Sage.

Kubota, R. (2017). Studying up, down, or across? Selecting who to research. In J. McKinley & H. Rose (Eds.) *Doing research in applied linguistics: Realities, dilemmas, and solutions* (pp. 17–26). New York: Routledge.

Law, J. (2004). *After method: Mess in social science research*. New York: Routledge.

Lunsford, A. A., & Lunsford, K. J. (2008). "Mistakes are a fact of life": A national comparative study. *College Composition and Communication*, 59(4), 781–806.

Johnson, R. B., & Christensen, L. (2016). *Educational research: Quantitative, qualitative, and mixed approaches*, 6th edition. Los Angeles: Sage.

Lerum, K. (2001). Subjects of desire: Academic armor, intimate ethnography, and the production of critical knowledge. *Qualitative Inquiry*, 7(4), 466–483.

Marshall, C., & Rossman, G. B. (2016). *Designing qualitative research*. Los Angeles: Sage Publications.

McKinley, J., & Rose, H. (Eds.). (2017). *Doing research in applied linguistics: Realities, dilemmas, and solutions*. New York: Routledge.

Mellor, N. (2001). Messy method: The unfolding story. *Educational Action Research*, 9(3), 465–484.

Paris, D., & Winn, M. T. (2013). *Humanizing research: Decolonizing qualitative inquiry with youth and communities*. Los Angeles: Sage Publications.

Patel, L. (2015). *Decolonizing educational research: From ownership to answerability*. New York: Routledge.

Prior, M. (2017). Managing researcher dilemmas in narrative interview data and analysis. In J. McKinley & H. Rose (Eds.) *Doing research in applied linguistics: Realities, dilemmas, and solutions* (pp. 172–182). New York: Routledge.

Ruecker, T. (2017). Publishing as an early career L2 writing scholar. In P. K. Matsuda, S. E. Snyder & K. D. O'Meara (Eds.) *Professionalizing second language writing* (pp. 66–79). West Lafayette, IN: Parlor Press.

Strauss, P. (1995). No easy answers: The dilemmas and challenges of teacher research. *Educational Action Research*, 3(1), 29–40.

Thomas, G. (1998). The myth of rational research. *British Educational Research Journal*, 24(2), 141–161.

PART 1

Getting started: navigating bureaucracies and recruiting participants

2

THE WHEELS OF BUREAUCRACY GO ROUND AND ROUND

Kendi M. Ho

Introduction

When I first heard the term *silo* referring to "specialization … 'stovepipes' … that impede cooperation in providing advice to policy-makers and service to citizens" (Aucoin, 1997, p. 293), I did not think that this metaphor would sum up my many years of experience as an English as a Second Language (ESL) instructor in adult education. Little did I know that the silo system of management and thinking within public education in a small community would chew up my hopes and dreams of doing research as an MA and Ph.D. student with adult English Language Learners (ELLs).

I had been teaching ESL and English as a Foreign Language (EFL) as an instructor in private language schools, as a tutor, and most consistently in the Community School for Adults (CSA) before I decided to enter the master's program at a local university. As a graduate student, I had been excited to study my own classroom and expand second language learning research in a population that is overlooked and understudied (Mathews-Aydinli, 2008; Tarone, 2010). In addition, it seemed like I would have had a shorter route for obtaining a data sharing agreement[1] for research as an employee for the state Department of Education (DOE) versus outsiders who were not employed within the DOE. Those outsiders had a longer process since they were required to receive written approval from the superintendent even before contacting any schools or offices regarding participation in research. According to the DOE website at the time, all I needed to submit with my application was the approval of the principal of the research site, a complete application, and a university Institutional Review Board (IRB) approved research application.

To ensure that my application process would go smoothly, I also decided to focus on a high priority area—English Language Learner (ELL) needs within the

General Education Development (GED) classroom.[2] Since the state DOE offered the online GED as its choice for high school equivalency testing, preparing ELLs for the new GED online examination seemed like a prime area for a needs analysis to reveal areas of interventions. Unfortunately, I both underestimated the impenetrable nature of silos and the mindset that they embody, and overestimated my own abilities as a novice researcher and graduate student without a position of power and influence.

In this chapter, I contextualize my experience so that readers may better adapt lessons learned to their own situations, then I discuss how researchers need to consider bureaucracy or governmental systems in all stages of their research and how these systems can be influenced in many ways, depending on the managers and leaders. I describe the hierarchy within my site in adult education and then elaborate on how I navigated within this bureaucracy numerous times by seeking to align with transformational leaders and administrators. Part of my attempt included showing the benefit research might be able to bring to the state DOE by applying for an Institute of Educational Sciences (IES) research grant in the GED classroom. This experience in adult education then informed my more successful attempt in education/training in public health, since my adult education research efforts were forced to shift. I conclude with advice and a discussion on how to maintain sanity, while achieving research with a community within the wheels of bureaucracy.

Context: public education hierarchies in a small community

Adult education for ELLs and Adult Basic Education (ABE) students throughout the US takes many shapes and forms. In general, programs within state education systems or community-based organizations can receive federal funding through the federal Workforce Innovations and Opportunities Act (WIOA), formerly the Workforce Investment Act (WIA). The funding requirements of providing equal opportunity to employees and applicants may determine the system that disburses the funding, like a state education system. Similar to a few other states, my research site for adult education was situated within the K-12 public education system rather than the state community college system. District superintendents report to the superintendent, who reports to the Board of Education (BOE). Members of the BOE are appointed by the governor for a limited term to give some account-ability to voters. Despite this intentional act, achieving goals (e.g., a data sharing agreement) requires an understanding of what greases the wheels of bureaucracy and prevents destruction of a research project.

One of the main challenges in any state is that each district faces different com-plexities while struggling within one bureaucratic system. For example, when our state budget for adult education was cut in half, the superintendent reduced the number of administrators overseeing the entire network of state adult community schools. This left some administrators in charge of schools in district areas that included large rural areas outside of their main school.

In a city with a small community feel where everyone knows everyone else by some degree of separation, disagreements and negotiations are handled differently than in a larger city where there may be more anonymity and less connectedness. For example, whenever I spoke with someone who may have worked in the DOE administration, they would often look over their shoulder to see who was watching and then speak to me in a softer voice. Even when writing this chapter, I often consider the potential consequences of what I say in the form of how people in positions of power might retaliate against me or my family. Although these questions of retaliation are always in my mind as I write, I remain optimistic that there are capable and transformative leaders within the state organization who can effect change. ELL adult education is an understudied area and I would like to continue to add to the knowledge base. As I will elaborate, I must respect those in power and work to build trust and relationships within this close-knit community.

Silos in K-12 public education

In this first pass through the wheels of bureaucracy, I elaborate on my three applications for a data sharing agreement and discuss the reasons for limited success in the third and final attempt. My first two attempts were needs analyses within the GED classroom where I hoped to suggest curricular changes to benefit ELLs. In my first application for a data sharing agreement, I discounted the numerous stories that I heard of failed attempts. I thought as an insider—ESL teacher in adult education—I would have more success with my application. I heard stories about how graduate students had left the university for other institutions in other states so that they could do research. At a local conference, I even heard a professor from a different department describe how he had his graduate student do research in Japan rather than in the same state as our university. I did not understand the magnitude of resistance to research that he was describing. I assumed that his students were outsiders, and, as an insider, I was determined to research my own classroom within my own context. I thought that the DOE would allow their own teachers to systematically find out what interventions were needed in their own schools. Moreover, my principal, the vice principals of other schools, and the GED instructors all verbally agreed to participate in my research. I did not think the wheels of bureaucracy would demand so much of my time in my graduate program and limit my ability to do research in my own classroom.

Data sharing agreement application: reality hits

Even before starting the application for a data sharing agreement with the DOE, researchers were faced with a dizzying *Research Routing Chart* to determine what the research application path would be. If the applicant required data that was not publicly available, there were thirteen of these process-and-decision pieces to navigate to determine how and what you needed to apply to do research. The flow chart had seven different colors and terminated its pathways with the following solutions that all seemed to end with the Data Governance Office (DGO):

(a) contact the DGO;
(b) have your instructor contact the DGO;
(c) contact the DGO to see if a formal agreement is necessary;
(d) have the inquiring school or office contact the DGO; and
(e) send a copy of the formal agreement to the DGO for review.

I eventually followed the advice of our university's IRB office to determine that I needed to contact the DGO.

The application process was burdensome because of the sheer amount of paperwork that was involved to complete the online application. This included the usual documenting of support from the school principal, graduate school advisors, completion of an online Family and Education Right and Privacy Act (FERPA) course, and approval from the university's IRB. However, for each data collection instrument, it was quite detailed in specifying:

(a) type of instrument;
(b) name of instrument;
(c) scope of participation;
(d) target groups;
(e) estimated time required to administer instrument to each participant/average number of minutes across all target groups;
(f) description of how the data collected by this instrument will be documented and analyzed;
(g) description of how this instrument will be administered (e.g., by whom, where, and when); and
(h) person in charge of administering this instrument.

It seemed to me that every cog in the wheel needed to be addressed before my application would move forward.

Once I had completed my instruments, plus numerous consent and assent forms, completing the online application took a few hours each day for about a week. At the time, an applicant could work on the online system for only an hour at a time and had to be sure to save their work or it would be lost when the system timed out. At the beginning, I was very nervous about the system because I would unexpectedly be kicked out with odd error messages:

Error: String or binary data would be truncated. The statement has been terminated.

Your application has been automatically saved. For assistance, please contact DOEresearch@xxxx.us. We apologize for the inconvenience.

I followed the instructions, but even the DGO representative was unfamiliar with such an error and forwarded my query to the tech team. I later received a forwarded email from the tech team explaining that I had entered too many characters in a field and they would be increasing the character limit. Although the error message had dumbfounded me for a bit, I was grateful for the assistance. Perhaps some of the wheels did work!

The most time-consuming part of the application was making revisions to the DGO's satisfaction. I mistakenly thought that since I had followed the exemplar application provided and the checklist for researchers, my application would be approved quickly. According to the research application rubric instructions that explained the scoring scale from one (exceeds expectations) through four (unsatisfactory), the application needed to be clear and consistent to receive a rating of one or two (meets expectations). However, my feedback on the rubric showed that a great deal of my application, particularly my assent and consent documents, scored a three (does not meet expectations) or a four. This was unfortunate, because the only guidance that I had for "unsatisfactory" was the following:

> Does not meet many of the stated expectations—one or more of the following are true:
> - Unclear.
> - Many inconsistencies or conflicting information appear.

I painstakingly had to move through this feedback, the exemplars, and my application to identify what was unclear. At one point, I made an Excel spreadsheet with one column with the error they noted in my application, another column with what their sample documents (e.g., consents and assents) showed, and then a general question to ask them to explain the difference. From my perspective, there did not seem to be much difference and I felt like I was moving as fast as a tiny snail slithering up a brick wall. Moreover, even if I had somehow managed to exceed or meet expectations that were somewhere beyond the exemplars, there was no guarantee of receiving an agreement. The next two steps to obtain a data sharing agreement, after demonstrating clarity and consistency, were:

(a) a review of the application's content area; and
(b) for the DGO to decide if they would recommend my application to the superintendent for approval.

As I crept through the application process, I slowly and eventually realized the truth of what the professor from another department said regarding graduate students not being able to do research within the state DOE. Now I understood why he recommended doing research in another context or with a publicly available dataset rather than in one's own classroom! Although my application was "expedited" because I was an employee, three months had passed, and the application was still in the review stage. I was starting to feel nervous because I had wanted to pilot my survey research before the end of the semester in order to graduate with my master's degree the following semester. I reached out to a professor in a different department at the university who responded that both of her students had been rejected after six to eight months. More importantly to me, one of those students was also an employee and also had an "expedited" application. Her sentiments that the system was broken were echoed in my contact with a professor from a different department who had a broader perspective. This professor wrote that the students were changing topics since the DGO process was delaying theses and dissertations by a year. At that time, they were recommending that students should work with publicly available databases. The professor's thoughts reflected to some degree the frustration and confusion of researchers or even those who work within the DOE who support systematic investigations to improve teaching, curriculum, and the overall education processes within schools. Also, by this time, my advisor told me two things:

(a) at least someone in the DGO was answering my questions; and
(b) I should change to another site if I wanted to graduate.

I decided to abandon trying to get the wheels of bureaucracy to turn, but left my application within the system in the hope that I could salvage it later. I became another casualty on the shores of the DGO, but I was determined to highlight ELLs in my context in research and eventually applied two more times. Each time I applied, I seemed to be inching closer to my goal of doing research in the DOE.

Second attempt, different angle

In my next attempt, the summer before my final semester in the MA program, I thought that showing the direct benefits of research, such as receiving a research grant award, would increase my chances of doing research in the school where I had been teaching for many years. Perhaps, I thought, it could add some gravitas to my efforts? A DGO representative who had helped me with my first application connected me to the grant writing office and also closed my withering initial application. I reshaped the same research proposal for a needs analysis to match the federal Institute of Educational Sciences (IES) Request for Proposals (RFP). I also noted that even in the IES application, researchers needed to include assurances that they had access to the data for the proposed research. The RFP stated that a common reason for failure was losing the participation of schools and districts. The IES grant writing webinar provided more information by instructing researchers to be sure to add detailed letters of agreement to show their access. With the help of two professors from my department, my principal's full support, and even the district superintendent's approval, I submitted my documents to the grant writing personnel in the DOE in time to meet the IES deadline and avoid the application submission process being slowed by an imminent hurricane.

The only document that was missing was the assurance of data. Although my principal became the principal investigator and the DOE submitted the IES application,[3] they would not give any letter of assurance that my university professors or I would have access to data in the school where I had worked for several years. This was one of the reasons we were not awarded the grant. This lack was highlighted as a major weakness in the IES feedback to the question "Do the commitments of each partner show support for the implementation and success of the project?" In the feedback detailing the proposal's rejection, both reviewers commented that no formal agreement for data sharing was in place, although part of the investigating team were housed within the department and had extensive experience in adult education. To highlight this point, one reviewer commented that, although there was a letter of commitment from the principal investigator to the superintendent, there was no letter or signature of the superintendent indicating approval of the study. The wheels of bureaucracy, at least in my mind, seemed to be turning in my favor to some degree. As in my previous attempt, my principal supported my efforts, but this time I also had the district superintendent's approval and the DOE grant writing team clarifying details of the application we submitted on behalf of the school. Later events would encourage me to try again.

Third attempt: the right place at the right time

Concurrent to my second application attempt, two timely events opened a door of opportunity. The first was a regular coming together of community leaders and members who were optimistic about change in the K-12 education system. Every year, a grassroots organization brought school leaders from different schools in the state to discuss changes within their school districts, schools, or classrooms. The conference that was held in the year of my IES application featured breakout sessions with guest speakers where the audience introduced themselves and asked the speakers to comment on an issue. When my turn to speak came, I described the hurdles and delays in applying for a data sharing agreement through the DGO and asked the guest speakers about the role of research in their schools. As we went around the room, I realized a BOE member also was in attendance. Later, he walked up to me, gave me his business card, and asked me to email him regarding my application. This introduction led to e-meeting others who informed me that the BOE had been working with the DOE to create an application system that was more open to research while still meeting DOE concerns about systematic investigation.

After I completed my master's research in the context of ELLs working entry-level health careers, I had two promising transitions that I thought could lead to more success in supporting ELLs. First, I enrolled in a Ph.D. program, where I hoped to gain more credibility in suggesting curricular changes. Then, in my first semester, I was asked by the vice principal of my school to take over the coordinator position of a grant-funded college and career readiness program that bridged ELLs and ABE students to community college certificate programs, degrees, or better careers. Previous to this conversation, those in charge of the grant had decided not to apply to extend the grant but decided that the community colleges would "gift" the program to the community schools for adults. Their reasoning was that the Workforce Innovations and Opportunities Act (WIOA), the federal funding mechanism, had redefined adult education and given the same mandate of creating career pathways for college and career readiness. I hoped that this could be a site for my dissertation research. Knowing that the BOE was creating a new, simplified application process, I made an appointment to talk with the interim DGO chief officer.

During a brief meeting with this officer, after I, with a quavering voice, told him my painful story, he replied with great empathy. He apologized and told me that he was creating a more streamlined application process than the existing process. The dizzying routing chart was dismantled since the interim chief officer reasoned that the university IRB's approval carried some weight in protecting privacy and confidentiality and the state DOE system did not need to add additional assurances. With this interim DGO chief officer and a streamlined application system in place, I received approval to do research in my classroom in three months rather than struggle and ultimately lose hope after eight months. After two failed attempts, including an IES application, over the course of almost two years, I had finally received a data sharing agreement. As the language arts instructor and coordinator of the program, I asked my students and my co-teachers to participate in my research. I finally collected data from my own classroom, including my students' work and their reflections on their learning.

Unfortunately, though, I underestimated the influence of a school administrator's relative who had been hired as part of the program's team. After one semester, I was informed that the program, which had been running successfully for over two years, would be closing permanently since the grant monies were gone. At the time, I thought that a certain individual made a decision to close this program. My reasoning was that there had been no conversation about looking for additional funding or other options for me to continue adapting the program, although WIOA had newly mandated that adult education programs should focus on creating career pathways for students. The scenario just did not make sense to me. All of the years of work to gain a data sharing agreement were now in ashes. My disappointment turned into disillusionment and I felt that I could no longer work in this environment that offered no more opportunities or explanations. I needed to pivot to another project outside the realm of K-12 public education. The influence of a single individual within the school seemed to be too much for anyone to question.

Bureaucracy: self-interest or public good?

Chalking up frustrating paperwork and strange administrative decisions to bureaucracy seems to be a cultural norm. In contrast to what we may feel, bureaucracy is a necessary part of governmental structures to guarantee fair treatment and continuity of administration (Bannister, 2001). As we may all know, this necessity can also impede innovation and likewise cause obstacles for any researcher, experienced or novice. Perhaps this is most notable in public administration, where there are innumerable turning gears for researchers to become entangled in or use to their advantage. Aucoin (1997) underscores that bureaucracy is not inherently outdated and cumbersome, but its problems stem from poor management or lack of change despite acknowledgement of the necessity to change. Indeed, the challenge is to

> design bureaucracy in ways that best adapt the requirements of hierarchy, specialization and standardization to serve the ends of democratic direction, control and accountability as well as the ends of effective public policy, productive public management and responsive public service.
>
> *(Aucoin, 1997, p. 292)*

This notion of bureaucracy serving democratic goals is also underlined by Olsen (2006), who suggests the rise of public accountability is pushing for an increased understanding of government administration and the public servants who work within it.

From this view of the fundamental workings of bureaucracy, I suggest that novice researchers need to be aware of their context and the individuals who work within the system. This includes the local as well as national hierarchy that not only defines their site but also the body that grants access to doing research within their site. For example, I fully understood the federal mandate and grant expectations that were guiding innovation and tried to align my research with these outcomes, and individuals within the administrative hierarchies helped me to move to where I needed to go or kept me going aimlessly round and round.

Navigating bureaucratic systems

Some have written that it is unfair to blame the system of bureaucracy for inflexibility, lack of innovation, or ethical failings and that it is more accurate to hold managers and leaders accountable for the actions or inactions of bureaucracy (Aucoin, 1997; Olsen, 2006). Leaders and managers are actors and even gatekeepers within bureaucracies. Their decisions can move organizational rules towards innovation, flexibility, and shared goals of improved community outcomes. Moreover, how leaders view their organizations and role is affected by their mental models or schema (Bolman & Deal, 2013; Senge, 2006).

However, researchers who are insiders, as I was, also need to consider their own frames and biases in interpreting the system and their position within the bureaucracy to understand more accurately what is happening as they navigate through the turning wheels. Senge (2006) and Oshry (2007) suggest that we have certain defaults and system blindness that cause us to blame others more readily than see our own role in the same system. I realized this only as I began research within public health and recognized the same wheels of bureaucracy were grinding. For example, an elders service program to which I was applying to do research suddenly and unexpectedly closed due to a shift in the state funding source. Although public health, like education, emphasizes evidence-based decision making within programs, the life of a program is determined by other factors (Weiss, Murphy-Graham, Petrosino, & Gandhi, 2008). Researchers should be aware that the programs they work with could lose funding and close quite suddenly after any change in policy or leadership. The difference in this new context of public health, from my experience with the DGO, was that the mindset of stakeholders was horizontal and shared versus vertical in that everyone was fighting for improved elderly care and they could see a place for an adult educator in their cause. They have what Senge (2006) would describe as a *shared vision*, which works within *systems thinking* to work collaboratively with other stakeholders within bureaucracy, *team learning* within their own organizations, and constant reflection of their own *mental models*. Through reflection on my own biases, discussion with other casualties who had also failed in receiving a data sharing agreement in the state DOE system, and persisting with research in other disciplines, I now have a better picture of the system I tried to navigate.

After hearing the comments of state DOE research representatives, I have begun to understand the mistrust and bad relationships that already existed and further thickened the silo walls. While I cannot speak for the graduate students who were casualties, I know that I had to be persistent in finding expertise from other insiders and also had to rely on those who were working to identify areas for change in order to build trust and relationships.

In navigating the various wheels of bureaucracy, I would encourage researchers to search out like-minded leaders in the community or the university to help identify potential pitfalls or ways of succeeding. With the benefit of 20/20 hindsight, I now see that the professors in other departments very wisely rerouted their graduate students to other sites for research. The experience of others can hasten research and spare a great deal of heartache and regret. More importantly, aligning with sources of power and influence can support gaining access and recruitment. Although I seemed to achieve this with the help of the BOE, the unpredictable nature of people can still lead to disappointment in research.

Finally, addressing the complex problems that we find in education needs multidisciplinary collaboration with multiple stakeholders outside of academia (Ortega, 2013). As researchers and practitioners, we need to reflect constantly on our own biases and practices (Richards, 1990; Senge, 2006) while considering that no agreement may be reached within a short time period. With persistence and support from the academic community and other stakeholders, shared vision can be developed and grow into collaborative partnerships with useful outcomes for the community.

Notes

1 In this situation, this is the written agreement between the researcher and the state Department of Education specifying the researcher's access to student or staff data in compliance with the Family Educational Rights and Privacy Act (FERPA).

2 In the US, adults without a high school diploma can earn a high school equivalence by passing a state approved high school equivalency test, like the GED. In 2011, the American Council on Education, a non-profit that administered the GED, collaborated with Pearson Education to revamp the test for the twenty-first century by creating an online assessment that was aligned to the Common Core with a focus on complexity using Webb's Depth of Knowledge. Because of the increased difficulty and cost, states began adopting alternative high school equivalency tests, such as Educational Testing Service's High School Equivalency Test (HiSET) or McGraw-Hill's Test Assessing Secondary Completion (TASC) (Porter, 2015).

3 IES specified that all grant applications must be submitted by an institution via the internet and using software found on Grants.gov.

References

Aucoin, P. (1997). The design of public organizations for the 21st century: Why bureaucracy will survive in public management. *Canadian Public Administration*, 40(2), 290–306.

Bannister, F. (2001). Dismantling the silos: Extracting new value from IT investments in public administration. *Information Systems Journal*, 11(1), 65–84.

Bolman, L. G., & Deal, T. E. (2013). *Reframing organizations: Artistry, choice, and leadership*. San Francisco: John Wiley & Sons.

Mathews-Aydinli, J. (2008). Overlooked and understudied? A survey of current trends in research on adult English language learners. *Adult Education Quarterly*, 58(3), 198–213.

Olsen, J. P. (2006). Maybe it is time to rediscover bureaucracy. *Journal of Public Administration Research and Theory*, 16(1), 1.

Ortega, L. (2013). SLA for the 21st century: Disciplinary progress, transdisciplinary relevance, and the bi/multilingual turn. *Language Learning*, 63(s1), 1–24.

Oshry, B. (2007). *Seeing systems: Unlocking the mysteries of organizational life*. San Francisco: Berrett-Koehler.

Porter, C. (2015). High-school equivalency degree loses its dominant position. *Wall Street Journal*, February 9. Retrieved March 1, 2019 from: www.wsj.com/articles/high-school-e quivalency-degree-loses-its-dominant-position-1423521427.

Richards, J. C. (1990). The dilemma of teacher education in second language teaching. In J. C. Richards & D. Nunan (Eds.), *Second language teacher education* (pp. 3–15). Cambridge: Cambridge University Press.

Senge, P. M. (2006). *The fifth discipline: The art and practice of the learning organization*. New York: Random House.

Tarone, E. (2010). Second language acquisition by low-literate learners: An under-studied population. *Language Teaching*, 43(1), 75–83.

Weiss, C. H., Murphy-Graham, E., Petrosino, A., & Gandhi, A. G. (2008). The fairy godmother—and her warts making the dream of evidence-based policy come true. *American Journal of Evaluation*, 29(1), 29–47.

3

RESEARCH METHODS FOR REACHING URBAN STUDENTS FROM GROUPS UNDERREPRESENTED IN STEM DISCIPLINES

Steven McGee, Randi McGee-Tekula, Lucia Dettori, Andrew M. Rasmussen and Ronald I. Greenberg

Introduction

In their quest for internal validity, researchers seek to minimize research interruptions. Many researchers adopt a strategy of reducing interruptions by avoiding research settings with a high probability of interruptions to research projects. These high-interruption research settings also tend to have a high percentage of low-income racial and ethnic minorities who are underrepresented in STEM disciplines (Shavers-Hornaday, Lynch, Burmeister, & Torner, 1997). Shavers-Hornaday et al. (1997) have identified a variety of research interruptions that can contribute to the underrepresentation of low-income minorities in research. For example, such students often end up attending schools that are marred by low performance on standardized assessments and that are under constant threat of sanctions. These conditions contribute to high levels of staff turnover (Allensworth, Ponisciak, & Mazzeo, 2009) and an overreliance on test preparation (Allensworth, Correa, & Ponisciak, 2008). For researchers who are pilot testing new educational programs, high staff turnover creates a burden to provide ongoing professional development for new teachers, and the overreliance on test preparation creates interruptions to the implementation of the educational program.

One consequence of this quest for settings free from research interruptions is the long-standing underrepresentation of racial and ethnic minority research subjects in educational (Usher, 2018), psychology (Graham, 1992; Henrich, Heine, & Norenzayan, 2010), medical (Shavers-Hornaday et al., 1997), and artificial intelligence (Lohr, 2018) research. Researchers seek to avoid the added costs of providing greater levels of support and thus fail to develop relationships with practitioners in low-income, high-minority settings (Shavers-Hornaday et al., 1997). A significant implication of this underrepresentation is that theoretical constructs and programs are based on biased samples and contexts that reflect dominant groups (Usher,

2018). In the field of artificial intelligence research, for example, facial recognition software is significantly more accurate in identifying white males than females or people of color (Lohr, 2018). This underrepresentation also results in medical treatments and educational programs that may have limited benefits for low-income, minority participants who are not represented in the research that led to the development of these treatments and educational programs. Therefore, while the treatments, algorithms, or educational programs may be effective under the right conditions, they are ineffective in low-income settings because they have not been adapted for marginalized populations. When marginalized patients and students do not respond to the treatments and educational programs in ways consistent with the normative models of the research, it creates a deficit view that reinforces marginalization (Usher, 2018) or contributes to outright racism and exclusion (Moll, 2010). This lack of effectiveness of outside programs reinforces the mistrust that individuals from marginalized populations feel towards external researchers.

In this chapter, we describe an effort to engage in research on an educational program designed to bring computer science to all children in the Chicago Public Schools (CPS). The Exploring Computer Science (ECS) program was initially developed for the Los Angeles Unified School District with equity as a core principle (Goode, Margolis, & Chapman, 2014). CPS was the first school district to adopt the program outside of Los Angeles (Margolis et al., 2013). In order to fully understand the impact of ECS on all students in CPS, particularly low-income, minority students, it was necessary for us to reconceive the ethics of research to go beyond a focus on "do no harm" and take a proactive ethical approach (Blee & Currier, 2011). Shavers-Hornaday et al. (1997) implore researchers to make an active commitment to recruiting participants from marginalized groups. They suggest offering incentives, developing relationships with the practitioners who serve those groups, and building trust by enhancing the applicability of the research. In the remainder of this chapter, we discuss examples of research interruptions we faced and our attempts to embody the principles of proactive ethics.

Context

In order to understand the context for the adoption of ECS, it is necessary to step back in time and explore the unmet need that called for a response. In the first decade of the twenty-first century, the number of students graduating with a computer science bachelor's degree dropped by about one-third from a high of 59,000 in 2004 to a low of 38,000 in 2009 (McGee, Greenberg, Reed, & Duck, 2013). Even though the social media age was dawning, with events such as the founding of Facebook in 2004, undergraduates' interest in becoming computer scientists was waning. University computer science faculty all over the country felt great concern about this falling enrollment and the growing shortfall of skilled computing graduates for an increasingly technological society (Cassel, McGettrick, Guzdial, & Roberts, 2007). University faculty saw a need for computer science to be offered more broadly at the high school level. In 2008, computer science faculty from Loyola University Chicago and University of Illinois Chicago joined forces, with support from the National Science Foundation (NSF), to promote computer science through hundreds of classroom visits to area high schools (McGee et al., 2013). These visits resulted in an increased interest in computer science, regardless of race or gender. However, many of the students lacked access to a computer science course in their high school.

In parallel, a small group of CPS computer science teachers noticed that access to high school computer science courses was only through AP classes at selective-enrollment schools and through the Information Technology Career and Technical Education (CTE-IT) track (Dettori et al., 2018). The vast majority of students had no access to computer science in CPS high schools. In addition, CPS administrative records show that there were racial disparities among those students taking AP computer science, with proportionally more Asian and Caucasian students and proportionally fewer African-American students in comparison to CPS students as a whole.

The Chicago area university faculty and the CPS teachers began working together in 2008 and discovered ECS the following year. The ECS curriculum and professional development model was designed to accomplish the goal of broadening participation by introducing the field of computer science and computational practices in a way that makes the field relevant, engaging, and stimulating for a diverse population of students and teachers (Margolis et al., 2012). The ECS curriculum is composed of activities that are designed to engage students in computer science inquiry around meaningful problems. The ECS professional development program prepares teachers to implement these inquiry-based activities, while also guiding teachers in building a classroom culture that is culturally relevant and inclusive of all students. The Chicago team felt that ECS would be valuable for broadening access to computer science in CPS.

By this time, the team had expanded to include another computer science faculty member at DePaul University, the head of CTE-IT at CPS, and The Learning Partnership. The team successfully formed the Taste of Computing project with funding from NSF's CS10K program in 2012. In support of the CS10K goal of training 10,000 new computer science teachers across the country, the Taste of Computing project successfully recruited 66 CPS teachers to complete the initial summer professional development. By the end of that summer, momentum was building for computer science education in CPS, and The Learning Partnership was poised to begin conducting research on the impact of the program on increasing the diversity of students taking computer science and improving student attitudes towards computer science.

Meanwhile, instability had been brewing in CPS for several years. The departure of the CPS CEO, Arne Duncan, for the Obama Department of Education in 2009 ended a long period of stability in district leadership and launched a tumultuous period of four CEOs in four years. These CEOs had to deal with the recurring effects of the 2008 economic crisis, which put tremendous financial strain on the school district, resulting in massive teacher layoffs and pay freezes. In the year that Taste of Computing started (2012), the district began holding hearings about the possible closure of 50 schools based on low attendance and low performance on the state exams (McGee, 2013). The bulk of these schools were located in low-income, African-American communities. Additionally, major changes came with the passing of IL Senate Bill 7 (McGee, 2012), which was designed to make the state eligible for Race to the Top funding (McGuinn, 2012). The bill enacted a collection of reforms. The most touted components that impacted teachers were:

- authorization for a longer school day in Chicago schools;
- increasing the difficulty of obtaining tenure;
- simplifying the process for revoking tenure; and
- increasing the percentage of teachers required for union members to authorize a strike.

There was also companion legislation passed prior to Senate Bill 7 that changed the teacher evaluation system to include standardized criteria for classroom observations and the use of student test performance. For many CPS teachers, these reforms seemed like a slap in the face. Not long after the launch of the Taste of Computing project, the CPS teachers went on strike for eight school days, interrupting the start of the school year and the start of our data collection (Liebelson, 2012).

The research design for the Taste of Computing was based on a two-phase recruitment process. The first phase involved members of The Learning Partnership team attending the ECS professional development in the summer of 2012. In order to facilitate the implementation of computer science using ECS, CPS waived the requirement that teachers needed a computer science endorsement to teach the course as long as they completed the ECS professional development program. In that first cohort of 66 teachers, only about half of the attendees held a certification in computer science, with the remaining teachers holding certifications in other subjects. At the beginning of the workshop week, attendees were invited to complete a background questionnaire, which covered their prior experience teaching computer science, demographic information, and their level of confidence in teaching the ECS curriculum. All of the teachers agreed to participate.

At the end of the week, all of the teachers completed an end-of-workshop feedback form, in which they were asked about their experience in the workshop and again were asked to rate their level of confidence in teaching the ECS curriculum. All but one person indicated that they were satisfied with the workshop experience (Dettori, Greenberg, McGee, & Reed, 2016). We saw a statistically significant increase in the confidence level from the beginning to the end of the workshop week. In open-ended comments, the teachers expressed appreciation for key components of the workshop, such as experiencing the curriculum from the perspective of the student, seeing how other teachers might implement ECS, and working in teams.

In the second phase of recruitment, we experienced the first sign of trouble. At the end of the workshop, we invited teachers to allow us to collect data about their implementation of ECS and the impact of the program on students' attitudes toward computer science. We received a mixed reaction from the teachers. Around half of the 66 teachers signed the informed consent form, agreeing to participate in the research. Of the half that turned down our invitation to participate in the student data collection phase, several told us that in their first year of implementation, they did not feel comfortable having anyone collecting data in their classroom. Even though the teachers as a whole rated their confidence level high by the end of the workshop, a number of them were still uncomfortable with the prospect of outsiders collecting data in their classrooms. The trouble continued after the strike ended in September 2012. Of the thirty or so teachers who had agreed at the workshop to participate in the student data collection, only seven responded to our requests to visit their classrooms to collect student assent and parental consent forms for their students and then followed through with collecting student surveys. Many teachers felt overwhelmed in the beginning of the school year trying to catch up after missing more than a week of class time due to the strike. It might also be the case that teacher mistrust of the district administration that had led to the strike had spilled over into mistrust in our data collection due to our connection with the district's central office. In the second year of the study, 28 new teachers completed the summer workshop, but only 12 responded to our request to collect data in their classrooms.

Given that the teachers who declined to participate in the research tended to come from schools with the lowest levels of performance in neighborhoods threatened with school closures, we ended up with a biased sample of students (see Table 3.1). The demographics of the overall population of students taking ECS with a Taste of Computing teacher closely matched the demographics of high school students in CPS. However, the demographics of the sample of students taking ECS with a teacher who agreed to participate in the research did not reflect the demographics of CPS. The study sample had a higher concentration of Caucasian and Asian students and a lower concentration of African-American students than in the overall population of students taking ECS that year. The study sample also had fewer special education and low-income students. In addition, students in the study sample had higher rates of attendance and higher scores on the CPS ninth-grade standardized exam (ACT EXPLORE) relative to the overall population of ECS students.

Incentivizing equitable representation of study participants

Within the subset of teachers who agreed to allow us to collect data about their students, there was a significant loss in the number of research participants. In our initial cohort of teacher study participants, there were 543 students who took ECS, but we were able to collect surveys from only 349 (65%). A little over one-third of the students failed to return their parent permission forms. The low-income,

TABLE 3.1 Demographic information about Taste of Computing study participants relative to all Taste of Computing students and all Chicago Public Schools high school students

Demographic information	Study sample	Taste of Computing	Chicago Public Schools
Hispanic	48%	42%	43%
African-American	12%	42%	43%
Caucasian	23%	9%	8%
Asian	13%	4%	3%
Female	47%	45%	–
Free or reduced lunch	65%	85%	85%
Special education	5%	14%	15%
English language learner	4%	5%	6%
Attendance rate	95%	89%	87%
EXPLORE score	19.5	15.8	16.0

minority students who are the target of programs like ECS are also more likely to have parents who are less involved (Bryk et al., 2010). By not returning parental consent forms, these students become underrepresented in the research and we run the risk of not being able to study the effect of the program on the very population we are targeting. Low participation is also a major factor that disinclines many researchers from working with marginalized populations (Shavers-Hornaday et al., 1997).

Seeking parental permission poses a dilemma for school districts. On the one hand, many IRBs provide a waiver of documentation of informed consent for research conducted in established or commonly accepted educational settings involving normal education practices, which is considered to be exempt from IRB review according to federal regulations (45 CFR 41.101(b)(1)). These IRBs allow researchers to send a letter to the parents with the details of the research that would normally appear in an informed consent document. Researchers can assume that students are a part of the research unless the parents or students object and ask to be removed from the study. However, for student populations that are most vulnerable and least engaged in school, there is not a reasonable assurance that the parents will actually see the letter and make a decision about whether to allow their children to participate. Therefore, urban districts, like Chicago, tend to require that researchers secure documentation of parents' informed consent to allow their children to participate in the research (Chicago Public Schools, 2010). Yet, if these same parents are unlikely to see the informed consent permission form that should be returned to the school, there will tend to be low return rates for many of the students targeted by the program.

This requirement to document parental consent combined with the low return rates of parental consent forms created a bind for us. We decided that the only way to increase the return rate was to offer an incentive to students for returning the forms. We wanted to ensure that the parents and students who were willing to agree to be in the study were included while providing the space for parents and students to feel free to decline participation. Following the recommendation of Shavers-Hornaday et al. (1997) for a proactive ethical approach, we decided to develop a student incentive to return the signed parental consent forms. This incentive did not induce coercion, since the parental consent forms provided boxes for parents to agree or decline participation. We set the threshold for incentive eligibility at a minimum of 90 percent of a given class returning the signed parental consent forms, regardless of whether a parent granted permission for their child to participate in the study. Within each class that reached the 90 percent threshold, a pizza (or healthy snack) party was provided to the entire class. According to federal cost principles, the allowability of using food as an incentive is ambiguous and subject to approval of the federal agency:

> Costs of entertainment, including amusement, diversion, and social activities and any associated costs are unallowable, except where specific costs that might otherwise be considered entertainment have a *programmatic purpose* and are authorized either in the approved budget for the Federal award or with prior written approval of the Federal awarding agency.
>
> *(Government Publishing Office, 2014, § 200.438)*

A proactive ethics pushes the boundaries of bureaucratic regulations that impede inclusion of all willing students and parents in the research. In some cases, program officers approved our pizza parties as an allowable cost, but in other cases they did not. These pizza parties often took place during lunchtime to minimize disruption to instruction. In addition, CPS recently enacted a healthy eating policy that precludes the use of food as a reward. In cases where food is disallowed as an incentive, we use five-dollar gift cards as an alternative incentive. We have found that the incentive seems to be most effective when the teacher embraces it by using daily reminders, such as starting each class period with a picture of a slice of pizza or a gift card on the projector screen. Without that teacher support, return rates are equivalent to having no incentive.

Developing trust through partnerships

Shavers-Hornaday et al. (1997) recommend that researchers develop relationships with practitioners who serve the marginalized communities that are the focus of efforts to broaden participation. Long-term partnerships can build trust with teachers since engagement is sustained over multiple years and teachers begin to see the researchers as advocates for them and their students, while at the same time maintaining objectivity as researchers. The Taste of Computing project was funded through a three-year grant from NSF and involved a partnership with the CTE-IT program in CPS. Over the course of several years, early adopters of the ECS curriculum became the facilitators of professional development. By actively participating in the research, these facilitators served as role models for new ECS teachers. During The Learning Partnership's recruitment at ECS workshops, the facilitators were able to endorse the research by highlighting its value and vouching for the minimal level of effort required to participate.

While this endorsement was beneficial, it was insufficient for reaching all teachers who were teaching ECS courses. Therefore, The Learning Partnership submitted a data request to the CPS Office of Research for data about ECS students. Since Taste of Computing was a project-level partnership with a CPS department, the Office of Research indicated that it could provide only anonymous data about the students. They would not provide The Learning Partnership with access to identifiable data through a data sharing agreement since the research was not related to a district-wide initiative. We were thus limited in the number of variables we could request as the risk of identifiability increases with the number of variables. For example, researchers could receive information about race and gender. However, if there was a particular class where there were only handful of students with a particular combination of race and gender, researchers could receive only aggregate data for that classroom. We were not able to connect this data to the survey data that we were collecting.

In addition to the limits on the number of variables, we found that the first dataset The Learning Partnership received from CPS was missing a significant amount of data. Based on the CTE office's direct contact with the teachers, we had a rough estimate of the number of ECS classes being taught. Yet, the data The Learning Partnership received contained significantly fewer classes. It turned out that not all schools were using the designated course code for Taste of Computing courses. For a variety of reasons, schools were implementing ECS under a variety of course names and course codes that did not appear in the official CPS course catalog. The CTE administrators performed an audit of course codes by examining the enrollment data at each school with an ECS teacher.

While The Learning Partnership and the CTE office had been laying the groundwork for a second request of anonymous data, national and local movements to promote computer science education had taken root. In 2014, Chicago's mayor, Rahm Emanuel, announced the CS4All initiative (City of Chicago, 2014). This was a first-of-its-kind push to ensure that every high school student in Chicago experienced at least one high-quality computer science course. Taste of Computing was no longer just a department-level project. It was now part of a district-wide initiative. This shift made The Learning Partnership eligible to pursue a data sharing agreement with the district that would provide access to student-level, identifiable data. In addition, The Learning Partnership received a grant from NSF in 2015 to study the implementation of the Taste of Computing project. The Learning Partnership now had the financial resources to conduct large-scale research on the initiative. The agreement provided access to information about all of the students who had completed any computer science course, including demographic information, test scores, and course performance. In return for that access, The Learning Partnership had to demonstrate that it had controls in place to protect the privacy of the data. In addition, access to the data was time-bound by the term of the research project. This time-boundedness created an urgency to complete analyses and publish results before the term of the data sharing agreement expired.

One immediate benefit of this data sharing agreement was that The Learning Partnership could re-examine its earlier research on the Taste of Computing project. The demographic data in the Taste of Computing column of Table 3.1 is based on the data secured from the CPS Office of Research, which allowed us to assess the level of underrepresentation of African-American students in our sample. In addition, we were able to connect the district data to survey data collected as part of the Taste of Computing research. The result was a publication by the Taste of Computing partnership about the 2012–2013 and 2013–2014 school years that demonstrated a correlation between students' perceptions of the personal relevance of ECS and the increased probability of taking additional computer science coursework in high school (McGee et al., 2017). These results were later corroborated in further research using the entire sample of students who completed an ECS course between 2012–2013 and 2015–2016. The students who completed an ECS course as their first computer science course were compared to those who completed traditional computer science courses as their first such course. These other courses had not been designed to be culturally relevant, in contrast to the ECS course. Students who completed an ECS course as their first course were twice as likely to complete another computer science course as students who took a traditional computer science course as their first such course (McGee et al., 2018b).

The computer science graduation requirement

Despite the positive results of the ECS implementation, less than half of the schools in CPS were offering computer science as of the 2015–2016 school year. To ensure that every CPS student had access to high quality computer science, the CPS School Board approved a resolution in February 2016 to enact computer science as a high school graduation requirement. The graduation requirement applies to students entering CPS as freshmen in 2016 and beyond. The vision outlined by the CS4All initiative in 2014 became policy in 2016. In the first year of the implementation of the new requirement, there was a 50 percent jump in the number of the schools offering computer science versus the previous year (42 in 2015–2016 to 64 in 2016–2017).

Despite this early success, significant challenges remained. Foremost among these was teacher turnover. In the first three years of implementation, about thirty teachers each year began teaching ECS after receiving their initial training (n = 90). However, three years after receiving their initial training, only about half were still teaching ECS. A second challenge came in the form of resistance to the policy. The CPS Office of Computer Science received anecdotal reports that some teachers and administrators were resistant to the new requirement because they either did not believe that computer science was important or felt that ECS was not a good choice for an introductory course. After the first full year of policy implementation (2016–2017), the Office of Computer Science began receiving further anecdotal reports sounding an alarm that the ECS course failure rate was extremely high. If true, a high failure rate would threaten the continued implementation of the policy. The need to develop a larger infrastructure for credit recovery of computer science through summer school or evening class during the school year would place an undue burden upon schools. In addition, prior research has shown that failing just one core class during a student's freshman year significantly increases the probability of dropping out of high school (Allensworth & Easton, 2007). A high failure rate for students taking ECS in their freshman year could threaten the progress the district had made in increasing the graduation rate.

In 2017, the Taste of Computing team formalized a researcher–practitioner partnership called the Chicago Alliance for Equity in Computer Science (CAFÉCS). It became a priority for CAFÉCS to better understand the extent of failure within ECS and the factors that affect the failure rate. As part of CAFÉCS's collaboration structure, the external partners meet with staff in the CPS Office of Computer Science on a monthly basis. At one of these monthly meetings, the partners developed joint research questions and hypotheses about the factors that may impact student failure rates. The Learning Partnership was able to use its district dataset to investigate these joint research questions using six years of data on over 14,000 students (McGee et al., 2018a). There was wide variability in the failure rate across implementations of ECS, but the overall average was 11 percent, which is consistent with other subject areas in CPS. There were two primary teacher-level factors that influenced the failure rate. First was participation in the ECS professional development. Teachers who skipped this had a failure rate that was twice as high as those who attended. Second was years of experience teaching ECS. As teachers gained experience teaching ECS, they steadily reduced the failure rate of the course. These results provided the district with empirical evidence to support the district policy that teachers should attend ECS professional development prior to teaching the course. They also provided evidence for principals to assign teachers to the ECS course over multiple years.

Conclusion

We started our narrative with a focus on balancing the needs of internal validity with the need to ensure that research opportunities reach all students. An overemphasis on the ethics of "do no harm" (Blee & Currier, 2011) can lead to the exclusion of important populations of students from the research. With the requirement to secure parental permission for student participation, our early research on ECS suffered from an underrepresentation of low-income, minority students. This underrepresentation was exacerbated by an unexpected teacher strike that interrupted the data collection for the first school year. In addition, teachers' mistrust of CPS that led to the strike spilled over into our data collection.

In subsequent school years, we sought to balance the ethics of "do no harm" with a proactive ethics as later characterized by Blee and Currier (2011): "A proactive ethics might push scholars to question the ethical stakes of what is not studied, the questions that are not asked, and the social groups and communities that are not the subject of research" (p. 404). The use of incentives to encourage the return of parental consent forms maintains the policy of ensuring that parents are provided a choice while at the same time ensuring that traditionally underrepresented minorities are well represented in the research.

At the heart of a proactive ethical approach is partnership between researchers and practitioners. The trajectory of the partnership from Taste of Computing to CAFECS provides an example of the kind of partnership that Shavers-Hornaday et al. (1997) recommend. It begins with an ongoing commitment on the part of the researchers and district administrators to work together on a vision of striving for equal outcomes for all students, particularly the marginalized. CAFÉCS is somewhat unique in the formation of the researcher–practitioner partnership as the partnership was initiated by the district, and external partners were added in a deliberate way (Coburn, Penuel, & Geil, 2013). We believed early on that the partnership could only grow at the speed of trust. We use the metaphor of barbecue to describe the formation of the CAFÉCS partnership. Proper barbecue occurs over low heat for a long period of time. The smoke slowly sears the outside of the meat without burning it and adds layers of flavor over time. This sear maintains ideal conditions for the meat to cook and develop flavor. Likewise, the early Taste of Computing relationships developed a community of practitioners that formed a protective layer of support around the program and created the ideal conditions to nurture its growth. As time passed, more layers of support were added. As Shavers-Hornaday et al. (1997) have identified, the development of partnerships involves a great deal of work that goes beyond traditional academic categories, and many academic researchers avoid pursuing such partnerships. Researchers must be willing to take on the research interruptions that the school districts face in return for higher-quality research that reaches all students. We are reaping the benefits of such a partnership in Chicago as CPS strives to use empirical evidence to ensure computer science benefits all students.

Acknowledgement

The authors were supported in part by National Science Foundation grants CNS-1738572, CNS-1738776, CNS-1738691, DRL-1640215, CNS-1543217, CNS-1542971, and CNS-0837769. Any opinions, findings, and conclusions or recommendations expressed in this material are those of the authors and do not necessarily reflect the views of NSF.

References

Allensworth, E., Correa, M., & Ponisciak, S. (2008). *From high school to the future: ACT preparation—too much, too late*. Chicago, IL: University of Chicago Consortium on Chicago School Research.

Allensworth, E., & Easton, J. (2007). *What matters for staying on-track and graduating in Chicago public high schools: A closer look at course grades, failures, and attendance in the freshman year*. Chicago, IL: University of Chicago Consortium on Chicago School Research.

Allensworth, E., Ponisciak, S., & Mazzeo, C. (2009). *The schools teachers leave: Teacher mobility in Chicago Public Schools*. Chicago, IL: University of Chicago Consortium on Chicago School Research.

Blee, K. M., & Currier, A. (2011). Ethics beyond the IRB: An introductory essay. *Qualitative Sociology*, 34(3), 401.

Bryk, A. S., Sebring, P. B., Allensworth, S. L., Luppescu, S., & Easton, J. Q. (2010). *Organizing schools for improvement: Lessons from Chicago*. Chicago: University of Chicago Press.

Cassel, L. B., McGettrick, A., Guzdial, M., & Roberts, E. (2007). The current crisis in computing: What are the real issues? Proceedings of SIGCSE '07, Covington, KY, March, 329–330.

Chicago Public Schools. (2010). *Research study and data policy*. Retrieved December 20, 2018 from: https://policy.cps.edu/download.aspx?ID=178.

City of Chicago. (2014). Mayor Emanuel announces major gains in Computer Science 4 All program. Retrieved December 21, 2018 from: www.chicago.gov/city/en/depts/mayor/p ress_room/press_releases/2014/dec/mayor-emanuel-announces-major-gains-in-computer -science-4-all-pr.html.

Coburn, C.E., Penuel, W.R., & Geil, K.E. (2013). *Research–practice partnerships: A strategy for leveraging research for educational improvement in school districts*. New York: William T. Grant Foundation.

Dettori, L., Greenberg, R. I., McGee, S., & Reed, D. (2016). The impact of the Exploring Computer Science instructional model in Chicago Public Schools. *Computing in Science and Engineering*, 18(2), 10–17.

Dettori, L., Greenberg, R. I., McGee, S., Reed, D., Wilkerson, B., & Yanek, D. (2018). CS as a graduation requirement: Catalyst for systemic change. Proceedings of SIGCSE '18, Baltimore, MD, February, 406–407.

Goode, J., Margolis, J., & Chapman, G. (2014). Curriculum is not enough: The educational theory and research foundation of the exploring computer science professional development model. Proceedings of SIGCSE '14, Atlanta, GA, March, 493–498.

Government Publishing Office. (2014). *Title 2: Grants and agreements: Uniform administrative requirements, cost principles, and audit requirements for federal awards*. Retrieved March 1, 2019 from: www.govinfo.gov/content/pkg/CFR-2014-title2-vol1/pdf/CFR-2014-title2-vol1 -sec200-438.pdf.

Graham, S. (1992). "Most of the subjects were white and middle class": Trends in published research on African Americans in selected APA journals, 1970–1989. *American Psychologist*, 47(5), 629–639.

Henrich, J., Heine, S., & Norenzayan, A. (2010). The weirdest people in the world? *Behavioral and Brain Sciences*, 33(2–3), 61–83.

Liebelson, D. (2012). What happened with the Chicago teacher strike, explained. *Mother Jones*, September 11. Retrieved December 18, 2018 from: www.motherjones.com/poli tics/2012/09/teachers-strike-chicago-explained/.

Lohr, S. (2018). Facial recognition is accurate, if you're a white guy. *New York Times*, February 9. Retrieved December 18, 2018 from: www.nytimes.com/2018/02/09/technology/fa cial-recognition-race-artificial-intelligence.html.

Margolis, J., Chapman, G., Goode, J., Dettori, L., & Lewis, D. (2013). *A tale of three ECS partnerships and why scalability = sustainability* [ECS Working Paper No. 1]. Los Angeles: UCLA. Retrieved December 18, 2018 from: www.exploringcs.org/wp-content/uploads/2014/04/A-Tale-of-Three-ECS-Partnerships.pdf.

Margolis, J., Ryoo, J. J., Sandoval, C. D. M., Lee, C., Goode, J., & Chapman, G. (2012). Beyond access: Broadening participation in high school computer science. *ACM Inroads*, 3(4), 72–78.

McGee, S. (2012). This year's outbreak of Illinois teacher strikes is oxymoronic. Blog post, November 9. Retrieved December 18, 2018 from: http://learningpartnershipnet.blogspot.com/2012/11/this-year-outbreak-of-illinois-teacher.html.

McGee, S. (2013). Rahm Emanuel's intuition-based reform. Blog post, June 5. Retrieved December 18, 2018 from: http://learningpartnershipnet.blogspot.com/2013/06/rahm-emanuels-intuition-based-reform_5.html.

McGee, S., Greenberg, R. I., Dettori, L., Rasmussen, A. M., McGee-Tekula, R., & Duck, J. (2018a). *An examination of the factors correlating with course failure in a high school computer science course* [Technical Report No. 5]. Western Springs, IL: The Learning Partnership. Retrieved December 21, 2018 from: https://ecommons.luc.edu/cs_facpubs/205.

McGee, S., Greenberg, R. I., Reed, D. F., & Duck, J. (2013). Evaluation of the IMPACTS computer science presentations. *Journal for Computing Teachers*. Retrieved December 18, 2018 from: http://www.iste.org/store/product?ID=2853.

McGee, S., McGee-Tekula, R., Duck, J., Dettori, L., Yanek, D., Rasmussen, A., Greenberg, R. I., & Reed, D. F., (2018b). Does Exploring Computer Science increase computer science enrollment? Paper presented at the American Education Research Association Annual Meeting, New York, April. Retrieved March 1, 2019 from: https://ecommons.luc.edu/cs_facpubs/201.

McGee, S., McGee-Tekula, R., Duck, J., Greenberg, R. I., Dettori, L., Reed, D. F., Wilkerson, B., Yanek, D., Rasmussen, A.M., & Chapman, G. (2017). Does a Taste of Computing increase computer science enrollment? *Computing in Science and Engineering*, 19(3), 8–18.

McGuinn, P. (2012). Stimulating reform: Race to the Top, competitive grants and the Obama education agenda. *Educational Policy*, 26(1), 136–159.

Moll, L. C. (2010). Mobilizing culture, language, and educational practices: Fulfilling the promises of Mendez and Brown. *Educational Researcher*, 39(6), 451–460.

Shavers-Hornaday, V. L., Lynch, C. F., Burmeister, L. F., & Torner, J. C. (1997). Why are African Americans under-represented in medical research studies? Impediments to participation. *Ethnicity and Health*, 2(1–2), 31–45.

Usher, E. L. (2018). Acknowledging the whiteness of motivation research: Seeking cultural relevance. *Educational Psychologist*, 53(2), 131–144.

4

CHASING THE TEAM

Participant recruitment strategies for qualitative research into student-athlete writers

J. Michael Rifenburg

Introduction

I didn't expect a *no*, at least a *no* given with such tired and annoyed eyes and body language that communicated frustration.

But my qualitative research into student-athlete writing practices took a different path because a first-year football player at Auburn University told me *no* as we walked side by side up the stairs, the hot sun of an Alabama August hitting us.

In summer 2008, I was midway through the two-year master's program at Auburn. The writing program director invited me to work with the Summer Transitional Enhancement Program (STEP). The basic concept behind the program is gaining traction across US higher education institutions under variously titled acronyms; in brief, programs like STEP identify a cohort of incoming students deemed at risk based on demographics, GPA, testing scores, and/or a host of other factors. The cohort matriculates at the university before the fall semester, lives in the dorms, and takes common first-year courses. STEP runs for eight weeks over the summer. During that time, students enroll in three academic, for-credit courses and participate in program workshops, seminars, designated study hours, and study groups. During the fall semester, the STEP students take classes together, such as a section of first-year composition, before getting mainstreamed for the spring semester. In my role, I monitored the three-hour blocks of study time in the library for the cohort of 18 students. I also co-taught a required success strategies class with a counseling psychology professor. In the fall, I co-taught the cohort's first-year writing course.

Most of the 18 students in this cohort of incoming students were student-athletes—specifically male, African-American football players. Auburn is known for its football team. The school competes in the Southeastern Conference (SEC), a top conference for college football where from 2000 to 2017 an SEC team claimed the national championship ten times, including in 2010, the year after I graduated. A graduate of STEP kicked the game-winning field goal. Because of the financial pressure to field a winning team, some schools, particularly Division I schools like Auburn, matriculate student-athletes who might not meet the academic acceptance scores. As a result, these students are labeled "special admits." All such students— not just student-athletes—have a talent or ability that will bring the university money, so the university waives test score expectations, but provides programs like STEP to support their success. Most special admits are student-athletes, and most of these student-athletes are male, African-American football players. I make this brief detour to say that many of the football players were academically struggling. I do not know which student-athletes, or which students in general, were special admits. Schools do not like to disclose those numbers. But when I sat down with these student-athletes during summer study hours, I saw their writing struggles.

The counseling psychology professor assigned a basic two-page response for the success strategies class. During study hours, the students leaned over their screens and began typing. I walked around the space to make sure all were on task. The students had been on campus for only two weeks. Outside, the summer sun had finally given way to a thick night. I came up to a student, a star football player, who was struggling with his paper. He had not heard of Microsoft Word and had typed out a few sentences on Notepad, the clunky, pre-installed text-editing software. We talked for a bit then I helped him locate Word and open a new document. I moved onto another player. Again, a highly recruited player. Again, writing struggles. Some struggles were with basic computer literacy, like the first writer, but most were syntactical and organizational. I spent my evening working closely with these two student-athletes, pushing them to generate ideas, to get words onto the screen. Their struggles were not just motivational or resultant of uninterest in a relatively insipid assignment. The student-athletes were working through some deep writing challenges.

Fast forward to the fall semester: all students in the STEP cohort enrolled in the first-year writing course. The lead instructor stressed one-on-one conferencing and revision. At the end of the semester, the students assembled a portfolio of their work. While I co-taught this class, I continued my own coursework with a class on writing pedagogy taught by Kevin Roozen. His research and teaching are committed to connecting seemingly disparate areas of one's literate identity—the curricular and the extracurricular. Through case studies, he reveals how a learner's engagement with non-school reading and writing practices are critical to their full literate development, even in ways unseen by the learner. In one case study, Roozen (2008) showed how a student's stand-up comedy routine helped the student perform better in a speech communication class. In another, Roozen (2010) introduced us to Lindsey, who keeps a prayer journal to help deepen her faith. Lindsey also took graduate classes in English literature. It turned out that Lindsey annotated her Bible and wrote in her prayer journal in the same way she annotated her literature books and wrote her notes. These findings led Roozen (2008) to argue, "extracurricular and curricular literate activities … are so profoundly interconnected that it becomes difficult to see where one ends and others begin" (p. 27).

Roozen's work came to mind when I sat down one-on-one with these football players. I wondered how the literate practices of football—reading and learning plays, for example—might connect with the literate practices stressed in our first-year writing course. With that, I had a thesis topic. With Roozen's guidance, I designed my study. I received IRB permission to interview first-year football players who were in both the STEP cohort and our first-year composition course. With the permission of the lead instructor, I pulled students out of class to ask about their football and academic literacies.

And now the interruption—an interruption that stalled and redirected my research trajectory for over five years.

I had already interviewed Sam (a pseudonym) twice. He was a first-year defensive back whose cousin played in the same position in the NFL. His role on the Auburn Tigers' defense was to cover the wide receivers and stop them catching the ball. Therefore, his job was preventative wherein he moved his body in reaction to his opponent's body. In thinking about academic writing and the rhetorical moves a writer makes to sketch an argument, Sam was anticipating and reacting to counter-arguments. I wondered if he might be able to transfer his knowledge in preventing his opponents from making a successful play to preventing his rhetorical opponents from making a successful argument. When he first granted me an interview, I didn't have my specific interview questions or research question fleshed out. I embraced, as I do now with my qualitative interviewing, an emergent research design where I work from an open-ended interview format (Creswell, 2014). I want the participant's responses to guide our conversation—and I use that noun intentionally; I very much want to craft a conversation with a person rather than interview a research subject. The upside of this approach is that I can productively react to false starts and tangents—the messiness of human conversation. The downside is that I often need to schedule follow-up interviews. After I chatted with Sam the first time, I transcribed our conversation. More questions came to mind.

I was walking to the first-year writing class when I saw Sam making his way up the stairs into Haley Center, one of the larger academic buildings on Auburn's campus. His backpack was slung over his shoulder. He was dressed in sweatpants, a T-shirt, Under Armour shoes. I pitched another interview to him. And he answered *no*. But as I wrote in the opening, the *no* was more than a *no*. It was a tired, annoyed *no*. The sort of *no* a participant gives to a researcher when the researcher is just too much. Sam's *no* started a landslide of more, as if his decision to turn down an interview request from his teacher emboldened the other student-athletes to say *no*, too. Sam dropped out of the study. Trey dropped out. So did Justin, Kris, Donte, Alex, and Casey. They allowed me to keep the interview transcriptions I had already compiled, but the data collection was at an end.

Professional organizations release important statements of research ethics. For my field of composition studies, the Conference on College Composition and

Communication's (2015) *Guidelines for the ethical conduct of research in composition studies* guides my research design (for full disclosure, I helped author the 2015 revision of the original 2003 statement). Statements like these rightly declare that participants can freely withdraw from a study at any point. These variously stated declarations are grounded in federal guidelines dictating the conduct of human subject research. The student-athletes in my study legally and ethically held the agency to make this decision. But, as I reflect on this moment, and as I reflect on moments where I more successfully wove student-athlete participants into my qualitative research, I find areas where my research design, particularly my sampling and recruitment strategies, may have planted the seed that eventually grew into participants' frustration with my research and, ultimately, their decision to withdraw from my study.

When seven first-year football players withdrew from the study that eventually became my MA thesis, I continued my work on student-athlete writers. I could keep their data but could not collect any more. But for my Ph.D. dissertation and my first few publications, I focused on NCAA academic policy (Rifenburg, 2016), the rhetoric of the term *student-athlete* (Rifenburg, 2015), and the construction of college football plays (Rifenburg, 2014). For the next five years after that *no*, I did not interview a single student-athlete, even though all my research, writing, and thinking were on student-athlete writers. I was afraid to try. I was afraid that I had encroached too much on this unique student population. I regained my confidence as a researcher in 2014 when I spent one year embedded in the men's basketball team at the University of North Georgia. I hung out in the locker room, rode the bus to away games, sat on the bench during games, and interviewed players throughout the year. And again in 2017 when I taught a class where 25 of the 26 students were student-athletes, and I interviewed three baseball players about their experience in the class.

My research trajectory followed this unexpected arc because I struggled to learn how to incorporate student-athletes ethically and legally into my research. I regained my research footing when I learned I was really struggling with sampling, recruitment, identifying, and working with gatekeepers and key informants.

Gatekeepers and key informants

Jones, Torres, and Arminio (2014) suggest that "participant selection ... is perhaps the most understudied and least understood dimension of the qualitative research process" (p. 106). They follow up this claim by pushing readers to see how sampling is tied into the larger picture of research design, and specifically how sampling leads to data collection methods like interview questions. After providing guidance on sampling criteria and sample size, Jones and colleagues land on sampling strategies. In this section, they introduce key terms guiding how I reapproached my qualitative work on student-athlete writers. They define sampling strategy as "a method that implies a plan for identifying those who may shed light on a phenomenon of interest to the researcher" (p. 115). For my work, the phenomenon of interest was clear, even when I was fumbling in the dark as a young qualitative researcher at Auburn: disconnects and synergies between the literate practices of football and the literate practices of first-year writing courses. I knew I wanted to ground my case study spatially (STEP at Auburn University) and temporally (summer and fall of 2008). I knew I wanted to focus on a specific population operating within this space and time (first-year football players). Because I identified my phenomenon and because I bounded my case study, I knew whom I wanted to interview. But that wasn't enough. I needed to gain access to these student-athletes. Glesne (2011, p. 57) invited us to understand *gaining access* as the gerund *gaining* implies: an ongoing action that

> involves acquisition of consent to go where you want, to observe what you want, talk to whomever you want, obtain and read whatever documents you require, and do all of this for whatever period of time is necessary for you to satisfy your research purposes.

A researcher's dream, indeed. Research projects rise and fall because of access. My work with the football players at Auburn got off the ground because I had *some* access. I worked with the student-athletes during the summer. I co-taught their class in the fall. To be fair, researching my own students—even though I was not the teacher of record—comes fraught with challenges. The CCCC *Guidelines* caution against researching one's own students. If one decides to ignore this advice, they suggest using "measures to avoid coercion or perceived coercion" (Conference on College Composition and Communication, 2015). Seidman (2013), too, cautions against such easy access. He writes "the easier the access, the more complicated the interview" (p. 44). The STEP cohort constituted this easy access. My easy access research project was interrupted not because I was interviewing my own students, however. Even though I had easy access, I had only partial access. I worked with only one dimension of these student-athlete writers. Student-athletes are a hyphenated population who balance *student* and *athlete*. I had access only to the *student* dimension of my research participants. For some research projects, this would work. But my phenomenon of interest—disconnects and synergies between the literate practices of football and the literate practices of first-year writing courses—demanded that I balance the hyphenated identity marker of student-athlete, that I gain access to the *athlete* aspect of my research participants' identity. I never did because I never negotiated with enough key informants (Patton, 2002) or gatekeepers (Seidman, 2013; Jones et al., 2014).

As the name implies, gatekeepers are an initial obstacle to the population a researcher wants to study. They typically provide initial approval or denial and then help the researcher make connections with the population. Seidman (2013) wrote that gatekeepers "control access to people [and] can range from the absolutely legitimate (to be respected) to the self-declared (to be avoided)" (p. 47). Once the researcher gains permission from (a) legitimate gatekeeper(s) and starts an initial conversation with the population, the gatekeeper(s) fade into the background and receive a nod of thanks in the acknowledgements section of the subsequent article, book, or presentation. Key informants operate more closely with the researcher and act as a liaison between the researcher and the research population. Patton (2002) described key informants as "people who are particularly knowledgeable about the inquiry setting and articulate about their knowledge—people whose insights can prove particularly useful in helping an observer understand what is happening and why" (p. 321).

At Auburn, I failed to identify enough gatekeepers or any key informants. Only three gatekeepers knew about my research: Auburn's review board on human-subject research; my thesis director, Michelle, who signed off on my IRB application, directed the first-year writing program at Auburn at the time, and initially recommended me to work with STEP; and Julie, a liaison between Student Affairs and the Athletics Department, who coordinated STEP in previous years. Who is missing here? Anyone in the Athletics Department—at any level. No coaches, no graduate assistant coaches, no athletics advisors, no one in athletics administration. Most high-profile athletics programs, like Auburn's, hire academic specialists to work with just one sport at a time. None of the personnel hired to support the academic side of the football players at Auburn knew directly of my work. Part of this decision was intentional. At the time, academics and athletics at Auburn did not play well together. One person within the Athletics Department had a reputation for being particularly thorny toward academics. This person worked as a high-ranking academic advisor for the football team and battled departments over student-athletes missing classes, needing to reschedule exams, failing to attend during office hours—all the common challenges that come with student-athletes balancing a full course load with a full athletic calendar. Both Michelle and Julie rolled their eyes when talking about this person, and they made the decision to keep them in the dark.

Michelle, Julie, and I made the decision to gain only the legally and ethically required level of permissions so my MA research could continue and I could complete it within a year. Legally and ethically, only the institutional board overseeing human-subjects research and the student-athletes themselves needed to know of my work. But, because I never enlisted anyone in the Athletics Department as a gatekeeper, I struggled to receive buy-in from the student-athletes and the depth and impact of my research suffered. Because I failed to identify enough gatekeepers, I never identified a key informant. As Patton (2002) explained, key informants help "an observer understand what is happening and why" (p. 321). For my research, a key informant might have been a person close to the student-athletes who could explain odd things I might observe, help me think through curious responses from the student-athletes, and encourage the student-athletes to find the time to talk with me. Here, a graduate assistant coach or an athletics academic advisor (many of whom are former student-athletes) would have worked well. These people are close to student-athletes but not too far up the chain of command (unlike gatekeepers); I could have worked closely with such key informants throughout my research. I was not a student-athlete at a high-profile school. I have never played football. I did not struggle academically or with my writing. I cannot read football plays. My positionality as a white, middle-class, male academic comes with limitations, and a key informant would have added depth and nuance to my research.

My research was interrupted because I did not develop these important relationships. When I picked up the student-athlete-focused qualitative thread of my research again at the University of North Georgia, I began with a key informant. I took the faculty athletics representative out to lunch.

Gatekeepers and key informants at the University of North Georgia

The University of North Georgia (UNG) is a five-campus regional university stretching across the northeast Georgia Appalachian Mountains and enrolling roughly 20,000 students. During new faculty orientation, I met the faculty athletics representative (FAR), who spoke briefly on athletics at UNG. The FAR is an NCAA-mandated position, a person who acts as a liaison between athletes and academics, and, depending on the specific university, serves a variety of positions. At UNG, Margaret Poitevint, an instructor in the Math Department, has served as FAR for many years. She advises student-athletes, attends a variety of NCAA conferences and meetings, and is an overall faculty advocate for the Athletics Department and student-athletes.

Margaret and I met for lunch a few months into my first semester at UNG. During the meal, I offered some vague ideas on interviewing players and coaches on a team. She picked up my offer with excitement, suggesting different possibilities and thinking aloud about which coach would be best to interview. We—more Margaret—landed on Chris Faulkner, the head coach of the men's basketball team. That afternoon, I was standing in Chris's office and pitched a year-long study of his team. I spoke of my background in college athletics and my interest in learning about how he teaches plays and how his players learn those plays. That afternoon, before I had even begun the necessary application for human-subjects research, Chris began talking with me about his players, his coaching philosophy, how he designs and teaches basketball plays. None of this conversation made it into the articles and book I authored on the team because Chris had not signed the consent forms. But in just one day, I had already gained more access to any college sports team than I had during my two years at Auburn and four years at Oklahoma. I gained this access because I connected with a key informant—a passionate advocate of student-athletes and faculty research.

Margaret helped me make sense of a world of which I am not a part. She updated me on the academic progress of student-athletes I taught, with the internal comings and goings of Athletics Department personnel, and with the current events animating NCAA meetings and conferences. She helped me make sense of NCAA academic policy, locate student-athlete data and Athletics Department data, and connect with new Athletics Department personnel. She also encouraged student-athletes to answer my emails requesting interviews and, when I designed a first-year writing class just for student-athletes based on learning theories of writing-related transfer, she encouraged the student-athletes to sign-up. Twenty-five did.

Margaret also served as a conduit to the gatekeepers: Lindsey Reeves, the athletics director, Derek Suranie, the associate athletics director, and Chris Faulkner, the head coach. I had only brief email communications with Lindsey and Derek, but both knew about and supported my work because Margaret advocated on my behalf. Through locating a key informant who led me to these three gatekeepers, I completed a book on student-athlete writers and published two articles on the men's basketball team at UNG. This work is full of the student-athlete experience: pictures I took of student-athletes during practice and sitting in my office working on their writing; basketball plays hand drawn by the players. A focus on the individual student-athlete experience was back in my research for the first time in almost a decade.

The 2014–2015 season with the men's basketball team at UNG was the most in-depth, ethnographically rich research I have undertaken. I sat side-by-side with the head coach on the bus traveling to a road game. I stood inside a team huddle during a timeout in a game. I hung out in the locker room as the coach delivered an impassioned speech during halftime. This deep dive was only possible because I identified and worked with gatekeepers and a key informant, all of whom operated at various levels within the Athletics Department. Margaret was my advocate with upper administrators. Besides shaking Lindsey's hand and exchanging a few pleasantries, I never had a substantial conversation with the head of athletics at UNG. But Lindsey approved my work through Margaret, whose energy and extroversion sold my research to the men's basketball coach. Margaret and I simply walked into his office, whereupon Margaret, with me standing in the doorway, pitched me and my work with her ebullient air. Chris and I subsequently formed a friendship. We still text and when one of his players passed away last year, right before the start of the season, we spent a long time talking in the hallway late one afternoon. But Chris is the head coach, a position that comes with a high level of responsibility and not much time to answer endless questions from an academic researcher over the course of the season. I also connected with the assistant coach, Josh Travis, and the graduate assistant coach, Josh Hawkins. The latter printed out practice schedules, explained drills to me during practice, talked with me in the Athletics Department hallway about the upcoming opponents. He encouraged the players to come by my office for interviews. In addition, I connected with the team's head physical trainer, Matt Daniels. This relationship came in handy. During a game, one of the players, Tanner Plemmons, dropped to his knees. An opponent's finger had caught him in the eye. Matt ran onto the court and helped Tanner to the bench. As the game continued, he conducted some quick eye tests. Tanner then headed to the locker room with Matt. He had partially detached his retina. Matt spent the whole ride home trying to locate an ophthalmologist at 11 p.m. on a Saturday night. Because I had connected with Matt, I had access, not to Tanner's personal medical data, but to the anatomical terms to describe an eye injury for my research notes. I learned about the recovery process and timeline. The year-long research project was predicated on developing and working within a network of relationships to learn about the mundane (when does practice start on Thursday?) and the medical (what might one's vision be like following retinal surgery?). This research happened through gatekeepers and key informants.

The possibilities of recruitment strategies

I quoted Jones, Torres, and Arminio (2014) earlier but return to their point: "participant selection ... is perhaps the most understudied and least understood dimension of the qualitative research process" (p. 106). In reading about research design from across a broad range of social science fields, I find many often cover sampling to the extent of helping readers think about who and how many to select as research participants and why. Jones and colleagues are correct in that I have not come across a social science research methods book that discusses gaining access in depth that speaks to the complex rhetorical moves a researcher makes to identify and then verbally connect with gatekeepers or key informants. For instance, does a researcher approach a gatekeeper in person or via email? How does a researcher differentiate between a legitimate gatekeeper and a self-declared gatekeeper (Patton, 2002)? What is the researcher's opening line and how specific do they need to be about the proposed work? What role—if any—does the gatekeeper play in the data collection, data analysis, writing, revising, and publishing of the research? How often does the researcher update the gatekeeper about the research, if at all? Sure, these questions don't come with definitive answers. But social science methodologies could do more than caution against easy access, opine on sample size, and encourage the use of gatekeepers and key informants.

When I have come across advice on the hows, it tends to be tucked tidily into a finished study. To be fair, such venues often do not allow more than this brief account. A leading journal in English studies, *College English*, published a special issue on digital humanities and historiography. Ridolfo's (2013) article in that issue stood out because of the care he showed in describing how, as a scholar at the University of Kentucky, he began a productive and reciprocal partnership with Samaritan elders in the Middle East. Ridolfo devoted five paragraphs to detailing the beginning of this partnership, even including his original email to Samaritan elder Benyamim Tsedaka and Tsedaka's email reply. Those paragraphs illustrated the serendipity of human-subject research (Goggin & Goggin, 2018), by which chance meetings can lead to fruitful partnerships. They also displayed the finesse a researcher needs on the front end of a project. As Milner (2007) argued, "how education research is conducted may be just as important as what is actually discovered" (p. 397). Even before writing interview questions, transcribing and coding the interview, writing up the findings, and placing these findings within existing literature and through a theoretical framework, researchers need to think through the rhetorically challenging task of locating and connecting with gatekeepers, key informants, and research participants. All researchers move through these processes, but they are often elided from the final published study. Ridolfo (2013) showed the front-end work he put into the project and this provided an insight into the hows of participant recruitment strategies.

My participant recruitment strategies are not definitive, nor transferable to all contexts. But despite the best efforts of research methods books that lay out the process as an easily digestible chapter-by-chapter heuristic, social science researchers need to do a better job of embracing, writing about, and discussing the messiness that is human-subject research. We can give direct advice on interview questions (Seidman, 2013) and coding data (Saldaña, 2012), so we write and read books on this topic. But participant recruitment strategies? That's messy work. Instead of jettisoning it from our research methods books, let's talk about it, because it is the foundation onto which we erect our methods, our findings, our implications. This collection is one important contribution to a small body of scholarship that invites us into the mess.

Our participant recruitment strategies develop first through partnering with gatekeepers and key informants. But as we move forward with identifying and developing these relationships, I end this chapter with a note of caution based on my research experiences: how we bring participants into our research via our gatekeepers and key informants will always be imbricated with issues of coercion and power dynamics. In my case, these issues are intensified by the racial component: I, a white academic, am researching at-risk African-American, male student-athletes. To undertake this kind of research, I need to adopt what Tillman (2002) refers to as "culturally sensitive research approaches" (p. 3). Like Tillman, Milner (2007) does not believe a researcher must come from the cultural or racial community in which they do their research as long as they are "actively engaged, thoughtful, and forthright regarding tensions that can surface" (p. 388). The United States has a long history of misrepresenting, exploiting, and ignoring people of color in education research and federally funded scientific research (Reverby, 2009). I step into research projects aware of this history, particularly how it might play out through issues of coercion and power dynamics animated by race. In my research, a head coach and athletics director (both of whom were white) directed student-athletes (most of whom were black) to me. Federal guidelines, professional organizational guidelines, and institutional guidelines clearly state the dangers of coercion in human-subject research. But these guidelines don't suggest researchers can eliminate coercion. Instead, for example, Title 45 of the Code of Federal Regulations states researchers should "minimize the possibility of coercion" (Government Publishing Office, 2011, § 46.116). I am not dismissing the very real problems that surface through coercion; nor am I making a fallacious argument that, since coercion will always be present, we shouldn't worry about it. What I am suggesting is that when educational researchers dive into the messiness that is human-subject research, we also jump into the messiness of human constructions and hierarchies. When my colleague and I interviewed army ROTC cadets at my university (Rifenburg & Forester, 2018), I needed the permission of the colonel, who then encouraged the cadets to talk with me. When I interviewed students who were minors, I needed the permission of their parents. When my colleague researched prisoners' writing (Berry, 2017), he needed the permission of the warden. And so on. As we encounter possible areas of coercion, we can take steps to grant our research participants more agency through allowing them to select their own pseudonyms, modify, delete, or add research questions, read and respond to early drafts of our findings, have a say in which images we include in public facing documents. Or we can create a space where participants gain agency so they can just leave the study whenever and for whatever reason. We can allow the participants' own language to guide the coding process through in vivo coding (Saldaña, 2012). We can ensure their speech patterns are represented stylistically and syntactically. The gatekeepers and key informants—the people who can wield undue influence—help researchers gain access to populations. But the gatekeepers and key informants do not play an active role in the data collection, analysis, and dissemination. It is through this process of inviting our participants into our research in concrete ways that discussions of participant recruitment strategies may dull—but never eliminate—the very real messiness of human-subject research exacerbated by a dominant race researching a marginalized one. Milner (2007) called for all researchers to be actively engaged, thoughtful, and forthright regarding tensions that can arise. The opportunities I touch on in this paragraph for bringing our participants more fully into our research—from design to circulation—answer his call. We speak back to issues of coercion and power dynamics intensified by race by bringing our participants into the mess with us and then collectively making sense of the work we are doing together.

References

Conference on College Composition and Communication. (2015). *Guidelines for the ethical conduct of research in composition studies*. Retrieved March 1, 2019 from: http://cccc.ncte. org/cccc/resources/positions/ethicalconduct.

Creswell, J. W. (2014). *Research design: Qualitative, quantitative, and mixed methods approaches*, 4th edition. Thousand Oaks, CA: Sage.

Berry, P. W. (2017). *Doing time, writing lives: Refiguring literacy in higher education*. Carbondale, IL: Southern Illinois University Press.

Glesne, C. (2011). *Becoming qualitative researchers: An introduction*, 4th edition. Boston, MA: Pearson.

Goggin, M. D., & Goggin P. N. (Eds.). (2018). *Serendipity in rhetoric, writing, and literacy research*. Logan: Utah State University Press.

Government Publishing Office. (2011). *Title 45: Public welfare*. Retrieved March 1, 2019 from: www.govinfo.gov/content/pkg/CFR-2011-title45-vol1/pdf/CFR-2011-title45-vol1.pdf.

Jones, S. R., Torres, V., & Arminio, J. (2014). *Negotiating the complexities of qualitative research in higher education*, 2nd edition. New York: Routledge.

Milner, H. R., IV. (2007). Race, culture, and researchers positionality: Working through dangers seen, unseen, and unforeseen. *Educational Researcher*, 36(7), 388–400.

Patton, M. Q. (2002). *Qualitative research and evaluation methods*, 3rd edition. Newbury Park: Sage.

Reverby, S. M. (2009). *Examining Tuskegee: The infamous Syphilis Study and its legacy*. Chapel Hill: Univeristy of North Carolina Press.

Ridolfo, J. (2013). Delivering textual diaspora: Building digital cultural repositories as rhetoric research. *College English*, 76(2), 136–152.

Rifenburg, J. M. (2014). Writing as embodied, college football plays as embodied: Extra-curricular multimodal composing. *Composition Forum*, 24. Retrieved March 1, 2019 from: http://compositionforum.com/issue/29/writing-as-embodied.php.

Rifenburg, J. M. (2015). "Student-athletes" and the rhetorical consequences of naming. *Present Tense*, 4(2). Retrieved March 1, 2019 from: www.presenttensejournal.org/wp-content/uploads/2015/04/Rifenburg.pdf.

Rifenburg, J. M. (2016). Supporting the student-athlete writer: A case study of a Division I athletics writing center and NCAA academic mandates. *Writing Center Journal*, 35(2), 61–87.

Rifenburg, J. M., & Forester, B. (2018). First-year cadets' conceptions of general education writing at a senior military college. *Teaching and Learning Inquiry*, 6(1), 52–66.

Roozen, K. (2008). Journalism, poetry, stand-up comedy, and academic literacy: Mapping the interplay of curricular and extracurricular literate activities. *Journal of Basic Writing*, 27 (1), 5–34.

Roozen, K. (2010). Tracing trajectories of practice: Repurposing in one student's developing disciplinary writing processes. *Written Communication*, 27(3), 318–354.

Saldaña, J. (2012). *The coding manual for qualitative researchers*, 2nd edition. Thousand Oaks, CA: Sage.

Seidman, I. (2013). *Interviewing as qualitative research: A guide for researchers in education and the social sciences*, 4th edition. New York: Teachers College Press.

Smagorinsky, P. (2008). The method section as conceptual epicenter in constructing social science research reports. *Written Communication*, 25(3), 389–411.

Tillman, L. C. (2002). Culturally sensitive research approaches: An African-American perspective. *Educational Researcher*, 31(9), 3–12.

5

NAVIGATING ADMINISTRATOR– RESEARCHER ROLES

Developing recruitment strategies for conducting programmatic assessment with diverse undergraduate and graduate writers

Tanita Saenkhum and Joseph Anthony Wilson

Introduction

Joseph was nearly finished interviewing a graduate student—we will call him Jibran—about his perceptions of a university's procedures for placing international students into academic English writing courses. As he wrapped up the interview, he felt that it had gone exceedingly well. Jibran seemed to possess a strong understanding of the procedures, and he had offered insightful critiques of our institution's English placement exam that were based on his own experience of taking it. However, when Joseph finally moved to the typical concluding question—"Is there anything else that you would like to share?"—Jibran countered with his own questions: "So, what do you think about my English? Do you think it's good? What do I need to do to sound better?"

Joseph's initial response was to assure the student that his spoken English was very good, and he listened while Jibran shared his struggles pursuing graduate studies at an English-medium institution. Through these questions and this conversation—which were unrelated to either placement or the content of the rest of the interview—Joseph learned that Jibran had initially misunderstood the purpose of the interview. Jibran had briefly glanced at an email invitation outlining the goals of the project, and Joseph had explained the consent form and purpose of the study in detail before the interview had taken place. Still, Jibran felt that the interview was designed to assess his English ability.

Another student, Jaimie, told Joseph that talking to a lofty administrator in a formal interview about a topic as sensitive as placement "sounded miserable." He elaborated:

> I hate tests: the GRE, the TOEFL, the IELTS, the placement exam, all of them. I thought to myself, "Why would I wanna talk about those?" Then I

saw that you were a graduate student too, and when you said you could come to my office to talk about it, I thought it could be a good thing.

These stories highlight two of the major student beliefs that initially hindered our ability to recruit students to participate in our research, which resulted in delays in data collection. In this chapter, we relate our experience of conducting research that aimed to incorporate students' perspectives into continual improvements of practices to place second language (L2)/multilingual writers (those whose first or strongest language is not English) into writing courses at the University of Tennessee, Knoxville. This research was designed to (re)assess our institution's English as a Second Language (ESL) writing program's English placement procedures, which use a combination of standardized test scores (TOEFL, IELTS, SAT, and ACT) as well as an in-house English placement exam (EPE). The study consisted of qualitative interviews of students, a systematic review of the program's standardized test score ranges, and an examination of previous and current in-house written EPEs.

This project and our other work on placement (e.g., Wilson & Saenkhum, 2017) have been guided by three principles: agency, reliability/validity, and ethics. Concerning the former, we want to ensure that our placement procedures offer students opportunities for agency, or "the capacity to act or not to act, contingent upon various conditions" in their placement decisions (Saenkhum, 2016, p. 11). For administrators and teachers involved in placement, reliability and validity have also served as crucial considerations when designing assessment tools (Crusan, 2002; 2010). We also maintain that assessment must be ethical. This involves ensuring that placement procedures are transparent and thoroughly communicated to students, that assessment tools are directly linked to an institution's course placement options (Leki, 1991; Weigle, 2007), and that placement procedures are informed by the results of published and in-house empirical assessment (Polio, 1998). With these guiding principles, we have proposed a sustainable framework for assessing placement that is continual and includes students' voices in programmatic placement decisions (Saenkhum, 2016; Wilson & Saenkhum, 2017).

Given our prior experience conducting programmatic research, we did not foresee major complications carrying out our project. Still, the problems introduced above led to nearly continual interruptions in our research—from participant recruitment through all stages of data collection. In what follows, we discuss the challenges and difficulties we encountered as we pursued our research, and we share some strategies we developed in order to overcome those issues. The chapter concludes by considering some implications that other researchers carrying out programmatic assessment research in educational settings may apply in their specific contexts.

Challenges and difficulties encountered

As we began this research, we encountered multilayered obstacles that stemmed from our dual roles as administrators and researchers as well as our research methodology. Moreover, recruitment regulations stipulated by our institution's Institutional Review Board (IRB) office negatively impacted the ways we communicated our study to students in our program. Finally, students' perceptions of their English proficiency impacted participant recruitment.

A combination of administrative status and research methodology

Throughout the process of designing this study, we discussed at length in our weekly meetings how our role as program administrators (Tanita as Director and Joseph as Assistant Director of the ESL writing program) might pose some ethical dilemmas to our research, especially with participant recruitment and in using interviews in data collection. In our case, we realized that power imbalances (Polio & Friedman, 2017) and/or power relations between an administrator–researcher and L2/multilingual student participants (Donahue, 2016) might have affected students' participation. Ironically, we worried that students who chose to take part in the study might feel coerced into participating, mainly to demonstrate that they were cooperating with university administrators. We presupposed that it was also possible that students might feel that they had to say positive things about the program in order to please us when expressing their views in interviews. This, in turn, could make them feel uncomfortable about sharing their opinions or criticisms of our administrative choices. As Polio & Friedman (2017) explained, these issues related to power imbalances "have an impact on interviewee behavior and the quality of responses generated by interview questions" (p. 184). Still, we both firmly believed that interviews were necessary for our project, as they would allow us to gain in-depth information about what students thought about the program's current placement procedures and their experiences both taking an English placement exam and the course in which they were placed. Research in our field has further noted that interviews necessarily "concern people's lives in the social world and therefore inevitably involve ethical issues … [They are] inherently interested in people's personal views and often target sensitive or intimate matters" (Dörnyei, 2007, pp. 63–64). With this in mind, our initial plans for this research accounted for potential ethical issues. Nevertheless, we did not predict that students might view our interviews with them as further evaluations of their English proficiency.

Institutional regulations

Our roles as administrators and researchers conducting program assessment research posed another challenge as we worked on our IRB application. We explained in our IRB protocol that we would contact the target participants by individually emailing them an invitation to participate in an interview about their experience taking the English placement exam. However, when the IRB office responded to our recruitment procedures, they restricted us from making initial contact with students directly. The letter from the IRB office reasoned as follows:

Enrollment in a course is a protected educational record, and so investigators should not have access to these students' names and email addresses. It is preferred that a recruitment email be sent to the course instructors with a request to forward it to their students.

This stipulation had nothing to do with coercion; instead, it related to our access to students' university email accounts and enrollment statuses. Although we understood the IRB office's concern, we were honestly frustrated. To this point, we had done everything possible to disassociate our research from students' evaluated performance in their English courses. The last thing we wanted was to have the students think that the research, particularly their confidential responses, would in some way get back to their instructors. Unlike the students' instructors, we had little contact with or authority over the students or their grades. Our detailed invitation email and consent forms noted that participation in/responses to interviews would not be shared with instructors. Still, we feared this language would not be enough to overcome any false associations between our roles and those of instructors—misconceptions students might justifiably conceive upon their instructors forwarding them the study invitation email.

We ended up sending an email to instructors of our target participants, asking them to forward a carefully crafted invitation to participate in our study to their students. Once students received the invitation through their instructors, those willing to participate could contact Joseph via email to set up an interview. With this recruitment procedure, only a few students responded to the initial invitation and two reminders. We wondered if the email had only reinforced the students' perceptions of the researchers as authority figures interested in evaluating their English.

Disappointed with our limited success, we reflected on the entire recruitment procedure, trying to rationalize why students did not wish to participate in the study. For graduate students, perhaps the nature of their academic work had already overextended them to the point that time for an interview simply did not exist. For four undergraduate students taking part in the study, English course placement likely served as an enigmatic process. Moreover, since all first-year students are required to take first-year writing courses, perhaps those who abstained from participating perceived little difference between their equivalent sections of first-year writing for multilingual students and the mainstream sections. However, we learned that our assumptions were only partially accurate, as the undergraduate students who agreed to participate in interviews were often misplaced and wished to voice their concerns. Other kind-hearted first-year students simply wanted to be helpful, even if they did not understand what "placement" meant until the project and consent form were explained to them in person.

Students' perceptions of their English proficiency and misconceptions about the study

As Joseph started interviewing a few students, we discovered dissonance between our intentions for and students' receptions of our project, similar to what Dörnyei

(2007) refers to as "a clash between the researcher's and participant's interests" (p. 64). First, students' lack of confidence in their spoken English abilities became apparent when Joseph conducted the first interview with an undergraduate student whom we shall call Azamat. This student associated the placement process with his tumultuous first few weeks in the United States, when he had quickly discovered that he had overestimated his English ability. With a nervous laugh, he told Joseph, "When I took [the placement exam], I'd just been three days here. It was just very soon. At that time, I'd just arrived here. I can't even talk to someone to get, like, a burger, or a combo meal, you know?" While Azamat had been unsurprised when he was placed into a course offered by the university's intensive English program as opposed to a regular first-year writing course, he was surprised when Joseph contacted him to talk about his placement experiences. Though friendly and eager to provide good feedback in his interview, his insecurity about his English ability was initially compounded by his recollection of an exam that had, for the past year, served as a tangible marker of his own perceived struggles with the language.

Azamat's willingness to participate in an interview with Joseph ultimately stemmed from an intrinsic desire to demonstrate his improvement in English since the placement exam by having a conversation with the very "top people" (his term) who designed and implemented it. As he went through the interview, he gradually became more talkative and comfortable as Joseph continually reiterated that his English was clear and his ideas understandable. He also acknowledged, however, that many of his peers shared his insecurity about their English ability. As researchers, we had not realized that conducting interviews in English might be problematic; nor did we suppose that students' language proficiency would affect our research methodology. Students, especially undergraduate students, tended to respond to questions with short answers. In consequence, and as a common approach to interviewing, Joseph often asked them to explain their responses in order to ensure that he understood what they really wanted to express.

Other students, such as Jaimie (see above), associated considerable anxiety with high-stakes testing, such as an English placement exam. Jaimie even noted that he had opted to attend our university because he had convinced his department to waive the Graduate Record Exam (GRE) requirement for admission due to his other credentials. Joseph was not aware of these struggles/anxieties until the interview, and he dedicated extra time to explaining the informed consent and participants' rights statements to Jaimie as a result. With a better understanding of both the research project's goals and the notion of informed consent, Jaimie offered a sharply critical perspective of the English placement exam and all other standardized exams. At the end of the interview, he thanked Joseph for providing him with an opportunity to share these opinions. Until this interview, he noted, he had never felt as though administrators cared about the struggles that international students face with standardized tests. Joseph's questions and apparent understanding of those struggles had meant a lot to him.

Joseph found that other students, especially graduate students, regarded their current English writing course as a punishment for a low standardized test (TOEFL or IELTS) score and/or failure to achieve a passing score on an optional English placement exam. For a few students, this perception motivated them to participate so that they could share their opinions of the exam and growth from a writing course they had found surprisingly beneficial. Others who held this perception instead sought to wash their hands of the whole process and opted not to respond (as communicated to us through their classmates who did participate). However, some students misunderstood that, by participating in an interview, they would have to discuss their low test scores.

Given these factors and circumstances, we had to decipher each of these causes over the course of a year of research, as each of our planned stages of data collection took significantly longer than anticipated to complete. Originally, we intended to interview 60 international undergraduate and graduate students who took an English placement exam in spring 2017 and fall 2017, and we hoped to complete individual interviews with each participant within the fall semester. However, it turned out that only six students were willing to participate in the interview process due to the reasons outlined above. We then had to extend our data collection to spring 2018, and we were able to recruit ten more students (see below for how we strategized our participant recruitment). Thus far, we have interviewed 16 students.

Periodically reflecting on these challenges as we conducted our placement assessment research, we returned to Dörnyei's (2007) remarks on research ethics in which he argues that "research participants need safeguards and researchers need informed answers to ethical dilemmas" (p. 71). Dörnyei (2007) also suggests, "what we need is a contextualized and flexible approach to ethical decision making, relying more on the researchers' professional reflexivity and integrity in maintaining high standards" (p. 72). We sought to maintain such high standards by translating our guiding principles for program assessment research, including placement—a desire to preserve student agency, reliability/validity, and ethics—to our assessment of our own research approach. This assessment practice ultimately proved vital for developing strategies to address the difficulties we encountered when engaging in programmatic assessment and educational research.

Strategies developed

We spent many hours in Tanita's office brainstorming different approaches to addressing issues related to participant recruitment, strategizing ways to collect data through interviews, and privately lamenting our frustrations with the IRB office. We found that these efforts helped mitigate the difficulties and challenges we faced during our research. As problems arose, we made some adjustments along the way in order to maintain our commitment to advocating for, promoting, and including the voices of diverse student populations (Saenkhum, 2016) in educational research as well as to comply with the IRB office.

As we hashed out various potential strategies, we kept returning to our major concern: that our association and administrative capacities with the ESL writing program might complicate participant recruitment—a concern that was exacerbated by the IRB office's requirement that we must recruit students through their instructors. We decided that Tanita should excuse herself from participant recruitment, given her role as Director of the ESL writing program. Instead, she asked Joseph to contact the course instructors of the target student participants, sending all email invitations to them. In all of this correspondence, Joseph highlighted his position as a graduate student who specialized in second language writing and writing program administration, and explained that he was conducting program assessment research. He also noted that his role as Assistant Director of the ESL writing program was funded in part by a research assistantship through the English Department, and that he did not have direct oversight of the program's instructors. Our rationale for adopting this approach was twofold. First, the course instructors would not feel that they were forced by their supervisor to take part in the recruitment. Second, by having Joseph communicate and conduct all of the interviews with the student participants, we hoped to mitigate the latter's discomfort with discussing exam scores as well as their perceptions of the university's placement policy with administrators.

After Joseph contacted the target students' instructors, we periodically reached out to them to see if they had distributed the consent forms and email invitations to their students. The instructors responded that they had done so, and asked if any students had opted to participate. Many of these instructors volunteered as raters for our spring and fall placement exams each year, and they often also expressed investment in improving the process/procedures. When we told them about our recruitment difficulties, they invited Joseph to their classrooms to explain the purpose of the study, the value that the program placed on students' perceptions, and his experiences as a graduate student researcher. We agreed that Joseph's visits to the classrooms might offer a friendly face that could potentially ease some students' anxiety or uncertainty about participation. Before we proceeded with this recruitment strategy, we revised and resubmitted our approved IRB protocol, explaining our rationale for the new recruitment plan. In this, we explained:

> In addition to recruiting student participants via their instructors as stated in our approved IRB, we will have Joseph Wilson (co-investigator) visit the target students' classrooms to introduce the study to the students and invite them to participate in an interview.

After our revised IRB protocol was approved, Joseph visited the classrooms of the target student participants. On the first of these visits, the instructor introduced him as "a graduate student in the English Department who researches second language writing." Although the students knew that Joseph was also Assistant Director of the ESL writing program, the "graduate student" title stuck. Joseph briefly explained the project and emphasized that students' participation would remain anonymous and that participation (or lack thereof) would not impact their grades in any way. This was to ensure that students did not feel pressured to participate by the presence of their instructor.

When Joseph asked if there were any questions, one graduate student immediately raised his hand and asked:

STUDENT: So, is this part of your graduate research then?
JOSEPH: Yeah, I'm a graduate student in the English Department, and placement is part of my research.
STUDENT: Well, I get that. I have a hard enough time even getting my own lab partners to help me with my research. You can put me down for this interview.

> Several other students laughed and nodded in agreement, and Joseph felt relieved. These students were all doing their own research and understood the process. He left the classroom with five students' contact information, all of whom ultimately participated in the study. Joseph then attended several other sections populated by international graduate students, where students offered similar responses and agreed to participate.

When Joseph visited sections of first-year writing that enrolled undergraduate students, he received a rather different reception. While the graduate students both understood that research is an essential component of academic work and largely viewed Joseph as one of their peers, the undergraduate students were initially unable to perceive the benefits of participating in a qualitative study. We further inferred from their timidity and unwillingness to refer to Joseph by his first name that they regarded him as a lofty authority figure. We therefore reconsidered how he should present himself to these students and frame the project. First, we decided that he should immediately highlight that he would not be sharing any information garnered from interviews with the instructors, and he should reaffirm that the instructors played no role in the research project. We wanted to ensure that students perceived the project as unrelated to their course, even though the IRB stipulations had precluded us from contacting them without first going through their instructors. We further decided to emphasize to students that participation would in no way impact their grades. Since fewer undergraduate students had chosen to challenge their placement by taking an optional English placement exam, more time was needed to explain both the concept of placement and how students' opinions might help with the assessment of placement procedures. In total, Joseph visited six sections of English writing courses that enrolled undergraduate or graduate international students.

Joseph followed up with all of the students who offered their contact information after his classroom visits, and some provided times when they would be free for an interview. Graduate student interviews often resulted in candid conversations about the program's placement procedures and the English placement exam. Most graduate students appeared quite comfortable sharing their experiences—either positive or negative. One explained his motivation to do so by saying, "When I realized that you were a graduate student like me, I went ahead and participated." Graduate students often offered such comments, and they represented a stark change from many students' initial hesitancy to take part in our study. Moreover, many graduate students (especially in the fall 2017 semester) wanted to ask Joseph questions about the university more broadly and chat about the aspects of US culture they found surprising, strange, or intriguing. Several asked to connect on social media, through which he was later invited to have a meal or hang out with their friend groups. Although all of the interviewees were aware of his role in the ESL writing program, this shift in attitude came as students realized that he was also their peer as a graduate student, and that he and Tanita both genuinely cared about improving the program for current and incoming L2/multilingual students through their research. At the time of writing (late 2018), Joseph considers many of these students to be his friends, although he kept a professional distance until after data collection so as not to influence the students' responses during their interviews.

During the interviews with undergraduate students, many participants informed Joseph that their initial hesitancy to take part in our study was tied to their lack of confidence in their own spoken English ability. In response, we reminded students that we were not there to judge their English proficiency, but that we hoped to improve our program's placement practices so that they could take courses tailored to their English proficiency needs. Their false perceptions were rarely linked to the consent form or the study title; instead, they were due to a perceived direct association between the study and the students' English courses. In nearly every interview with individual undergraduate students, they would ask Joseph something to the effect of "How is my English?," "Can you understand me?," or "Is my speaking alright?" In response, Joseph would praise the students for their English ability, highlighting the fact that they were succeeding in university-level English-instructed courses. Phrases like "Your English is great, and I'm not here to critique it" or "Your English is so, so much better than my Chinese" quickly ameliorated any concerns the students had about their English proficiency. A few undergraduate students even asked for pointers on how they could improve their fluency, and explained that one of their motivations to attend the interview was to practice their speaking with an experienced English teacher.

Conclusion

The opening stories of Joseph's interactions with two students—Jibran and Jaimie—highlight two of the major student beliefs that initially hindered our ability to recruit students to participate in our research. Jibran misunderstood the purpose of the interview, believing that participation would offer him an "authoritative" evaluation of his English proficiency. To that end, he was willing to overcome the sensitivity he associated with talking about his placement. Jaimie, on the other hand, associated his negative feelings about standardized testing with the administrators who required these exams, so the idea of talking to those administrators was unappealing to him. In these cases and many others, student participants perceived the power relations between themselves and us, as researchers–administrators. This dissonance posed challenges as we conducted our program assessment research, especially with L2/multilingual students.

By sharing these difficulties and the ways that we addressed them, we want to provide other researchers with insights into the complications that may arise when conducting research into sensitive administrative, educational, and/or policy topics in relation to their diverse L2/multilingual student populations. Our experience conducting program assessment research as administrators demonstrates that researchers with a higher status than participants need to consider how these power imbalances influence research productivity. As evidenced in our case, at first some student participants did not agree to be interviewed, partly because the email invitation was sent to them from administrators of the writing program via their course instructors. This hierarchical power impacted students' decision-making. As a result, we were able to convince only a few students to take part in the interview. However, more were willing to participate after Joseph visited classes to introduce the project and once they realized that he was also a graduate student conducting research as part of his studies. This suggested that how we positioned ourselves played a significant role in students' involvement and engagement in our research.

In a few cases, we also found that students struggled to comprehend the legalistic, IRB language used in consent forms, and we decided that we could have made the form more accessible. Terms such as "placement procedures" and "assessment" carried different connotations for some students, especially undergraduate students, who were less aware of the university's different first-year writing course options and placement practices. With this in mind, when Joseph visited the target participants' classrooms, especially those of undergraduate students, he felt the need to explain in detail the goals of the study, the nature of their involvement in the research, and the ways that involvement could contribute to the program's improvement of placement practices.

Working on this project enabled us to become more aware of "the effects of language of the interview" (Polio & Friedman, 2017, p. 185), which have not been a focus of discussion in research methodology in fields such as second language writing research. Our project collected interview data from students whose first or strongest language was not English, and we conducted the interviews in English. However, we did not realize that, as Polio & Friedman (2017) have pointed out, the use of interview language can cause issues related to communication, including students' tendency to provide very brief answers. In order to ensure that students' answers reflected their actual attitudes toward our institution's placement procedures, Joseph often asked them to explain and elaborate on their responses.

Communication-related issues also connected to students' lack of confidence in their spoken English; we provided a combination of continual encouragement during the interviews as well as several reminders that we were not trying to evaluate students' English proficiency. Joseph often stressed the goals of the study as separate from the students' coursework and testing and provided frequent encouragement to them about their strengths in speaking English. We decided that this was necessary at all stages of data collection—from introducing the study via email or in person, to carrying out the interviews, to responding to students' questions after the interviews. We realize that students' language proficiency is not always an issue, but we urge researchers working with diverse student populations to consider "its potential effect on interviews," as suggested by Polio & Friedman (2017, p. 186).

We also found that Joseph's dual roles as graduate student and Assistant Director of the ESL writing program allowed us to reduce the distance that students generally perceived between themselves and their administrators. As a graduate student himself, Joseph was able to create a low-stakes environment in which student participants were willing to share their honest views about our institution's placement procedures with someone they often perceived as a peer. From this experience, we recommend that researchers working from positions of authority—program administrators and policy makers or otherwise—collaborate with trained graduate students.

Although we were unable to remove the obstacles to our research, the strategies we developed aided us in mitigating these issues and enabled us to pursue reliable, valid, and ethical research. As we found that conducting programmatic assessment research inherently raises issues related to power relations, we encourage other researchers to maintain cognizance of these issues as they design their research methodology and consider who should participate in various areas of data collection, participant recruitment, and so on. We hope that our experience will provide other researchers with some guidance in how to examine sensitive administrative, educational, and/or policy topics in relation to their diverse student populations.

References

Crusan, D. (2002). An assessment of ESL writing placement assessment. *Assessing Writing*, 8 (1), 17–30.

Crusan, D. (2010). *Assessment in the second language writing classroom*. Ann Arbor: University of Michigan Press.

Donahue, C. (2016). What is WPA research? In R. Malenczyk (Ed.), *A rhetoric for writing program administrators* (pp. 446–459). Anderson, SC: Parlor Press.

Dörnyei, Z. (2007). *Research methods in applied linguistics*. Oxford: Oxford University Press.

Leki, I. (1991). A new approach to advanced ESL placement testing. *WPA: Writing Program Administration*, 14(3), 53–68.

Polio, C. (1998). Examining the written product in L2 writing research: A taxonomy of measures and analyses. Paper presented at the Symposium on Second Language Writing, Purdue University, West Lafayette, IN, September 25.

Polio, C., & Friedman, D. A. (2017). *Understanding, evaluating, and conducting second language writing research*. New York: Routledge.

Saenkhum, T. (2016). *Decisions, agency, and advising: Key issues in the placement of multilingual writers into first-year composition courses*. Logan: Utah State University Press.

Weigle, S. C. (2007). Teaching writing teachers about assessment. *Journal of Second Language Writing*, 16(3), 194–209.

Wilson, J. A., & Saenkhum, T. (2017). Continual assessing placement procedures for multilingual writers: A sustainable framework for placement. Paper presented at the Council of Writing Program Administrators Conference, Knoxville, TN, July.

PART 1 DISCUSSION QUESTIONS AND ACTIVITIES

Discussion questions for Chapter 2: The wheels of bureaucracy go round and round

1. Kendi Ho's chapter describes multiple attempts to gain access to the data needed for research. What was the most surprising aspect of these attempts to apply for a data sharing agreement? Would you have done the same? Why or why not?
2. Thinking about a future research project, how will you gain access to the data you desire? Does the project involve multiple sites? Are you an insider or outsider at the data collection site(s)? What do you need to do to gain access to complete your research project? Who can help you gain access? If you cannot gain access, what is an alternate plan for your study?

Discussion questions for Chapter 3: Research methods for reaching urban students from groups underrepresented in STEM disciplines

1. Steven McGee, Randi McGee-Tekula, Lucia Dettori, Andrew M. Rasmussen, and Ronald I. Greenberg describe how their initial dataset was not representative of the students in their study site. Thinking about your own research, are there individuals who are less likely to participate in your study for reasons similar to theirs?
2. How might an emphasis on the ethics of "do no harm" contribute to this inequity?
3. McGee and colleagues detail their proactive ethics approach, which involved incentives such as a pizza party if 90 percent of the students in a particular class returned their consent forms, regardless of whether they agreed to participate in the study. Taking a proactive ethics approach, how might you encourage equitable participation and representation in your study?

Discussion questions for Chapter 4: Chasing the team: participant recruitment strategies for qualitative research into student-athlete writers

1. J. Michael Rifenburg describes the importance of gatekeepers and key informants. Who are some gatekeepers and key informants that can help you during sampling and recruitment of participants in your own research project?
2. Imagine you are sitting down for your initial face-to-face meeting with a gatekeeper. Pitch your research project to this gatekeeper, keeping in mind that they might not understand the jargon of your discipline and may look upon you with skeptical eyes. How would you describe your credibility as a researcher? How would you describe the anticipated benefits of your research? How would you describe what it is that you want to research?
3. What issues of coercion do you anticipate encountering with your research participants? How might you navigate these issues?

Discussion questions for Chapter 5: Navigating administrator–researcher roles: developing recruitment strategies for conducting programmatic assessment with diverse undergraduate and graduate writers

1. Tanita Saenkhum and Joseph Anthony Wilson recount their experiences as administrators conducting programmatic assessment and placement research, which posed several challenges related to power relations, recruitment, and data collection. Considering your own research plans, what power dynamics or hierarchies are present? Who is in a position of power over your participants? As a representative of a university, are you in a position of power?
2. What are some ways these power dynamics might affect your study?
3. What are some other strategies you can plan to overcome potential issues tied to power imbalances in your study?

Part 1 activity

Beyond the IRB: ethics of (non-)participation in research

When preparing an IRB protocol, researchers are asked to explain how their research process will protect the privacy and confidentiality of participants. Often, new researchers get trapped in what can feel like the classic carnival whack-a-mole game, with each protection bringing up new management concerns. This activity will engage the reader in a contextual analysis of their planned methods and data management strategies. Using role-play to reveal potential repercussions should privacy or confidentiality be breached, readers should consider the limitations to the scholarly and worldly significance should they opt for less risky (e.g., exempt) approaches.

Scenario 1

A writing teacher completing her doctorate wants to research how students respond to different types of peer review—where students read and give feedback on each other's work—in her classroom. She plans to have students complete traditional peer review in the classroom in a face-to-face format, followed by a fully online version, and finally a hybrid (online and face-to-face) version. Her IRB places special restrictions on research on her own students, saying she cannot know who consented to participate in a study until after the semester.

Role-play a discussion between the student and her advisor exploring how she might modify her project to meet this requirement and explore what alternatives she might have. Explore the advantages and disadvantages of each approach you come up with in the role-play.

Scenario 2

A research team is interested in observing classrooms at a local high school and interviewing teachers and students about their learning experiences as part of a project focused on how undocumented immigrant students are being supported in their schools. The district IRB mandates that the team obtain parental consent forms from every student in each class they plan to observe. To complicate this process, the principal informs the team that the term "investigator" in the consent forms may scare off parents who are nervous about crackdowns on undocumented immigration.

Role-play a discussion between the research team members on how they might continue with their study and collect a meaningful sample of participants. What modifications might they make to their study? What arguments might they make to the IRB to get them to reconsider their policies?

PART 2

Relationships across contexts: geographical, cultural, political, institutional

6

THE PREDICAMENTS OF "BEING THERE"

Conflict and emotional labor

Romeo García

Introduction

In 2014, I was a graduate student at Syracuse University preparing to do qualitative research. In scope and breadth, it would be multi-sited. Both the idea that there is a rhetoric of the everyday (Cintron, 1997; Duffy, 2007; Guerra, 1998) and that culture can be read as a text (Geertz, 1973) inspired me to conduct a study on place-based rhetorics, literacies, and identities in the Lower Rio Grande Valley (LRGV) of Texas for my dissertation. One research method I found appropriate was what Aaron Hess (2011) calls *rhetorical ethnography*. This works from already established fundamental principles. One central principle is that ethnography requires the researcher to "be there"—that is, to be present at the research site (Conquergood, 1991; 1992). It is from intimate involvement and engagement with subjects that it is possible to gain insight into the complexities of meaning-making practices and knowledge productions. According to Hess (2011), rhetorical ethnography additionally relocates and resituates advocacy front and center in order to address power dynamics and carry out social actions for tangible social changes.[1] My research would bring me back home to the LRGV. I had two goals in mind: to create awareness about the material conditions in the LRGV; and to advocate for local pedagogical practices and curricula designs. My research required me to be there in the LRGV.

My research would consist of observations, interviews, and shadowing across two central sites: Harlingen, Texas; and a local institution of higher education. To do such research, I would be required to submit an Institutional Review Board (IRB) application. For approval, I was asked to submit, amongst other things, research site(s) and cross-institutional contacts. Anticipating such requirements, I spent the preceding year establishing contacts, selecting sites (a first-year composition classroom, a learning center, and institutional archives), reading literature on qualitative research, and meeting with committee members who had conducted their own qualitative research. I was optimistic. Not only had I prepared, but I was familiar with the research site. In fact, I was born and raised in the region. My return to the LRGV, however, would be marked by interruptions, such as identity conflict, being-at-the-site conflict (bureaucratic conflict), and emotional labor. In fact, I forewent one research site because it was so fraught with bureaucracy. This demanded I be adaptive. My research experience did not go as planned. Sure, Karen O'Reilly's (2009) *Key concepts in ethnography* prepared me for understanding the role of gatekeepers and the complexities of conversations (see also Davies, 2008), while Robert Emerson, Rachel Fretz, and Linda Shaw's *Writing ethnographic fieldnotes* (Emerson, Fretz, & Shaw, 1995) prepared me for documenting my experiences and engaging in reflexivity so as to learn from experiences (see also Brewer, 2000), but experiencing the messiness that is research is a different thing. Throughout the research process, I learned that research interruptions and adaptability are part of the messiness of research.

Identity conflict

I set out to navigate two sites, one being Harlingen. I was optimistic about returning to the LRGV for research. I saw myself as one of them still. How could I not be? I still spoke the language and identified with both the people and the place. Such identification motivated my research. Quickly I realized I was wrong. Wrong in the sense that I truly believed I had not changed and that the people there would see that. The first scene here focuses on the predicament of being there—in Harlingen—and the struggles I faced as I grappled with people not seeing me as one of them.

> Fieldnote 1: On the way to el Valle …
> "Un otro mundo," la gente like to say. A different world. A sad world, marked by tragedy and hope. There is the history of settler colonialism that continues in the present through international borders and internal check-points. The LRGV is essentially boxed in. A stuck people. Ask a denizen of the LRGV, ¿Quien eres?, and more often than not they will say, "Pos, soy Mexicano." But ask them about the world beyond the Valley and many only know that world beyond via movies, books, stories, or the questions encoun-tered at the checkpoints 70 miles north of the LRGV: ¿De donde eres … a dónde vas … y tu papeles? Suddenly, the certainty of identity is undermined by the question ¿Pos quién soy? Those roots that have been tested over time stand as a reminder of hope.

"Somos del Valle," Jose from Las Palmas, Texas, told me as he sat down at a public library with me in the fall of 2015. "Ya sabes," he continued. I smiled. "Claro que sí," I said. I knew exactly what he meant. There is something special about those palm trees Jose pointed at throughout the interview, even if they are not native to the LRGV. "Sé que no estaban acquí," acknowledging my smile, "pero no importa." "¿Por qué?" I asked curiously. "Ya sabes," he responded, "pero es difícil de explicar." I have often thought about why it is so hard to explain what it means to be from the LRGV and how to make sense of how a non-native tree such as the palm can come to represent a place and people. Jose, sipping on some RC Cola, rescued me from my own reflection of memories when he asked, "¿Qué piensas, profesor?" I had to explain to him, once more, I was not a professor, at least not yet. He laughed. "You made it though. !Qué suerte!" To "make it" can mean to escape the LRGV or to be successful. Both are subjective. "I was thinking about the palm trees that mark our return every time to the LRGV," I responded to Jose. "Sin pasaporte," I continued. We both laughed. Today, there is a threat to uproot the palm trees. And the people of the LRGV have protested. The white officials say, "Those palm trees are not even native." As Jose would say, "pero no importa." La gente, like those palm trees, are neither from here nor there, and yet, "Valley." And that is partially the beauty about the LRGV—no importa if one is neither from here nor there. So long as one can identify with those palm trees, there is a foundation for identification.

"Soy del Valle y somos Valle … what does that even mean?" I asked Jose. He countered with a question: "¿Pos quién eres?" And it was that question that took me back to both Syracuse and the airport in Austin, Texas. You see, Jose was an anomaly. He responded to an online call for interviews to be conducted at the public library with compensation. Before him, I had little success recruiting participants. So, contemplating Jose's question, I was taken back to Syracuse.

I had been thinking about how people would "see" me. I pondered these very thoughts at the airport in Austin. While awaiting my sister to pick me up, I had a conversation with a friend. It reminded me that, while people were happy that I was doing well, they sensed a "difference" within me. "¿Quién es?" "Romeo," I responded. "Who?" "Romeo!" "!Pos chingao! ¿Que onda ese?" Oscar said while still surprised. "Nada homeboy, no mas aquí mismo," I said. Disappointed in how I responded, he said, "Chale, I hear your doing good, don't bullshit me." He continued, "You coming down o que?" "Yeah," I responded. "Pos puro party at my canton," he said, laughing. I laughed too. "I am going down to do research," I said. There was a pause. "Wacha, Mr. Researcher ay que no." We both laughed. "You're different ese, a changed man, ¿que no?"

When my sister picked me up from the airport, one of the first things she told me was, "You look different." "¿Como?" I responded. "Just," she said. The whole drive, I kept thinking about how I was different. Could it be the music I now listened to? Could it be the way I dressed now? Could it be the way I spoke? What was different about me? Could distance have created change? I was still the same! I was still Romeo García del Valle. Soy Valle. I repeated this to myself over the five-hour drive. Changed, though, I was, and others could see that difference in me.

"Mira mira, es Romeo," Antonio said to me as I picked up my rental car. "Where've you been, homeboy? Some people say you doing good. I am happy for you bro." He continued, "I hear you are coming down to do research." Oscar must have told him. Small town. "You prolly don't kick it no more, homeboy. Right?" I knew what he meant. "I'm down," I replied. I wasn't, though. "No manches, wacha, Dr. García, still down for some virongas. Híjole, education don't got you all fucked up," he responded. "Give me a call," I said, as I gave him my number.

Week 1. No call. Week 2. No call. Week 3. No call. I reached out to a member of my committee who reassured me to be patient. "It takes time," he told me. But time was not a luxury I had. Every day I was not interviewing meant more interruptions. These were interruptions I could not afford. I would not be able to stay longer or revisit after my allotted time. Week 4. Finally, a call.

"¿Quieres toke?" was the first thing I heard when I answered the phone. I knew it was Antonio. I didn't know how to respond, though. All I knew was that I had tried and tried for weeks to reach out to people I knew; but in a small town, people talk. Perhaps I was different and had changed. "Rafa told me you passed by the shop to get faded up." "Simon," I responded. "¿Pos quieres toke?" he asked once more. I didn't say "yes," but I did say I'd bring over some carne and beers. "Orale, I'll see you in a few." I sensed he knew I was dodging that question. But who could refuse free meat and beer?

"Be careful with what you say, he might be recording," Antonio said, laughing as I settled into his house, finding my seat at the table. "I gathered up all the homeboys," he told me. Many of my friends were indeed there. They were all telling me the same thing. "You made it ese." I hadn't made it. If anything, I was just arriving onto a field that knew very little about me or the work I planned to do. "¿Otro vironga?" I was continuously asked. They wanted to see if I was still down and if I could still kick it. We spent the night until the morning platicándole. We laughed. At times we got frustrated. We laughed some more. Reminisced on good times and the struggle. It took weeks of interruption to get to this point. And it would take weeks of conversation before they would actually let me interview them. In fact, this research scene was the culmination of three carne asadas.

Re-immersing is not a given. It can result in interrupted research. To everyone who knew I was down in the LRGV, I was different—I had changed. For all the happiness they expressed for me, the fact was that, in changing, I was no longer an "insider." The people who did not know me were more welcoming, but still approached me with hesitation, for I drove a "fancy" rental car, dressed differently, and even spoke differently. Instead of "isn't," I would say "is not"; and instead of "ora" (short version of orale), I would say "OK." These were habits taught to me in school, where I was criticized for using too many contractions. They picked up on these differences. Still Prieto. Still had all my tattoos. But I had "made it" in their eyes—I was simply el profesor.

In the weeks it took to get that call on the fourth week, I started adapting. I stopped driving everywhere. I started walking, the way I used to walk on my way home from school, to my grandma's house, and to my friends' homes. I started talking con los vecinos. I stumbled across a neighborhood garden, where I began helping them plant. I continued to walk and talk. I walked to the barber shop.

"¿Qué onda loco?" an acquittance of my friends, who ended up owning the barber shop, said to me with surprise as he saw me. "Hey," I responded. "No te chifles ese," he said as the "Hey" caught him off guard. I realized it a little too late but waited for the next time I could show folks I still was Valley. I walked, talked, and listened. In the process of it all, I learned how to unlearn and learned how to re-listen.

Being-at-the-site conflict

I noted earlier that during the cross-institutional IRB process I made contact with folks in the LRGV who worked across institutional sites, such as a university first-year writing classroom, a learning center, and the archives. The plan, for the first two sites, was to do observations, conduct interviews, and shadow students. My contacts were Elaine, who was the professor of the first-year writing class, and Sandra, who was the learning center director. Both had expressed interest in my research and in me conducting research at those specific sites. Things changed, however, when I arrived on campus. The second research interrupted scene here focuses on the predicament of being on campus and pursuing the learning center as one research site. The end result was two weeks of research interruptions.

> Fieldnote 2: Nothing goes as planned …
> Day 3: Everything was going as planned until today. Sandra expressed concern with my presence on campus, to both Elaine and some other faculty and administrators. I received an email from Elaine this morning stating that we have to put a pause on things until things are sorted out. I can't be on campus until then.

Sandra called into question my presence on campus after our in-person meeting on my second day of research. In fact, she had expressed to others, including Elaine, that there had been a serious breach of protocol. Elaine had forward to me the email Sandra sent to her, which also included other faculty members and administrators. In it, Sandra identified me as a "volunteer." (I will never know why she did this because I had previously presented her with my IRB credentials, which clearly distinguished me from a volunteer.) A volunteer is different from a researcher and it requires additional paperwork and clearances. I assured Elaine that I was a researcher and that I did have cross-institutional IRB approval. Still, she expressed hesitance and noted that we would have to "reassess" my research tasks on campus because of this serious breach. I was told I could not do my research on campus until all this was sorted out. Things got even messier and more complicated as time progressed.

I reached out immediately to the IRB office at both my home institution and the institution I was visiting for assistance. They confirmed to me via phone and email that I was classified as an external researcher from an outside institution whose IRB had been approved and deferred to my home institution. I submitted this information to both Elaine and Sandra. Three days had passed and I still could not conduct my research. Sandra, meanwhile, continued to identify me as a "volunteer" to others. Elaine recommended that I should continue to have the IRB people reach out to Sandra and go to the Provost's office to straighten everything out. In both instances, I was assured of my rights as a researcher and the policies that protected said rights. Even after the being re-notified of my status, Sandra still expressed concerns. This resulted in an additional week of research interruptions and sorting out things.

Sandra made the argument that my research would violate FERPA policies. This was despite the IRB offices at my home institution and the institution I was visiting confirming otherwise. It would be further confirmed by the Provost's office. I had been approved for human subjects research that included interviews, observations, and surveys in and across the university, the classroom I was observing, and even the learning center. Still, Sandra was not satisfied. Two weeks later, though, everything was finally sorted out. I would be invited to conduct research at the learning center. I decided to visit the learning center, despite my hesitation to do so. In preparation for the visit, I was sent numerous emails by Sandra, warning me about using a "recorder" during interviews and a request to sit in during those interviews. I agreed. Halfway through, realizing that every response was mitigated by Sandra's presence, I decided to conclude the interview early. Ultimately, I decided to leave this research space and drop it altogether as part of my research, as it was fraught with animosity and unproductive resentment.

I had had similar experiences previously. In upstate New York, for instance, while attending an event for undocumented farmworkers, a colleague and I were confronted by a faculty member (Linda) who claimed that the space and the people belonged to her. She stated that any questions we had for the folks there needed to go through her. The similarity between Linda and Sandra is the pursuit of management and control of space and bodies. I did not need Sandra's permission to conduct interviews with her colleagues or students. Still, I agreed to her conditions because at the time collecting data was more important. I dropped this research space because the data would have an extra layer of complexity that would be unproductive to my research.

Emotional labor: recruitment, interviews, and writing

Recruitment

The majority of my research would focus on observations, conducting interviews, and shadowing students within a first-year composition classroom taught by Elaine. Students were receptive to who I was and why I was there. However, they didn't necessarily "trust" me. Building "trust" took time. Time, of course, is not the researcher's friend. It took time, nonetheless, for students to participate in my study. And, as they participated, they shared stories, which I must say resulted in interruptions during the interviewing and writing-up processes. My last research interrupted scene here focuses on the emotional labor that comes with recruitment, interviews, and writing.

> Fieldnote 3: Research is emotionally taxing …
>
> Hola gente, my name is Romeo García. Soy del Valle. Harlingen, Texas. I only want to take a moment of your time. First, I want to begin by telling you a little bit about myself. Some time ago, I was like you, sitting at a desk, a freshman. But I was in a world I had not known before, and everyone knew I was an outsider. I struggled. I was not academically prepared, they told me. I was conditionally admitted to the university. I struggled. But now I am here, translating that struggle into research questions such as how can we improve curriculum and pedagogical practice to ensure that we are not just enrolling "Hispanics" but making sure they graduate?

Introductions matter. The script above is part of what I read to students when asking them to participate in my study. Recruitment, however, can be a difficult process, especially when time is a constraint. I had only one semester to dedicate to researching in the LRGV—just five months. For the first month, I struggled to recruit participants, particularly students. I felt my research being interrupted. Every week that I couldn't conduct an interview was time lost, research lost. In the third week, I reached out to my mentors, because I felt that everything had gone wrong. Working with students would be at least one chapter of my dissertation. I remember asking my mentors, "How can I write that dissertation chapter without any interviews or discussions with students?" They reassured me of both the messiness of research and the importance of allowing the research process to continue. Being in that situation, however, it was difficult to imagine how anything good could come out of it if there was no data to analyze, interpret, and discuss.

There was emotional labor in struggling to recruit students. It wasn't that students did not inquire about my study. Students were interested, but there was hesitation. They would consistently ask what the information I gathered would be used for. And this question would emerge despite reassurances that the information would help improve and develop pedagogies, theories, and curricula to better meet the needs of students like themselves. There was also hesitation about potential repercussions for speaking about their experiences in the classroom and institution. Students would often ask if they would get in trouble for speaking out, despite assurances that anonymity would be guaranteed. Building "trust" takes time. It took about a month to convince students that I would not do them any harm.

Interviews

In the fourth week, students suddenly started volunteering to be interviewed. I felt this was because I dedicated weeks to relating to them, mentoring them, and making myself as available as necessary (and possible) to answer their questions and assure them of anonymity. I would end up conducting interviews with 35 students, each of which was one and a half to two hours long. These interviews were held primarily in open spaces, such as the library, the hallways, and near stairwells. The optimistic side of me initially thought it might be a good idea to book interviews back to back. I thought it would be somewhat like holding student–teacher conferences. What I did not anticipate was the emotional labor. Holding back-to-back interviews is taxing enough, but hearing the stories of students adds an extra dimension of complexity. Therefore, I decided to do just one to two interviews per day. Below, I offer an example of the emotional labor involved in listening during interviews, then an example of the emotional labor associated with transcribing and writing up data.

There was significant emotional labor in the process of interviewing participants. Students were talking about experiences that had affected them—experiences, I must say, that situated their sense of urgency to pursue higher education. They believed that it would provide a better life for them and, eventually, their families. Students were asked a range of questions. Below are some responses to the question: "Which experiences have had an impact on your life?"

ERICA: I used to hate working at Peter Pipers, sir, when the Winter Texans would come. They don't like Mexicanos. One time, some gringo and his wife came up to me and asked if I understood English. "DO … YOU … UNDER-STAND," he said it like that, sir. "¡Yo sé inglés gringo!" [I know English white man!], I first said, and then I said it in English … Maybe you will find someone, my family tells me. I'm Mexicana you know, so I know what that means in terms of the expectations of having to stay home and take care of mi abuela or doing home thing. I didn't want to be or feel stuck. Why couldn't I go to college? I needed to take care of grandma, they told me, which I had done for a long time. When I told them I had applied for school outside the Valley, they guilted me. I had dreams, sir. You know. It feels good to be outside of this damn place sometimes. They refused to sign the paperwork I needed to go and they said the only way I could go to college was if I stayed near and if I visited weekly. I agreed. But this was not my dream.

OLIVIA: When people hear me say I am Mexican American, sir, all they think about is how I am Mexican. That is what they hear first. And, to add, I am from the Valley, so I am nobody to them, because both Mexicans and the Valley has a bad rep, you know. When I say I am Hispanic they do not look at me or treat me differently. It means I can go places, without having people speaking to me dumb or speaking down to me.

ABRIENDA: When I was younger, I moved to the US because I wanted to go to school in the US. I had to stay with my aunt. She gave me a mattress—not a bed, just the mattress! She placed it outside the restroom in the hall, I had no privacy, or a closet; I had to put my clothes on plastic bags, next to the old mattress. Besides no privacy, her daughter used to inspect my bags and take my earrings, necklaces, or anything she liked that was mine. It doesn't matter how difficult things get, though, I know it is not impossible. No quero parar.

Everyone has their own expectations for me, but I have my own too. I will be a good wife, a good mother, but just on my own time. I risk it all, you know, to travel back and forth from Mexico and the US. But I do it because I see my future is just a hand's reach away.

SANTANA: I was so proud when I got accepted in college, sir. The first in my family. My life didn't start out as well as I would have liked. My mom with no job was stuck with my sister and me constantly struggling to keep food at the table. I remember having to grow up pretty fast and for a six-year-old learning how to steal wasn't the greatest skill to be proud of. And here I am now, though, and I don't know what to do. I am working a full-time job, because I have family shit to deal with, but now my grades have suffered. I am literally failing all my classes, sir. And they have already told me they are going to kick me out. I will work, like my family has always done, but I thought I could be so much more.In listening to these stories, there was no way to set my emotions aside or to be objective. I could relate to every emotion expressed to me. For instance, my mom, like Erica's family, contemplated not signing my FAFSA forms to go to college. When Santana discussed his situation, I was taken back to when I was an undergraduate, seeing many of my friends being kicked out of school for the same reasons. Santana ultimately joined the army and reached out beforehand to seek my advice. But who was I to dissuade him? All I could do was offer advice and provide reassurance.

Many, if not all, the interviews stimulated intense emotions. For nearly half of them, there was some kind of research interruption, which could be measured in terms of minutes, hours, or days. I asked many times throughout the interviews whether students would like to stop or whether I should stop recording. While every participant wanted to continue, the ways in which they came to terms with the emotions of the interviews differed from student to student. Some needed only a couple of minutes, while others needed hours. For the latter, we would agree to take a break and meet up later. Then, there were some students who needed days. I had one central concern for these students—their wellbeing.

The writing process

The students' stories had an impact on me, especially during the writing process. Can we ever, I thought many times, claim to write outside of the places we occupy (physically and figuratively) and the interactions and exchanges we have with others on a daily basis during the research process? I struggled to write daily, but not because I had nothing to write about. Often, I would play the audio files of the interviews while writing. In listening and reading along, I would be transported back to my data collection, sitting in the library or another building, talking with students about life and their educational experiences. I have trained my hands to keep typing even when reflecting, so they typed while I was transported back into those interviews. But whenever an emotional story was shared, I would stop writing. I began to wonder, in those moments, if I was the only one who recognized and acknowledged a type of haunting that came with conducting interviews and undertaking participant observation. Can we ever write without reexperiencing those voices, bodies, or stories of the past?

Those voices, bodies, and stories never left me. They haunted me. Therefore, every time I wrote, I thought about how students were affected, especially in terms of their desires and abilities to attend college. For instance, I agreed with a young woman who said, "My gender should not determine if I should go to school." And I thought about the students who had to leave school to provide for their families. I remember one telling me, "School is a privilege, I gave it a try, but now my family needs me." Who was I to tell him he was wrong? I could acknowledge that this reality brought him sadness. And such stories have often reminded me of how ill-prepared my field is to address the needs and concerns of Mexican-American students. Culturally informed pedagogies are just one aspect of attending to this population. If we are not mindful of everyday factors, such as familial obligations, what use are those classroom pedagogies? And for all those students who have not successfully completed higher education, they too haunt the school, the department, the educators, and the system of higher education. I felt this haunting in writing about students and their experiences. I found myself often having to come to terms with those emotions.

I wanted to do more for students, but I could not. I wanted to help more, but I had limited resources. All I could do was offer to listen, and I still provide that option for them today. And I remember how my listening, even if it was to collect information from them, made them feel. It is something like a secret, though. I know what took place. I know how it has affected me. But the vulnerability that transpired in those moments, as well as during the writing process, is something I cannot fully comprehend. I remain indebted to those moments. Pause. We'd take a deep breath. Release. Still not quite ready to continue. Extended pause. More time was needed to ingest those emotions. Release. "Pos eso es la vida." This was a dicho I often heard: "That is life." It was not a concession to oppression or hegemony or anything along those lines. La gente del Valle often say, "Pos eso es la vida," to recognize a reality that haunts, but that does not define them necessarily to a particular outcome. We continued our interviews, like I continued my writing, not simply to "get through," but to advance a memory of hope. And hope is what my research with local Mexican-American communities has been about.

Final thoughts

I do research. My research requires me to be there or to be present within the research sites. The researcher identity can create predicaments. I've named a few in this chapter, such as identity conflict and being-at-the-site conflict. The reason I shared several research interrupted scenes was both to expand upon the messiness of research and to illustrate the adaptability required of the researcher. I would like to conclude with two final thoughts on mess and being there.

Mess happens. No one ever said research is easy. One can prepare, as I did, by reading all the literature and having critical conversations with dissertation committee members. I was truly optimistic that returning to the LRGV to conduct research would be an easy task. I learned the hard way that research does not always go as planned, as discussed in the above sections. I would argue such experiences contribute to the insider/outsider debate that is still so contentious (Surra & Ridley, 1991). Such contentious debates still influence perspectives of what comprises "real" research (Bennoune, 1985; Rosaldo, 1993; Zuberi & Bonilla-Silva, 2008; Bonilla-Silva, 2012). "Insiderness" cannot be assumed. And even if it exists, it cannot guarantee objectivity (Harding, 1995; Griffith, 1998), claims of bias (Burgess, 1984; Serrant-Green, 2002), role conflict (Asselin, 2003; Brannick & Coghlan, 2007), and/or unchallenged assumptions (Hockey, 1993; DeLyser, 2001; Hewitt-Taylor, 2002) and unreliability (Sikes & Potts, 2008; Woodward, 2008). If the experiences outlined above attest to anything, it is that insider and outside frames are not mutually exclusive frames of reference (Naples, 1996; 2003; Chavez, 2008). In fact, the accounts above illustrate how I moved in and within both frames (Dwyer & Buckle, 2009), requiring critical interrogation into my positionality (Labaree, 2002; Kuwayama, 2003; Kusow, 2003; Ganga & Scott, 2006; Wray & Bartholomew, 2010). Research requires adaptability. While doing research, I learned some things that I offer now as advice.

"Native" identity cannot guarantee certainty. People will read a body differently, whether positively or negatively, because the degree of difference is more obvious and internalized. Don't feel bad. Adapt, but remember, empathy and mindfulness are two central principles. IRB approval cannot guarantee smooth sailing. Some people read the identity of the researcher negatively, whether just or unjust, because ultimately research calls attention to limits. Adapt, but remember, if one site falls through, that does not automatically mean the end of research. Thick skin cannot guarantee objectivity. We are human beings. As human beings we are not emotionless. We internalize feelings with all kinds of experiences. Adapt, and remember, it is all right to experience emotions throughout the research process. Self-care is important for the researcher. Research can cause anxiety, because it can be stressful. We all cope with stress and experiences differently. My only advice here would be to exercise self-care during the research process. Practice self-care as a form of intentional interruption. Whether that interruption is measured in hours or a day, self-care is needed to ensure mental and physical health. It is not an act of selfishness. Rather, it is a way of adapting the mind and body to new conditions.

In all, I am not sure there is anything I could have done differently with regard to preparation. How was I supposed to anticipate and/or even prepare for Sandra, the learning center director? I could not. And no matter how messed up it all was, ultimately, that was her center. What I learned (and what I hope is the most important piece of advice) is that, because research takes time, it is important not to rush the process. Admittedly, this is hard to do, but trust in the research process. Research interruptions are part of the messiness of research. If nothing else, they provide great source material, which will inevitably help the next researcher as they prepare to do their research.

Note

1   Previous conversations on critical ethnography and the relationship between rhetorical and ethnographic studies helped lay the foundation for this concept (see Brown, 2004; Gorzelsky, 2004; Thomas, 1993).

References

Asselin, M. E. (2003). Insider research: Issues to consider when doing qualitative research in your own setting. *Journal for Nurses in Staff Development*, 19(2), 99–103.

Bennoune, M. (1985). What does it mean to be a Third World anthropologist? *Dialectical Anthropologist*, 9(1–4), 357–364.

Bonilla-Silva, E. (2012). The invisible weight of whiteness: The racial grammar of everyday life in contemporary America. *Ethnic and Racial Studies*, 35(2), 173–194.

Brannick, T., & Coghlan, D. (2007). In defense of being "native": The case for insider academic research. *Research Methods*, 10(1), 59–74.

Brewer, J. (2000). *Ethnography*. Philadelphia, PA: Open University Press.

Brown, S. G. (2004). Beyond theory shock: Ethos, knowledge, and power in critical ethnography. In S. G. Brown & S. I. Dobrin (Eds.) *Ethnography unbound: From theory shock to critical praxis* (pp. 299–316). Albany: SUNY Press.

Burgess, R. G. (Ed.). (1984). *In the field: An introduction to field research*. London: Routledge.

Chavez, C. (2008). Conceptualizing from the inside: Advantages, complications, and demands on insider positionality. *Qualitative Report*, 13(3), 474–494.

Cintron, R. (1997). *Angel's town: Chero ways, gang life, and the rhetorics of everyday*. Boston, MA: Beacon Press.

Conquergood, D. (1991). Rethinking ethnography: Towards a critical cultural politics. *Communication Monographs*, 58, 179–194.

Conquergood, D. (1992). Ethnography, rhetoric, and performance. *Quarterly Journal of Speech*, 78(1), 80–97.

Davies, C. A. (2008). *Reflexive ethnography: A guide to researching selves and others*. London: Routledge.

DeLyser, D. (2001). Do you really live here? Thoughts on insider research. *Geographical Review*, 91(1–2), 441–453.

Duffy, J. (2007). *Writing from these roots: Literacy in a Hmong-American community*. Honolulu: University of Hawaiʻi Press.

Dwyer, S. C., & Buckle, J. L. (2009). The space between: On being an insider–outsider in qualitative research. *International Journal of Qualitative Methods*, 8(1), 54–63.

Emerson, R. M., Fretz, R. I., & Shaw, L. L. (1995). *Writing ethnographic fieldnotes*. Chicago: University of Chicago Press.

Ganga, D., & Scott, S. (2006). Cultural "insiders" and the issue of positionality in qualitative migration research: Moving "across" and moving "along" researcher–participant divides. *Forum: Qualitative Social Research*, 7(3). Retrieved March 2, 2019 from: www.qualitative-research.net/index.php/fqs/article/view/134/290.

Geertz, C. (1973). *The interpretation of cultures*. New York: Basic Books.

Gorzelsky, G. (2004). Shifting figures: Rhetorical ethnography. In S. G. Brown & S. I. Dobrin (Eds.) *Ethnography unbound: From theory shock to critical praxis* (pp. 73–98). Albany: SUNY Press.

Griffith, A. I. (1998). Insider/outsider: Epistemological privilege and mothering work. *Human Studies*, 21, 361–376.

Guerra, J. (1998). *Close to home: Oral and literate practices in a transnational Mexicano community*. New York: Teachers College Press.

Harding, S. (1995). Strong objectivity: A response to the new objectivity question. *Synthese*, 104(3), 331–349.

Hess, A. (2011). Critical-rhetorical ethnography: Rethinking the place and process of rhetoric. *Communication Studies*, 62(2), 127–152.

Hewitt-Taylor, J. (2002). Insider knowledge: Issues in insider research. *Nursing Standard*, 16 (46), 33–35.

Hockey, J. (1993). Research methods: Researching peers and familiar settings. *Research Papers in Education*, 8(2), 199–225.

Kusow, A. M. (2003). Beyond indigenous authenticity: Reflections on the insider/outsider debate in immigration research. *Symbolic Interaction*, 26(4), 591–599.

Kuwayama, T. (2003). Natives as dialogic partners: Some thoughts on native anthropology. *Anthropology Today*, 19(1), 8–13.

Labaree, R. V. (2002). The risk of "going observationalist": Negotiating the hidden dilemmas of being an insider participant observer. *Qualitative Research*, 2(1), 97–122.

Naples, N. A. (1996). The outsider phenomenon. In C. D. Smith & W. Kornblum (Eds.) *The field: Readings on the field research experience* (pp. 139–149). Westport, CT: Praeger.

Naples, N. A. (2003). *Feminism and method: Ethnography, discourse analysis, and activist research.* New York: Routledge.

Olson, D. H. (1977). Insiders' and outsiders' views of relationships: Research studies. In G. Levinger & H. L. Rausch (Eds.), *Close relationships: Perspectives on the meaning of intimacy* (pp. 115–136). Amherst: University of Massachusetts Press.

O'Reilly, K. (2009). *Key concepts in ethnography.* London: SAGE Publications.

Rosaldo, R. (1993). *Culture and truth: The remaking of social analysis.* Boston, MA: Beacon Press.

Serrant-Green, L. (2002). Black on black: Methodological issues for black researchers working in minority ethnic communities. *Nurse Researcher*, 9, 30–44.

Sikes, P., & Potts, A. (Eds.). (2008). *Researching education from the inside: Investigations from within.* London: Routledge.

Surra, C. A., & Ridley, C. A. (1991). Multiple perspectives on interaction. Participants, peers, and observers. In M. Montgomery & S. Duck (Eds.) *Studying interpersonal interaction* (pp. 35–55). New York: Guilford Press.

Thomas, J. (1993). *Doing critical ethnography.* London: SAGE Publications.

Woodward, K. (2008). Hanging out and hanging about: Insider/outsider research in the sport of boxing. *Ethnography*, 9(4), 536–560.

Wray, S., & Bartholomew, M. L. (2010). Some reflections on outsider and insider identities in ethnic and migrant qualitative research. *Migration Letters*, 7(1), 7–16.

Zuberi, T., & Bonilla-Silva, E. (2008). *White logic, white methods: Racism and methodology.* Lanham, MD: Rowman & Littlefield.

7

RESEARCHERS OR SERVICE PROVIDERS?

A case of renegotiating expectations in a research–practice partnership

Victor R. Lee, Mimi Recker and Aubrey Rogowski

Introduction

Research–practice partnerships (RPPs) have become an increasingly recognized form of interventionist educational research (Coburn & Penuel, 2016) that seeks to improve practice through long-term research engagements with organizations that are doing the day-to-day work of interfacing with communities, such as social services offices, hospitals, and schools. These are dubbed in the RPP literature "practice organizations," which distinguishes them from those that can reflect upon, evaluate, and study the work of such organizations, dubbed "research organizations." The hope is that, with RPPs, members of the research organization and the practice organization will work together to identify challenges within educational practice and utilize research tools and expertise and collaboratively develop new testable solutions in situ (Penuel, Fishman, Cheng, & Sabelli, 2011). For example, a community college system working with a group of researchers to establish networked improvement communities (e.g., Bryk, Gomez, Grunow, & LeMahieu, 2015) can be considered to be a form of RPP. Similarly, a project that involves interfacing with school district personnel and multiple classroom teachers in a particular subject area could represent another (e.g., Cobb et al., 2013). The work described in this chapter resembles the latter arrangement in that it describes a partnership between university researchers and school librarians at several schools within one rural and semi-rural school district.

Where this particular school district-level project encountered a need for a course correction was in the nature of the partnership. As stated in various documents describing best practices for RPPs, maintaining the quality of and trust within the partnership is one of the critical dimensions (Henrick et al., 2017). Power imbalances must be mitigated such that all parties collaborate and contribute to the articulation of consequential questions and the development of solutions, with different partners contributing complementary expertise. When this involves high-stakes subject areas such as mathematics or literacy, one can imagine how pressures facing different members of the partnership could devolve into power imbalances.

Yet, as described in this chapter, we also found that a partnership with a group of educators in a collaborating school district whose work was considered to be of much less relative importance also needed that constant nurturing and negotiation. The particular educator population was school librarians, and the dynamic that we encountered was one where those from the research organization became viewed as service providers rather than partnering researchers.

In this chapter, we articulate why this perception emerged and how we responded. Our story begins with some background on librarians in our partnering school district. In short, the librarians already had much to do beyond working with university researchers. In addition, there were organizational changes afoot that became consequential while all waited to learn if funds to pursue this RPP were going to become available. By the time funds were available, the key players from the district had changed because so much of how the district was organized also changed. The new librarians who were involved were responding to these changes and defaulted to seeing the university as doing what it had always done before: provide outreach services. These factors are all discussed in more detail to help set the context that gave rise to this research–practice partnership interruption. Following that, we describe how all needed to find a new way to renegotiate how the relationship would proceed. In doing so, some underlying concerns surfaced that prevented this RPP from being as productive as everyone had hoped. The chapter then concludes with a brief summary of where the partnership has gone since the interruption.

Contextual forces influencing the partnership

The changing role of school librarians in the school district

While teachers are the most obvious personnel who would be employed by a school district, the operation of a school involves a tremendous diversity of educators and other staff. School librarians are among those other personnel. Their professional space typically consists of a library or media center, which may also extend into or include a computer lab. Historically, school librarians were expected to obtain some form of certification or accreditation, such as a master's degree in library and information science or a school library media endorsement. In our partner district, middle school librarians are expected to have the latter. Within the partnership, two of the librarians were working towards this endorsement during the project period, while the third had already received hers. The first two librarians also had classroom teaching experience, while the other did not. Thus, while all three brought varying levels of experience to the role, all were relatively new to the job of being a full-time librarian.

The evidence of the positive impact that the school librarian has on a school is rapidly growing, even when controlling for student income levels (Lance & Kachel, 2018). Specifically, students designated as "at-risk" show the greatest benefits when a librarian is present in the school. Yet, as school budgets get stretched, we have noted a recent trend of trimming school library personnel in the surrounding school districts where we conduct our research. Consequently, fewer experienced librarians with prior certification and credentials remain, especially in elementary schools. During library observations, it was usually one person who was tasked with managing all of the many school library activities at each school without support from paid assistants. The researchers did not realize the full extent of the myriad demands on librarians until after the partnership was underway.

At the school district level, librarians are supervised by an assigned district coordinator whose main responsibility is another subject area. Their work with the librarians is secondary and often does not get the attention that other subject areas receive. In our case, while the district coordinator felt favorably about the role of school libraries, these were not the most pressing concern. The librarians were not directly dealing with areas subject to high-stakes testing. The target audience for district professional development is comprised of classroom teachers, which left school librarians with little support or professional development. Within each of the schools where we conducted our research, we learned that there was limited understanding among many school personnel and the general public about the many and varied responsibilities of the librarians. For instance, in interviews, librarians were amused at how some of their teacher colleagues would comment enviously that the librarian role looked much easier and quieter than classroom teaching. The librarians, some of whom had prior classroom teaching experience, felt that school library work had equal or greater demands, given their varied and continually changing responsibilities. In our own observations of school librarian work practices (Phillips, Lee, & Recker, 2018), we have seen them take on activities and ongoing projects as diverse as:

- advising student clubs;
- co-developing disciplinary instruction with teachers;
- coordinating the school yearbook;
- managing school identification cards;
- leading weekly information instruction;
- acting as emergency substitute teachers;
- overseeing homeroom students;
- developing media collections;
- managing electronic communications systems;
- handling internal school fundraising;
- assisting teachers with tech support;
- mentoring individual students;
- running afterschool clubs;
- managing standardized test administration; and

- developing rotating sets of activities and programs for students who drop into the library during recess, lunch, and immediately before and after school hours.

These activities were all in addition to handling materials circulation. Moreover, school librarians are the only educators in the school who individually oversee a space that every student, regardless of grade level, visits and uses during the school year. In sum, school librarians handle numerous responsibilities that are not necessarily completely understood or recognized within their schools. These additional responsibilities were not anticipated when the partnership was first established.

The waiting period between proposing and doing research

Pivoting toward the researcher side of our partnership, we consider how educational researchers work toward and with external funding. Many educational researchers are personally familiar with the nature of funding cycles. A request for proposals is released and investigators put in many hours to conceptualize a pressing research project and provide documentation that they hope will be deemed worthy of funding. To make their argument, and in some cases respond to specific funding agency requirements, researchers often bring in collaborators from other disciplines or institutions, or partners from outside the university. With RPPs, those partners are expected to be practice organizations. Furthermore, that partnership is intended to be more than a practice organization's agreement to serve as a research site. It is supposed to reflect a true partnership and involve thoughtful plans for reciprocity in the relationship.

For the particular project described in this chapter, the research team began conversations with local practice organizations with whom there were existing relationships. These included public and school libraries. Those conversations involved one of the school districts with which the university researchers had worked previously. As was typically done with grant-funded project proposals, the researchers initiated discussion about the project solicitation and the opportunity for the two organizations to work together. In this case, the goal was to identify ways to improve the support for school library personnel in conceptualizing and implementing STEM-oriented maker programs for adolescent youth in the library setting. This support could come in the form of professional development activities, activity plans, and frameworks for optimal program design and implementation (e.g., Lee & Recker, 2018). Initially, there was strong interest and commitment from both school librarians and district personnel.

Then came widespread school and district restructuring.

Several months typically pass between grant submission and notification of funding. During those months, the partner school district was responding to rapid student population growth and decisions made years earlier to build additional schools. At the time of the project, the additional schools were in the midst of completion. This led to numerous staffing changes at all levels. Teachers and administrators were moving to different schools. Coordinator assignments at the district office were changing. Most specifically impactful for this project, the district added a new middle school, shuffled grade-level assignments in schools, hired new school librarians, and moved the primary contacts to new district positions outside of the scope of our project. By the time that the research team, whose university was administering the grant, received notification that funds were coming, the landscape of partners had changed almost completely. All of this meant that partnerships needed to be reestablished.

Research–practice partnership interrupted

Reestablishing relationships

Once new district contacts had been identified, the research team, which had stayed fairly stable, immediately met with them, described the funded project to them, and offered them the option of joining. Their response was positive, with the new district contacts and the new librarians excited about the proposed vision of library maker experiences.

The project was originally planned as a staggered rollout. The first phase of work involved members of the research team observing library personnel and the programs they already offered. This was to understand what made for effective, comparable school library programs. The researchers learned a great deal about the activities that took place in libraries and what contributed to highly attended and enthusiastically received youth programs in these spaces (Lee et al., 2017). The second phase, which began six months later and lasted for a whole year, included working with a subset of librarians who would help design and pilot some new maker activities supported by program resources and materials.

During these two phases, which lasted a total of 18 months, the researchers hosted centralized professional development meetings so the school librarians could meet together for co-design activities. The librarians also hosted the researchers at their libraries to meet and observe the space. The conversations during these meetings generated ideas for STEM-oriented maker programs. Yet, when the project began to expand, and as the district reorganization proceeded with new personnel assuming their new positions and responsibilities in various school libraries, the researchers discovered that an unexpected perception was forming. Namely, it seemed that the librarians were looking to the university-based researchers to design and lead the programs with the school youth. This perception developed partly due to the time constraints the librarians were facing and their unfamiliarity with STEM-oriented maker programs. For instance, on one occasion, after an observer from the research team arrived for research observations, the librarian expressed relief and then left the research team member to lead an after-school library activity so the librarian could catch up on other work. On another occasion, a different librarian, feeling overwhelmed, asked a member of the research team to run a multi-week afterschool club in her library that her principal had assigned to her at the last minute. It was a sign of trust in the research team members, but also took that particular visitor by surprise. When the researcher mentioned it to her fellow team members, there was a long discussion about the status of the partnership and why things had unfolded in this way.

Service providers rather than partners

In response, the research team began to examine past correspondences, observations, and notes to identify why the university-based team seemed to be taking on the role of visiting service providers rather than partners. One reason was clearly the district restructuring, which brought in an almost entirely new set of district personnel than those who had been involved in conceptualizing the grant proposal. From the university researchers' vantage point, we assumed it had been clear that the librarians were going to work as partners in design and would be instrumental in reflective work on what all were learning through the partnership. However, this partnership was one that had been remade after the project had been awarded funding in light of a number of other changes that had been going on in the district. While there were plans to proceed, Coburn, Bae, & Turner (2008) have noted that external partners—particularly those that come from research bodies— may be viewed as having a privileged status that often invites some deference in conversations and tentative agreements. This does not necessarily mean that what those external partners suggest will ultimately be taken up in practice.

Second, in looking at our fieldnotes of the many activities and responsibilities of a school librarian, the research team recognized and appreciated further that participating in a project with the university was simply one additional responsibility amidst many others for each school librarian. While the university team could commit several hours each week to think about and reflect on the practices of librarians and how STEM-oriented maker programs could be designed, tested, and supported, that was a privilege that the practitioner partners did not have in their busy work schedules. For example, the school librarians do not have preparation periods. Rather, they are among the school staff members who make it possible for the classroom teachers to have preparation periods as their students complete librarian-led lessons. Before school began, the partner libraries were crowded venues, attended by dozens of students with diverse needs and interests. After school, they were host to school-affiliated clubs. Lunchtimes were heavy traffic periods, too, and moments when our partner librarians had their attention pulled in competing directions. When scheduling meetings, design sessions, and observations, there was continual uncertainty about whether those meetings would remain as scheduled because some unexpected conflict for the librarian would often emerge.

Stated simply, librarians were very limited in the time they had to engage in similar kinds of design, planning, and reflective work as the university researchers. Amidst the district restructuring, this may have been even more limited as many personnel were new, and entire faculties and staffs were renegotiating their roles and responsibilities. From the university perspective, there was appreciation that the school district was able to offer staff professional development days where the library personnel could miss district scheduled professional development activities in order for all to meet and do joint work as the project progressed. Still, these took place infrequently enough that much of the important negotiation regarding when project activities would take place was rescheduled and had to be accommodated within complicated and dynamic schedules.

A third influence the university researchers identified was how the school district understood the university as a larger institution. The research team was based at a major research university that employs many local residents, many of whom obtained their training there in a variety of fields. For the school district, it was common for university outreach activities, whether they were externally funded or part of university extension efforts, to take place with and through the schools. For example, university student clubs would do outreach activities that involved demonstrations at assemblies or in some of the classrooms. Funded research projects that had outreach components would set up afterschool programs with the schools that were fully staffed and led by university personnel. Free professional development was provided from some science departments as a way to do outreach work.

Thus, our project, which required a collaborative relationship, was an unfamiliar model for the school district. In reviewing some records of interactions between the researchers and library personnel, the research team observed that there was some conflation between the research team and other university outreach groups that had been in contact with the school. For instance, one librarian asked a university researcher when she would begin setting up for an afterschool computer coding program organized by the university's computer science department—a different department from the one involved in the RPP. On another occasion, a librarian had assumed a research team member would facilitate a library-based activity, whereas the team member had only planned to conduct observations and a debrief. The librarian later explained that she had assumed our team was going to operate the same way that another university group conducted their district activities. The other team bought in their own equipment and ran the entire activity, such that the librarian felt her presence was unnecessary.

Finally, as mentioned earlier, while the libraries and their activities were appreciated, they were not a central focus for the school district. Often, library services were seen as a possible place for budget cuts to help address limited and already stretched resources. In practice, this meant that librarians were often left on their own with respect to their daily activities. While there were no shortage of commitments and expectations placed on them from teachers and fellow school staff, their work and how it was executed were left open to individual interpretation. The librarians did not receive mandated curricula, required materials, or planning guides, as would be the case for math, language, art, or science teachers. For example, librarians revealed that they had to submit some media literacy assessment scores to the district, but how many and how they were obtained were left up to each librarian. Some tried to ask a few teachers to bring in their students to complete the assessment. Others asked handfuls of youth who visited their libraries to do the assessment throughout the year. Standardizing how libraries did this was not a concern from the district perspective. Having some data was enough. The assessments were feedback for each librarian but not coupled with any district-promoted action plans for what, if anything, to change.

When considered in terms of the nature of the RPP, this perspective raises questions about where partnerships should invest their energy. The common language associated with RPPs that centralizes design and implementation work involves joint focus on "persistent problems of practice" (Fishman et al., 2013, p. 136). In this partnership, there was recognition of both an opportunity (i.e., to enhance the activities and experiences provided by school libraries) and a need (i.e., limited expertise and lack of models, which would benefit from researcher involvement). However, the press for this particular opportunity—to do more with libraries—was modest. It was one of many areas of improvement that the district was addressing. It was also one commitment of many that the librarians were facing. There did not seem to be a lack of interest or desire from the librarians to be involved in the partnership; rather, they lacked bandwidth and press from the entities that wielded the most centralized authority in the district (Coburn, Bae, & Turner, 2008).

Thus, there were four major factors leading to librarians perceiving the university researchers as service providers. The first was related to staffing and personnel changes. More was going on that was beyond the control of librarians or researchers, and that led to an unexpected reset. Second, there had not been a deep enough understanding among the researchers about the demands placed on librarians in terms of ongoing and spontaneous responsibilities and duties. The researchers had thought the partnership and its activities would be at the forefront of the librarians' minds. In reality, it was one of many issues that the librarians were trying to manage. Third, prior engagements with different university groups, combined with all the competing responsibilities, led to the university researchers being mistaken for other groups from their institution. The university most often did outreach through the schools. That applied also to the libraries. With various university groups contacting the schools and having involvement with the libraries for a number of reasons, it was not obvious what the researchers were doing that was different from what any other university-based group had done in the past. This was in conflict with the goal of RPPs. Finally, at the district level and with ongoing personnel changes, there was little immediate press for this partnership, as what the libraries were doing was one of many ongoing concerns centrally. At all times, districts are faced with numerous competing requests for attention and resources. Researchers may see their school-based work as essential—and even worth promoting in their marketing and public relations—but, for schools, it is but one of many pursuits in a complex district system with little mechanism to privilege one RPP above other obligations.

Having observed all of this, the research team began to identify strategies that could be used to renegotiate our relationships and ensure that the needs and concerns of all parties were being met.

Renegotiating the partnership

The research team pursued three strategies to renegotiate the partnership: reestablishing the focus of the partnership; delineating new boundaries; and validating and building upon the librarians' existing work.

Reestablishing focus

Initially, the research team tried to have clarifying conversations with their librarian partners. However, these were difficult to schedule and implement in light of the ongoing and many commitments each librarian faced. The conversations typically took place while the librarian was working and tending to other responsibilities, as that was the closest that each had to free time during the work day. It was not entirely clear to the researchers that these conversations were altering the relationship or the direction of the work, so the university team adopted another approach to reestablish focus.

For one of the district-wide professional development activities, and with the support and facilities provided by the school district, project leaders convened a session where all were asked to commit to reflect further on the partnership and the intended work of co-designing STEM-oriented maker programs. The goal was to reduce perceived asymmetries in status and also orient each person toward concretizing their thinking about the partnership, program design, and program development so all could jointly discuss ideas.

At the beginning of that pivotal meeting, the researchers shared some observations with the librarians they had made about effective library-based maker programs, emphasizing low-threshold activities and how to think about STEM integration. Then everyone, including the research team members, was asked to complete the two tables shown in Figure 7.1. The purpose of first table was to encourage everyone to reflect on their unique contributions so that, when ideas were subsequently shared, there would be more clarity about the meaningful contributions each party was making. The main purpose of second table was to generate a series of program ideas quickly. This involved encouraging everyone to reflect on what might count as a library-based program, to think about how each of these could be realized, and to see this as an exercise to produce several ideas and pursue only those that seemed feasible and attractive to the librarians but also one that the researchers could inquire about and learn from.

The group generated several new program planning ideas, such as the "Lego Wall" and "Tinker Toys" suggestions in Figure 7.1, building terrariums from empty soda bottles, and making paper circuit greeting cards for the holiday season. With respect to the first table, one librarian wrote that the university was bringing "Ideas + experience" (her underlining), while she was bringing a "small amount of knowledge." This demonstrated a disconnect in what the librarian felt she was contributing relative to what the reserchers felt she was bringing. Other librarians offered similar responses. In response, members of the research team commented

What unique resources is the university team bringing to this partnership?	What unique resources am I bringing to this partnership?

Program idea	Resources needed	Where resources can be obtained	When and how to implement the program	How to evaluate it
Lego Wall • hands on, spatial	time, building know how, lego's photos, glue	online,	before school lunch study hall	visually, ask students
Tinker toys • hands on, spatial	legs	walmart	before school lunch study hall	visually, ask students

FIGURE 7.1 Reflection instrument designed to help reestablish focus, elicit perceptions, and reduce asymmetries in the RPP, including an adapted version of one librarian's handwritten responses

that the librarians knew much more about what youth were interested in, what were reasonable crowds and activity types at different times of the school day, connections that could be made to other teachers and to materials in the library, and also that the library was providing valuable space for students to convene and exhibit their work. They also stressed that the librarians' knowledge of how to put together programs in the library was instrumental in helping to inform the researchers about which resources were more or less useful. This conversation revealed that the librarians felt that they did not have much to offer the partnership. The researchers assured them that seeing things in all forms, especially when this was new and challenging, was very valuable and more informative than seeing things that were easy for them. The project could not be successful if the librarians were already doing activities like the ones that were being conceptualized and implemented.

Delineating new boundaries

Opening the conversation about the different contributions that the research team and the librarians were bringing to the partnership also helped to reassert the project's primary concern. Specifically, this was to see how different materials and approaches led by the librarians could be made useful and accessible for maker learning activities. It appeared that this message was being mutually re-understood and re-appreciated. This is illustrated below in an excerpt from an interview that was conducted a few months after the reappraisal of the relationship had taken place. The librarian was asked about the quality of the partnership between the university and the library, and she responded:

> [We're] busy in the library, and we want to get with you [the university team], and you want to get with us, but you're busy too. So, it's just having

the time to get together and collaborate. You've done a good job of giving us so many great ideas and showing us how different things work that I would have never thought of. And then it's been good as a partnership because then we can actually put it in and see if kids really like it or not. Because some things you think that they will, they don't, and some things you don't think they will, and they do. So, it's been good to know that.

(Librarian 3, May 2018 interview)

This particular librarian had been especially helpful in that some activities the research team had seen pilot tested at another library did not test well in her library. Specifically, a different school library had been very enthusiastic about using Osmo-based apps that would allow for tangible interactions and tangible coding experiences. At the library where Librarian 3 worked, the Osmo was seen as too juvenile and unsuitable for the interests of youth at that school. This was informative for understanding the breadth of the Osmo system's appeal for different library settings.

Also with respect to Librarian 3, the research team had been interested in potentially using a loom as a resource in libraries for introducing computational thinking. This idea had been mentioned early in the partnership. However, using a loom was seen by other libraries as being too time intensive to configure, and the STEM connections were not obvious to many. Librarian 3, however, wanted to try the loom as she found crafts had strong appeal with her students. Subsequently, it was a tremendous success at her library, particularly with young men. The librarian reported enthusiastically about how much it was used and that it would be better to have multiple looms at a single station, as there was a lot of conversation taking place while the boys were weaving. The positive response to the loom in that library inspired the research team to revisit possible connections between loom patterns and computational thinking, which Librarian 3 expressed interest in pursuing and running (see Lee & Vincent, 2019). The successes and obstacles she had encountered were indeed providing valuable information.

Over time, the researchers described the positive reception some of their earlier reporting of work on the project has received at national conferences. This impressed the librarians and gave them a sense that their involvement was purposeful and making a valuable contribution to education research in general (Henrick et al., 2017). As they had grown used to thinking of their space as one that was used for outreach rather than knowledge generation, this was a new way of recognizing their own importance to the partnership. This realization seemed to bring some relief and renewed enthusiasm among the librarians.

The project was reestablishing itself as a safe space for taking chances and reporting frankly to one another what the experience was like and what was being learned. New regular meeting arrangements were made so that when a librarian had anxiety about participating, the university team could be sounding boards and help the librarians think through possible challenges. In the end, the boundaries had been reset with respect to what was expected, what aspects of librarian work were considered interesting, and that the university team was not looking strictly for success. They wanted to be advocates and champions for the librarians when appropriate, but also trusted partners.

Validating and building on practitioner work

Having realized that there was some underlying anxiety about how they could contribute to this project and finding that an important part of our work was to strengthen the relationship, the researchers sought to encourage and validate the efforts that had already been made by the librarians in developing and launching new programs in their libraries. Part of this encouragement involved decreasing any perceived disconnects between what we saw the librarians doing and what STEM-oriented making would involve. The university team did this by strategically using photo-documented records and introducing a framework for educative maker activities (Bevan, 2017). In that framework, three categories of educative maker activities with decreasing levels of activity structure were identified: assembly; creative construction; and tinkering. The researchers prepared a slideshow of existing activities that were conceptualized and launched by the librarians and linked them to the framework. The goal was to decrease any perceived disconnects and uncertainty with regards to what the librarians provided to students and what was associated with making in the research literature.

For example, following the response of one of the librarians to the reflection instrument (see Figure 7.1), the research team showed how efforts to provide students with Lego and K'Nex construction sets (Figure 7.2) were consistent with assembly-oriented making. Seeing their ideas as validated by official literature and seeing images of other librarians' work gave the librarians ideas about what they could do in their own libraries. As they were rarely in each other's company, the opportunity to learn what others were doing and then imitate (or remix, in maker lingo) successful initiatives was received very favorably. Similarly, the research team made a point of publicly showcasing librarians' successes when venturing into new maker territory. For example, one librarian with no prior circuitry experience made her first paper circuit (Figure 7.2) using program guides the researchers designed after testing early versions with the other librarians. With her permission, the research team then emailed pictures of this project to the other librarians, who greeted the images with enthusiasm and encouragement. This led to the creation of a mailing list of librarians so further successes could be shared and any questions could be posed to one another.

A partnership closer to what was envisioned

Since the reappraisal and the resulting renegotiation strategies, the perception from librarian interviews and researcher disclosure is that the RPP has become much healthier. Additional evidence for this is that the librarians have since undertaken a variety of maker programs and increasingly become more confident maker

FIGURE 7.2 K'Nex construction sets—an approachable form of assembly-oriented making that was popular with the librarians (left); and paper circuit holiday cards—a new maker experience for one librarian that instilled personal pride (right)

program facilitators in their libraries. In the past year, since the researchers and librarians reappraised and responded to the changes in the partnership, the librarians have launched 19 maker programs involving over 320 youth. This does not include maker activities that librarians left out on tables for use by students wandering into their libraries—a regular offering that the researchers learned about from watching the librarians at work. The librarians conceptualized new programs, including balloon car races, e-textile badges for backpacks, and light-up classroom decoration contests. The perception of the district office has been favorable as well, with some of the senior administrators boasting to outside consultants about the innovative activities taking place in middle school libraries. At this point, we believe that the project is increasing our knowledge of how school library maker activities can be effectively structured within the constraints of limited resources and competing demands. Had there not been recognition that the researchers were seen as service providers, this progress would not have been made.

In understanding how this perception emerged, the researchers needed to critically examine why the partner librarians might see the university team as providing a stand-alone service rather than as partners. RPPs are becoming more commonplace in the education research community, and we believe this makes our story useful. It is important for partnership teams to be responsive to broader changes that impact staffing and roles. Beyond that, researchers should understand that their immediate concerns for a given project represent a small fraction of what educators are trying to accomplish every day. While researchers may be devoting substantial time and effort to reflecting upon the nature of the RPP relationship and what the research community can learn from a given project, that luxury of time may not be an option for the members of the practitioner organization. Practitioners are in situations where they must continuously act and manage several parallel and competing commitments. This is a constraint the research community needs to recognize and respect. Furthermore, the ways in which researchers view their work can be very different from how the practitioner partners understand and view what universities are trying to accomplish. While researchers may feel that goals and understandings are mutually shared, the diverse set of initiatives and histories that district-based partners bring to the relationship play an important role in what they see and expect from a university. In this case, the university had often been a service provider rather than a genuinely interested party. For RPPs to be productive in the future, researchers need to acknowledge that this happens, continually monitor roles and expectations, and then respond accordingly.

Acknowledgements

This work was supported by Institute of Museum and Library Services grant number RE-31-16-0013-16. We thank Jenny Hansen, Whitney Lewis, and Abigail Phillips for their invaluable help, as well as our partnering librarians and school district.

References

Bevan, B. (2017). The promise and the promises of making in science education. *Studies in Science Education*, 53(1), 75–103.

Bryk, A. S., Gomez, L. M., Grunow, A., & LeMahieu, P. G. (2015). *Learning to improve: How America's schools can get better at getting better*. Cambridge, MA: Harvard Education Press.

Cobb, P., Jackson, K., Smith, T., Sorum, M., & Henrick, E. (2013). Design research with educational systems: Investigating and supporting improvements in the quality of mathematics teaching and learning at scale. *Yearbook of the National Society for the Study of Education*, 112(2), 320–349.

Coburn, C. E., Bae, S., & Turner, E. O. (2008). Authority, status, and the dynamics of insider–outsider partnerships at the district level. *Peabody Journal of Education*, 83(3), 364–399.

Coburn, C. E., & Penuel, W. R. (2016). Research–practice partnerships in education. *Educational Researcher*, 45(1), 48–54.

Fishman, B. J., Penuel, W. R., Allen, A. R., Cheng, B. H., & Sabelli, N. (2013). Design-based implementation research: An emerging model for transforming the relationship of research and practice. *National Society for the Study of Eeducation*, 112(2), 136–156.

Henrick, E. C., Cobb, P., Penuel, W. R., Jackson, K., & Clark, T. (2017). *Assessing research-practice partnerships: Five dimensions of effectiveness*. New York: William T. Grant Foundation.

Lance, K. C., & Kachel, D. E. (2018). Why school librarians matter: What years of research tell us. *Phi Delta Kappan*, 99(7), 15–20.

Lee, V. R., Lewis, W., Searle, K. A., Recker, M., Hansen, J., & Phillips, A. L. (2017). Supporting interactive youth maker programs in public and school libraries: Design hypotheses and first implementations. In P. Blikstein & D. Abrahamson (Eds.) *Proceedings of IDC 2017* (pp. 310–315). Stanford, CA: ACM.

Lee, V. R., & Recker, M. (2018). Paper ircuits: A tangible, low threshold, low cost entry to computational thinking. *TechTrends*, 62(2), 197–203.

Lee, V. R., & Vincent, H. (2019). An Expansively-framed Unplugged Weaving Sequence Intended to Bear Computational Fruit of the Loom. In P. Blikstein & N. Holbert (Eds.) *Proceedings of FabLearn 2019*. New York: ACM.

Penuel, W. R., Fishman, B., Cheng, B. H., & Sabelli, N. (2011). Organizing research and development at the intersection of learning, implementation, and design. *Educational Researcher*, 40(7), 331–337.

Phillips, A. L., Lee, V. R., & Recker, M. (2018). Small town librarians as experience engineers. In V. R. Lee & A. L. Phillips (Eds.) *Reconceptualizing libraries: Perspectives from the information and learning sciences* (pp. 158–169). New York: Routledge.

8

REPRESENTATION AND EMOTION

Researching in the rural US in a politically polarized time

Todd Ruecker

Introduction

Three days after Donald J. Trump won the 2016 US presidential election via a campaign rife with anti-immigrant discourses (e.g., Steudeman, 2018), I sat on my bed hesitating. I had just drafted an email to the teachers at the rural school where I was conducting research on the literacy and language learning experiences of immigrant Latinx students.[1] I had left the school's town to head home early that week because I was exhausted and demoralized, both as a US citizen and as a researcher. Hours away from the school, I felt the need to do something to address the hateful comments I regularly witnessed against the students I was working with. Expressing concern in person to a few teachers and administrators did not prompt the response I had hoped for. Normally, I would have asked someone else to read my email before sending. But I had already thought extensively about my response on the several-hour-long drive home the day before. Wanting to get my voice out there as quickly as possible, I clicked "send." With that decision, I brought an abrupt end to a three-year project exploring the literacy and language learning experiences of Latinx students in six rural schools in the Southwestern US.

I originally grew interested in rural education research several years ago after listening to documentaries on National Public Radio and reading articles in the *New York Times* with headlines such as "As Small Towns Wither on Plains, Hispanics Come to the Rescue." Despite rapid demographic shifts being recorded in rural communities around the US, I found rural schools and especially their immigrant populations were largely ignored in the literature, something I initially attributed to the logistical challenges of researchers securing funding and then finding the time to travel to rural schools with immigrant populations. One challenge I did not fully consider was the personal challenge of crossing ideological divides at a time when they've become increasingly hardened.

Through exploring a particularly challenging moment when I was disinvited from future visits, this chapter engages with the ethical and personal challenges researchers may face when researching in ideologically foreign communities in a polarized era.

I set out to visit six schools over three years throughout the state where I taught, New Mexico. Due to feedback I received early on from a grant reviewer, I eventually set a goal to visit schools outside the state to gain a broader picture of rural education for immigrant students. Although I did not fully realize it at the onset of this study, New Mexico is a unique state with a longer history of diversity than some of the surrounding states. The state constitution and other laws give special protections to English and Spanish speakers, such as the requirement that all election materials must be printed in both languages (Baker, 2013). Most of the small New Mexican communities I visited were majority Latinx, with many residents in the northern part of the state tying their lineage back to Spain and claiming the term "Hispanic" (see Roberts (2001) for an in-depth profile of a school and community in northern New Mexico). The communities I visited in southern New Mexico saw a larger predominance of more recent immigrants and migrants who tended to identify as Mexican or Mexican American. Despite an increased tendency as a state to vote for the Democratic candidate in the last few presidential elections, many counties in the largely rural state trend towards Republican candidates. Having visited three schools in Republican New Mexico counties, which went between 60 and 70 percent for Trump in the 2016 presidential election, I did not anticipate the challenges I would face when crossing state lines for the final site of my study.

Prejudice, emotion, and interruption at Plains High School

During an initial phone conversation with the principal of Plains High School (PHS),[2] I received word that their immigrant and migrant ESL population had doubled in the last few years and that the principal was really interested in ways to help those students, something I was promising to assist with as part of my research. Soon after, I drove hundreds of miles to meet with him face to face, a practice I have found vital for building trust with rural administrators when seeking project approval. After an explanation of my IRB protocol ("I'm interested in examining how schools are supporting the language and literacy needs of their immigrant students as well as the challenges they face in doing so") and my interest in targeting ESL students, the principal further explained how they had recently lost their ESL teacher of 20 years and the person they had hired over the summer quit before even starting. My initial impression was one of an administrator who wanted to help a diversifying student population but didn't know where to begin.

I made it to PHS a week before the 2016 presidential election. As a vegetarian in a county largely dependent on animal agriculture and a progressive in a county that reliably votes upwards of 80 percent Republican, I continually felt out of place. This feeling of being an outsider pervaded throughout this project for a few different reasons. For one, the very design had me constantly going to new schools for a short time, so I was never able to get too comfortable in any one place. Also, I constantly felt I had to conceal parts of myself because our worldviews were often very different and I did not want to jeopardize our relationships and my funded research project. This feeling of discomfort is often an inherent part of ethnography because the ethnographer enters a liminal space where they "are always partially subject, partially researcher; partially participant, partially observer; partially self, partially other" (Brueggemann, 1996, p. 33). While being an embedded, fully integrated member of a community has certain advantages, such as the depth of knowledge one is able to obtain about that community and their practices, it is also limiting. As Ladson-Billings (2000) wrote, "epistemology is linked intimately to worldview" (p. 258). It takes work (or a different perspective) to see phenomena that people embedded in a particular community or worldview may not see.

The first 20 minutes at PHS were a bit of a whirlwind that illustrated the myriad challenges and responsibilities facing many rural ESL teachers. I first ran into the ESL teacher, Ms. Johnson, in the hallway talking to a history teacher who had handed her a student's writing explaining that it wasn't good and that the student could understand and write down dictated notes but not write well in English. The history teacher had written an unexplained low grade on the paper but no other comments before giving it to Ms. Johnson. We walked back to Ms. Johnson's classroom and she told me that the students were failing in a lot of their classes and teachers didn't know how to deal with them, noting that she and only one other teacher, an English teacher, were TESOL certified. She explained students would get in trouble with other teachers for using Spanish and she had to explain that some of them simply couldn't speak English. She talked about how she would sometimes end up doing the assignments with her students and have them copy, just so they would get a grade. It was clear that Ms. Johnson, like many teachers but especially rural school teachers, had a lot of responsibilities and was struggling with good intentions to find her place in a radically new role (she had just moved from elementary school to teaching high school senior English and ESL classes).

I quickly learned that Ms. Johnson had been brought into teaching the ESL classes without a curriculum, the previous teacher having simply worked one-on-one with a small ESL population as they completed work from other classes. She was advised by the previous teacher just to give participation grades in ESL because it was easier. Understanding the need for more structure, she was piloting a program sold to teachers via a workshop and based largely on drilling students in "standard English pronunciation" and vocabulary, but it was the only curriculum she had learned about. Like some of the other schools I had visited, PHS had also purchased a subscription to the language program Rosetta Stone, but Ms. Johnson hadn't started using it because of her reservations about the software. Outside quick and basic phonics lessons, the ESL classes were mostly study halls where the teacher helped students keep up with work from other classes, ranging from algebra to a research paper for another English class. This is the tradition that had been established and, even though Ms. Johnson had reservations about it, she found it hard to challenge what the other teachers had come to expect, given her newness in the school.

Meanwhile, outside of the ESL classroom, I witnessed an environment some-times accommodating, sometimes indifferent, and, at worst, hostile to the immi-grant ESL students. One the one hand, Spanish classes were celebrating *Día de los Muertos* and some of their altars were on display in the school library. Likewise, Ms. Wilson, the English teacher with a TESOL certification who had worked in a neighboring district with a history of diversity, was always conscious of supporting immigrant students. She constantly thought of ways to accommodate her ELL (English language learner) students, having them do work alongside the other stu-dents by providing texts at lower Lexile levels or providing a Spanish translation alongside the English. She would use her own money to buy dictionaries for them and shared resources with Ms. Johnson to use in her classroom. The way she talked about Ronald Reagan during one class presentation to illustrate ethos gave me a hint that she was strongly conservative, although this wasn't made clear until I saw her flash a bracelet adorned with Republican elephants right before we sat down for an interview on election day.

At the other end of the spectrum from Ms. Wilson was a history teacher from out of state who had a reputation of losing patience with ESL students, forcing them to stand and speak when they didn't want to, or, as some students mentioned to me, laughing at them and allowing others to laugh at them. At history exam time, I saw several ESL students pleading with Ms. Johnson for permission to take the exam in her class because they would take longer than everyone else in the history class and didn't feel safe there.

Outside of the sanctioned spaces of Spanish classes, there was a clear English-only culture in the school and town, something that the one immigrant student I managed to interview noted had been exacerbated in recent years: "A mi el año pasado me tocó mucho, o sea, me ofenden por hablar Español."[3] While the stu-dent clearly noted that overt language prejudice was rare among teachers, she described an instance in which a coach chastised her for speaking Spanish: "Me gritó muy feo enfrente de todos los alumnos no más por hablar Español con otra niña que no sabía hablar Inglés."[4] While I did not witness teachers making hateful comments, I did hear some from students. A particularly telling moment occurred where a student sweetly replied, "Sí señorita" to confirm something a teacher had said to the class in English. A student quickly said, "Speak English—we're in America!" and another girl affirmed this by saying, "Thank you for saying that." I remember angrily taking notes about this incident and suppressing my urge to chastise the students, whom the teacher hadn't heard. Although I mentioned something to the teacher after class, I kept silent among the students, knowing that whatever I came out with would be angry and aggressive. These overt aggressions as well as microaggressions—such as short written comments on boards with anti-immigrant Trump campaign slogans—only increased towards the election.

I discussed these comments with Ms. Johnson and Ms. Wilson. While they expressed sympathy, they were either not interested or were uncomfortable about challenging the status quo (they were both new at the school). As a researcher, I kept thinking of other ways to intervene. I hated the thought of coming across as the kind of researcher I always tried to avoid being: the university professor who comes to judge schools and their teachers while listing the many things they're doing wrong. However, I also felt uncomfortable sitting idly by in the face of racist actions.

Around this time, I interviewed the principal. Unsurprisingly, the election came up: "If Trump gets elected and Trump stays true to his claim, he said that he's gonna take all that … that fed regulations and put them on the local school districts. Now, to me, that would be wonderful." He continued by detailing his frustration with all the regulations and associated paperwork, giving the example of his son-in-law, who was a teacher in a neighboring state. Internally, my mind was racing. Throughout this interview and my visit, I maintained an apolitical face and sought common ground by sharing my concerns about heavy-handed federal and state interventions in education under administrations from both parties.

As the election approached, student comments about building a wall on the US–Mexico border increased. I came to dislike some of the students who wrote and shouted these statements, and became increasingly frustrated with the way they were ignored or unaddressed by staff members. Confident, like many, that the town's favored candidate would lose, I started to look forward to seeing the hateful comments silenced after the election.

Consequently, November 9 was very different than I had expected. After a lonely and sad election night spent in a cheap motel room, I was dreading going into school to hear the emboldened comments of some of the students. I overheard celebratory conversations among staff and administration as I signed in at the front office. As I fought back tears, multiple people greeted me with a chipper "How are you?" Inside, I was completely demoralized. Externally, I mustered an underwhelming "fine" or "OK" while struggling to maintain my detached researcher persona in front of people who were clearly celebrating the previous night's result. Any sadness I noticed was largely limited to the faces of the immigrant students and Latinx custodial staff members. The ESL class that day became a study of curriculum decisions completely divorced from students' life worlds. During the class, Ms. Johnson played Hillary Clinton's concession speech without thinking or acknowledging what it meant to her students. Inadvertently, she even had a lesson about feelings that didn't go as expected:

MS. JOHNSON: What makes you sad?
STUDENTS: Trump winning.
MS. JOHNSON: What makes you angry?
STUDENTS: That Hillary Clinton didn't win.
MS. JOHNSON: What makes you tired?
STUDENTS: When the election finishes.
MS. JOHNSON: What makes you sick?
STUDENTS: When Donald Trump becomes president.

After these exchanges, Ms. Johnson quickly silenced the students by saying she didn't want to hear about the election. I looked around to see glum and scared faces in the classroom. The message: your real feelings are not welcome here. She would routinely post a question of the day before each class, which students answered by sticking post-it notes on the board. Today's question read, "What is one word that describes the election last night?" A number of posts declared "Bye," which I interpreted as saying good riddance to the immigrant students, but equally they could have been tongue-in-cheek references to upcoming deportations. Others read "Trump train" or "Lit,"[5] while several simply said "Sad" or "Doomed."

Throughout the morning, I heard exuberant Trump comments in the hallway. Ms. Johnson explained that one of her students had complained that he was going to get in trouble because he wanted to hit a student who told him to start swimming. Her only response to the student was not to fight back and avoid getting in trouble. While unintentional, the message was clear: be silent and take the abuse; you're a minority here. A number of the immigrant students clearly looked down, depressed, and afraid in their classes, and I was sad with them. Midday, a PA announcement reported the results of the school vote, which had gone 76 percent for Trump. It ended with the only statement I heard that day dealing with potential fallout from the election, calling for healing in the local and national community. I could only imagine what some students were thinking upon hearing that 76 percent of students had voted for a candidate who had vowed to deport members of their families.[6]

I stayed silent through much of this, sharing my dismay with the students in Spanish, and at times failing to fight back tears. I expressed my concerns to a couple of teachers and the principal, none of whom (in my view) seemed to understand the severity of the situation and how their ESL students felt marginalized. After a few days away from the school, I decided to take a stronger stand that aligned with my interests in effecting change through my work. My perspective was shaped by previous studies I had read: Norton's (2013) work on language learner "investment," which posited an intimate connection between an individual's social history and their desire to learn the target language; Valenzuela's (1999) work on Latinx students rejecting a schooling system that forced them to reject their culture and language and Bashir-Ali's (2006) and Ibrahim's (1999) work on ESL students resisting the dominant culture and language taught by their schools. With work like this in mind, I sent a message to all the teachers I had visited, first thanking them for letting me enter their classrooms, but then calling out the comments I had heard in the school. Here is the email in full:

> I'm writing first to thank you for letting me visit your classrooms these past couple weeks. I'll be away for the next two but plan to return at the end of November for a couple more weeks.
>
> As you know, my work focuses on how ELL students (especially immigrant and migrant students) are being served in rural secondary schools. [PHS] is the

6th school I have visited as part of this project so I was taken aback and dismayed by the racist and hateful comments I saw expressed against Latino students during my visit, something I have not come across in the more conservative counties I have visited in New Mexico. Regardless of how you voted in the election, I'm sure you agree that hateful comments in your school and community against your students is unacceptable. I'm sure you agree that conservative (and especially Christian) do not equal hate.

Before the election, I heard aggressive comments about English only and about building the wall. A girl in the elementary school had gone to the principal worried about what might happen to her family after the election. The day after, I saw students tell others they're going to be deported and should start swimming as many of the Latino students (and at least one custodial staff member) were stunned with horror and sadness in their faces. I interviewed a student who has lived in [Plains] for over a decade and considered it home who told me about increased hate she has faced over the past year.

I'm writing this because different people expressed to me the concern that a number of the ELL students were unmotivated and messing around in class regularly. While there are certainly multiple causes to this, one of them is likely feeling unwelcome in the school and the community and resisting education (and to some extent, English instruction and speaking) is one reaction to this. We can develop curriculum for the ESL program or work to adapt materials for different students, but if students feel unsafe and unwelcome, this work will only go so far.

As teachers of language, I encourage you to make it clear to all your students that discrimination is unacceptable and that diversity of cultures and languages is a valuable trait in a community. I encourage you to call out students when you see examples of discrimination and educate them on the wrongness of these acts and also to the valuable role the Latino population plays in the [Plains] community and school. You might use some class time to have productive discussions around these topics.

I should let you know that on my way out of school this week, I expressed some of these concerns to [the principal].

Thank you again for welcoming me into your classrooms and your school. As always, I enjoyed seeing talented teachers taking diverse and creative approaches to instruction and have learned a lot from spending time in your classrooms.

I immediately received angry reactions from two teachers who were deeply offended and withdrew from the study. Several hours later, I received a message from the principal noting that my email "was unprofessional and self-serving" and that "you were collecting data for your research not coming to preach to us." Unsurprisingly, I was told I wasn't welcome back. Most of my individually sent apology emails for the way I delivered the message went unanswered. Although I had recovered a bit from the post-election shock, I immediately retreated into another state of numbness, wanting to escape a world that seemed to be falling down around me as a person and as a researcher.

Upon rereading the original email in a calmer state of mind the following week, I realized that my "generous" reading of the situation could have been easily construed as preachy and offensive, and I have often thought about how I could have communicated my concerns differently. While I stand by my belief that the comments made by other students were offensive, left unaddressed, and contributed to the immigrants' disengagement from their classes, I also recognize how different dynamics impacted my attempt to communicate across Republican/Democrat and rural/urban cultures—dynamics I'd like to reflect on here.

Challenges representing oneself and one's research

As I have written elsewhere (Ruecker, 2017), one challenge researchers face is building good relationships with schools and teachers who are often suspicious of the motives of an external researcher. This is exacerbated by conducting research within rural schools that may be hours away or even in a different state, compounded by ongoing characterizations of academia as a bastion of liberalism. Throughout my time making connections with schools in counties that were mostly very conservative during this project, I never found the divide a huge obstacle until I made it so glaringly obvious with my post-election email. This was perhaps due in part to the way I looked—my whiteness may have indicated I held a similar worldview to those in my study sites, albeit my status as a university professor could have simultaneously contradicted that assumption.

One might argue I gained access to schools under false pretenses by downplaying my critical perspective and focusing on my general interest in improving the literacy and language learning experiences of immigrant students. As mentioned earlier, as part of my initial contact with administrators, I shared my full IRB protocol as well as lists of interview questions. I typically shared my CV, too. A closer review of these materials would have revealed the profile of a critical scholar interested in issues of difference, with articles such as "'White native English speakers needed': The construction of privilege in online English language teaching recruitment spaces" and interview questions such as "Have you noticed any demographic shifts in the community and school since you've been here? How has the community reacted to these shifts if there have been any?" and "What role do you see Spanish (or another language spoken by students) playing in your classroom and/or the school context?" However, as we know, school administrators are overworked and likely relied more on what I told them in our face-to-face meetings than what I provided in the emailed few dozen pages of written documents.

One point I was forthcoming about during my initial contacts was that I would provide my support and expertise during and after my visit to help the schools better serve their immigrant students. During our first conversation, I recall the

PHS principal declaring that he really wanted to know how to help their ESL students. Perhaps if I had been clearer about my critical perspective from the beginning, then school staff would have been more open to critical discussions about power and prejudice. On the other hand, I may have had a harder time finding schools that would support my study.

The dilemma of how to represent oneself and one's research to those being researched has been explored especially within sociology, most notably by Carolyn Ellis, whose book *Fisher folk* (Ellis, 1986) was based on a study of the lives of people in a rural community. Ellis was accused of downplaying her role as a researcher as she returned to the community over a period of several years, becoming a close friend to many of the members while continuing to take notes and treat them as research subjects, without regularly reminding them that she was still researching their lives (see also Allen, 1997). As Ellis described in a confessional article written nine years after the publication of *Fisher folk* (Ellis, 1995), she had assumed that those she studied would never read her book and how she described them; however, the community did learn about the book and a number of individuals were offended by the ways they were portrayed and by the fact that she was profiting from them under the guise of friendship. As Ellis (1986; 1995) noted, people in the community were notoriously suspicious of strangers; without getting to know them as a friend, they would have been unlikely to open their lives up to her. Other sociologists were known to use somewhat disingenuous or outright deceptive practices to gain access to research sites and subjects. For instance, Robert Jackall, the author of a book titled *Moral mazes* that focused on managerial ethics, had reportedly been rejected by 36 companies as he tried to find a site for his project. Apparently, he ended up working with "a public-relations expert to devise a project description that would sound acceptable to a CEO," which advertised a study focused on "the effect of chlorofluorocarbon regulation on corporate practices" (Allen, 1997). In another confessional piece, Leo (1995, p. 121) described how he changed his appearance and adopted a particular persona to ingratiate himself with police interrogators:

> For example, I feigned conservative politics; I openly shared their bias against abortion and in favor of the death penalty; I affirmed their antipathy toward homosexuality; and I described my intimate relations with women in the same crude manner and sexist language that is common in police culture.

I feel my efforts differ significantly from those discussed above in that I always had a clear identity as a researcher in the schools I visited. As mentioned above, in response to my email, the PHS principal reminded me that "you were collecting data for your research not coming to preach to us," indicating that I was welcome in the school to collect my data, leave, and write what I pleased. While I never denied personal beliefs, I arguably hid parts of myself and my interests in introductory and subsequent conversations. In reflecting on this, I think of the dissonance between theories of functional literacy and my own belief in social/

contextual literacy. Proponents of functional literacy instruction see literacy as a decontextualized skill that is largely divorced from any external social reality (e.g., Selber, 2004; Street, 1995). Based on the way I presented myself and my project, I positioned myself as a researcher concerned with functional literacy, the mechanics of teaching and learning. I tended to downplay my interests in the sociopolitical contexts surrounding literacy and language instruction—interests that could have been discerned through reading my previous work. When I made suggestions focused on curricular decisions, such as the need to invest in teaching resources or to find a way to divide students into classes based on their language abilities, my feedback was well received. However, when I made suggestions that did not narrowly focus on the classroom (e.g., the school should address prejudice against immigrants), I was perceived as having breached my boundaries and the promises I made in regard to my research. While my email could certainly be construed as preachy, I felt my attempts to express these concerns in a more productive and tactful way had been politely ignored. As both a human and a researcher, I was naturally concerned about how the students in the other schools I visited were dealing with the election results; however, concerned that follow-up interaction would prompt the same response and possibly lead to the loss of more data, I kept my distance.

Emotionality

I have shared this story in a few different venues: at a fellowship retreat; as a rejected conference proposal; and as an earlier version of this essay, which was rejected after review by two different journals. Reactions have been polarized. For instance, several listeners and reviewers have told me that they appreciated my level of honesty and willingness to share the story. On the other hand, some reviewers have questioned my ability to write objectively about this experience because of the emotionality I expressed. Reviewers who discourage any semblance of emotionality and the resultant subjectivity help uphold the hegemony of a sanitized research tradition in which a researcher experiencing emotional reactions may perceive themself as "deviant" (Cook, 2009, p. 278). My initial reaction in revising was to remove some of the rawer emotional descriptions included in earlier drafts; by providing a more sanitized and less emotional account, I would likely stand a better chance of publishing this piece. If I chose to sterilize it too much, however, I believed an essential element would be lost. As McKinley and Rose (2017) noted, sanitizing research reports can deprive "researchers of valuable insights from which we can grow and allow novice and experienced researchers alike the chance to learn from our pitfalls, mistakes, and follies" (p. 14). As referenced in Chapter 1, Prior (2017) detailed the emotional reactions he had to some of the research he was pursuing: "I was not just exposed to emotionality by vicariously 'reliving' participants' narratives through repeated data analysis; I was also (re) exposed to emotionality by reliving the intensity of the interviews and the fieldwork" (p. 176). In arguing that we needed to rethink our methods to capture some of the mess of the world around us, Law (2004) similarly argued that we may "need to know them through 'private' emotions that open us to worlds of sensibilities, passions, intuitions, fears, and betrayals'" (p. 3).

Echoing other ethnographic researchers (e.g., Brueggemann, 1996; Murchinson, 2010), a mentor at the fellowship retreat reminded me that an ethnographic researcher becomes the data collection instrument and one should realize that there is only so much they can handle. Research can be deeply human and even emotionally destructive to oneself or others. On one hand, I found myself thinking that I was collecting rich data at the type of site I originally envisioned when developing this study: a rapidly changing immigrant population, a teacher thrown into teaching ESL with insufficient training, and tensions between long-time community members and recent immigrants. On the other hand, the activist part of me who had participated in a number of protests over the years and had a worldview shaped by extensive readings in critical race theory was appalled and wanted to act. I simultaneously felt upset with myself for fetishizing the data I was collecting— data that was documenting harm being done to the students I wanted to support. This internal wrangling was compounded by the fact that I was already emotionally distressed through spending extended periods of time away from my family while having to cope alone with an extremely depressing election result. Feeling powerless but compelled by my interest in improving the lives of the students I was working with, I lashed out. The email was a way to vent my frustration and anger.

Looking back at that email, I can clearly see that it was foolish to send such a confrontational message; however, in the emotional state I was in at the time, it seemed rational and measured. As I was dealing with the aftermath of the email, I recall my partner saying, "You didn't call them racist, did you?" While it may accurately describe a particular situation, "racist" is a polarizing word that can arouse strong reactions and shut down a productive conversation across ideological boundaries. As Lopez (2016) noted in an article, calling white people racists can simply harden divides instead of promoting the change we'd like to see. My tenuous relationship with teacher participants was severed and emotions heightened as I immediately set up a binary by using the term "racist"—an egregious accusation to many white people, even if true (DiAngelo, 2011)—and patronizing comments about perceptions of conservative Christian communities. I failed to emphasize the good work the school was doing, such as hiring a full-time ESL teacher, providing her with a budget to buy curricular materials, and implementing sheltered instruction training for teachers. My budding collaborative relationship with the ESL teacher, Ms. Johnson, was immediately severed after the email. I never heard from her again.

When I set out to design this project, I thought about the different reasons why research on rural education was lacking: distance from home, ideological differences, and cost of travel. In the future, I'll be more conscious of the personal toll a study will have on me as I plan the study and pursuing self-care where needed (Prior, 2017); if I'm not in an emotionally sound place, then I stand to jeopardize relationships with participants and any broader project I'm working on.

Moving forward

In envisioning this project, I was shaped by a research philosophy that sought benefit not only for myself as a researcher but also for those being researched—a philosophy influenced by the work of Schensul & Schensul (1992), Bleich (1993), and Faber (2002), and one I have discussed elsewhere (Ruecker, 2017). Bleich (1993), for instance, described "socially generous research," which aims to contribute "to the welfare of the community or society being studied" (p. 178). Valenzuela (1999) described times when she took a risk by approaching a teacher or administrator regarding concerns about how her study participants were being treated. As part of this project, I aimed to provide feedback to teachers and administrators after my visit as well as observation letters for the files of most of the teachers with whom I collaborated closely. At another school, I completed a recommendation form for a teacher seeking another job. At a third, I helped a recent immigrant with his English after school. I also gave regular feedback on students' writing at several school sites.

This give-and-take process of researching was occasionally fraught with tension. I recall having debates with a teacher at one school about their overdependence on computers in the classroom, although she was quick to clarify that she was just trying to encourage a productive discussion. The principal at that school pushed back against my feedback memo, asking me to redact parts that "had nothing to do with my study." My conversation with the PHS principal before my departure was extremely awkward. When expressing my concern about the results of the election and explaining why I felt the students were scared, he downplayed them by pointing to a Latinx staff member who had lived his whole life in the community and had joked about being deported. The aim was clearly to reassure me that Trump would not deport every immigrant.

As I write about this experience more than a year after the event, I'm still wrestling with the fallout of that visit. I recognize I became one of the voices I have always strived to avoid being—attacking teachers and telling them what they're doing wrong. Perhaps if I had been at the school for a longer period of time and had managed to establish more meaningful relationships, things could have been different. I'm also concerned that my comments might have increased community feelings of antipathy towards the students I intended to help. Finally, my behavior certainly placed a roadblock in the way of any future researchers wanting to study education in Plains by increasing the mistrust members of the school community had for university researchers like myself.

On the other hand, writing at a time when President Trump has separated immigrant children from their families, encouraged the use of tear gas on families at the border, and used DREAMers as pawns in a game to secure funding for his border wall, I would have regretted not saying anything. Any strong message I chose to send, even if more tactful than the fateful email, could have put my research at risk. I chose to take a stand, rather than sit idly by, because my interest in helping improve the lives of immigrant students is more important to me than simply collecting data and writing it up for publication.

Acknowledgment

The author would like to acknowledge funding from the Spencer Foundation/ National Academy of Education. Any opinions, findings, and conclusions expressed are those of the author and do not necessarily reflect the views of the funding agencies.

Notes

1 While I recognize the difference between immigrant and migrant students, I will use "immigrant" throughout this paper for conciseness. I also use the phrase "English as a Second Language" (ESL) when discussing students in connection to a specific class while also recognizing the limitations of this term.
2 All location and participant names are pseudonyms.
3 "I felt it a lot in the past year, that they get offended by me speaking Spanish."
4 "He yelled at me very ugly in front of all the students just because I was speaking Spanish with another girl who didn't know how to speak English."
5 "Trump train" was a self-identifier for people who were "on board" with the Trump campaign. "Lit" is a slang term that could be equated to "awesome" in this context.
6 Hateful chants and statements were not confined to rural schools in the aftermath of the election; for instance, a "Build the Wall" chant in an overwhelmingly White Detroit suburb went viral (Stafford & Higgins, 2016). Also, some of the Trump voters in the school I talked with noted that their votes were not primarily driven by immigration policy and they didn't expect him to carry out his promised action on that front.

References

Allen, C. (1997). Spies like us: When sociologists deceive their subjects. Retrieved May 15, 2017 from: http://linguafranca.mirror.theinfo.org/9711/9711.allen.html.

Baker, D. (2013). Spanish not "enshrined" as official NM language. *Albuquerque Journal*, June 9. Retrieved May 15, 2017 from: www.abqjournal.com/208492/spanish-no t-enshrined-as-official-nm-language.html.

Bashir-Ali, K. (2006). Language learning and the definition of one's social, cultural, and racial identity. *TESOL Quarterly*, 40(3), 628–639.

Bleich, D. (1993). Ethnography and the study of literacy: Prospects for socially generous research. In A. R. Gere (Ed.) *Into the field: Sites of composition studies* (pp. 176–192). New York: Modern Language Association of America.

Broockman, D., & Kalla, J. (2016). Durably reducing transphobia: A field experiment on door-to-door canvassing. *Science*, 352(6282), 220–224.

Brueggemann, B. J. (1996). Still-life: Representations and silences in the participant-observer role. In P. Mortensen & G. E. Kirsch (Eds.) *Ethics and representation in qualitative studies of literacy* (pp. 17–39). Urbana, IL: NCTE.

Cook, T. (2009). The purpose of mess in action research: Building rigour though a messy turn. *Educational Action Research*, 17(2), 277–291.

Delpit, L. D. (1995). *Other people's children: Cultural conflict in the classroom*. New York: The New Press.

DiAngelo, R. (2011). White fragility. *International Journal of Critical Pedagogy*, 3(3), 54–70.

Ellis, C. (1986). *Fisher folk: Two communities on Chesapeake Bay*. Lexington, KY: University Press of Kentucky.

Ellis, C. (1995). Emotional and ethical quagmires in returning to the field. *Journal of Contemporary Ethnography*, 24(1), 68–98.

Faber, B. D. (2002). *Community action and organizational change: Image, narrative, identity.* Carbondale, IL: Southern Illinois University Press.

Ibrahim, A. (1999). Becoming black: Rap and hip-hop, race, gender, identity, and the politics of ESL learning. *TESOL Quarterly*, 33(3), 349–369.

Ladson-Billings, G. (2000). Racialized discourses and ethnic epistemologies. In N. K. Denzin & Y. S. Lincoln (Eds.) *Handbook of qualitative research*, 2nd edition (pp. 257–277). Thousand Oaks, CA: Sage.

Law, J. (2004). *After method: Mess in social science research.* New York: Routledge.

Leo, R. A. (1995). Trial and tribulations: Courts, ethnography, and the need for an evidentiary privilege for academic researchers. *American Sociologist*, 26(1), 113–134.

Lopez, G. (2016). Research says there are ways to reduce racial bias: Calling people racist isn't one of them. *Vox*, November 15. Retrieved May 15, 2017 from: www.vox.com/identities/2016/11/15/13595508/racism-trump-research-study.

McKinley, J., & Rose, H. (2017). *Doing research in applied linguistics: Realities, dilemmas, and solutions.* London: Routledge.

Murchinson, J. (2010). *Ethnography essentials: Designing, conducting, and presenting your research.* San Francisco, CA: John Wiley & Sons.

Norton, B. (2013). *Identity and language learning: Extending the conversation.* Bristol: Multilingual Matters.

Prior, M. T. (2017). Managing researcher dilemmas in narrative interview data and analysis. In J. McKinley & H. Rose (Eds.) *Doing research in applied linguistics* (pp. 172–181). London: Routledge.

Roberts, S. (2001). *Remaining and becoming: Cultural crosscurrents in an Hispano school.* Mahwah, NJ: Lawrence Erlbaum Associates.

Ruecker, T. (2017). Stranger in a strange land: Conducting qualitative research across borders. In S. A. Mirhosseini (Ed.) *Reflections on qualitative research in language and literacy education* (pp. 45–58). Cham, Switzerland: Springer.

Schensul, J. J., & Schensul, S. L. (1992). Collaborative research: Methods of inquiry for social change. In M. D. LeCompte & W. L. Millroy (Eds.) *The handbook of qualitative research in education* (pp. 161–200). San Diego, CA: Academic Press.

Selber, S. A. (2004). Reimagining the functional side of computer literacy. *College Composition and Communication*, 55(3), 470–503.

Stafford, K., & Higgins, L. (2016). Royal Oak students chant "build the wall". *Detroit Free Press*, November 10. Retrieved May 15, 2017 from: www.freep.com/story/news/local/michigan/oakland/2016/11/10/royal-oak-middle-wall-viral/93582256/.

Steudeman, M. J. (2018). Demagogery and the Donald's duplicitous victimhood. In R. Skinnell (Ed.) *Faking the news: What rhetoric can teach us about Donald J. Trump* (pp. 7–21). Exeter: Societas.

Street, B. (1995). *Social Literacies: Critical approaches to literacy in development, education and ethnography.* New York: Routledge.

Valenzuela, A. (1999). *Subtractive schooling: US–Mexican youth and the politics of caring.* Albany: State University of New York Press.

9

CRISS-CROSS APPLESAUCE, "WHERE ARE YOU FROM?" AND OTHER INTELLECTUAL CHALLENGES

Ilene R. Berson, Michael J. Berson, Aaron Osafo-Acquah and Joyce Esi Bronteng

Introduction

This chapter focuses on the methodological challenges encountered by an international team of Ghanaian and US researchers as we engaged in a comparative multi-case study of civic education in kindergarten classrooms serving low-income students in the US and Ghana. To ensure inclusivity of community contexts, we jointly developed a research design that privileged Ghanaian discourse while also critically challenging the binary distinctions between Indigenous and Western forms of knowledge. This collaborative dialogue led to our culturally responsive adaptation of a video-based research methodology for use in kindergarten classrooms. Researchers have used video-cued interviews as a method to address asymmetrical power relations inherent in exchanges between children and adults (Christensen, 2004; Rogoff, 2003) and create conditions that privilege children's "interpretations about the motives, goals, and values" (Fleer, 2008, p. 113) of the young participants who are the main actors of interest (Dockett, Einarsdóttir, & Perry, 2011; Einarsdóttir, 2007). Our research strategies invited children and teachers to provide their insights and co-analyze recorded videos of their classrooms. We also relied on this participatory research approach to counter social injustices in the research enterprise that typically marginalize epistemologies among people of the Global South.

Despite careful planning and shared decision-making, we found that cross-national research posed unique dilemmas. It necessitated an interdisciplinary approach that integrated multiple methodological and theoretical tools to transcend traditional knowledge production and effectively accomplish the goals of the project. Each step of the research revealed tacit structures and discourses that traditionally subjugated Indigenous knowledge and favored Western forms of interpretation. The process of conducting the research provided our transnational team of researchers with unique opportunities to reconceptualize the design and implementation of inquiry that honored multiple perspectives and confronted the traditional exclusivity of the research enterprise.

Although our research plans intended a straightforward multi-site study in two countries, we discovered that the enactment of the methodology required a lengthy and rigorous process of reflective discourse and refinement. Each stage of the research revealed new complexities that required members of the research team to "translate" across cultural chasms. In this chapter we detail our team process as we learned to navigate these issues and accept the extra time to develop shared understanding, build trust, collect data, and interpret the findings.

Planning for our cross-national research

Our planning process began with the selection of a research topic that had trans-cultural relevance. The team unified around a common research theme of young children's citizenship formation.

Ghana is a sovereign multinational state located along the Gulf of Guinea and the Atlantic Ocean, in the sub-region of West Africa. The country comprises eight main ethnic groups: Akan, Mole-Dagbon, Ewe, Ga-Dangbe, Gurma, Guan, Grusi, and Mande-Busanga. The Ghanaian culture is built upon the belief of one nation, one people, with a common destiny, so even with the numerous traditions of the various ethnic groups, they are bound by common values, beliefs, and norms.

Cape Coast, the area where the study was conducted, is located in the central region of Ghana and serves as the capital city of Cape Coast Metropolitan area. Its population was officially recorded as 169,894 in the 2010 National Census. The main occupation of the people is fishing. Within this context, the "communal and community legacy is highly celebrated but the legacy's foundations have been rocked by modernity, urbanization, and the social isolation of people from their cultural and ancestral roots" (Marfo, Biersteker, Sagnia, & Kabiru, 2008, p. 204).

Despite a commitment to early learning, Ghanaians struggle with how best to educate their children to participate as citizens in a democracy. In Ghana, the national agenda includes initiatives to promote civic engagement among children and youth as part of the country's poverty eradication policies (Arnot et al., 2009). Educators in schools across Ghana face a challenge as they prepare "citizens who can consider problems in a global context" yet "develop Ghanaian solutions" to those problems (Wilson, 1999, pp. 94–95). This duality of citizenship represents the tension between Western values, which focus on citizens as contributors to economic development, and non-Western understandings of citizens as a collective community with a shared identity, caring for one another, and upholding traditional cultural values (Oduro, 2009; Pence & Shafer, 2006; Twum-Danso, 2010).

From the very inception of the project, our international team of Ghanaian and US researchers collaborated on the construction of a research protocol to study the situated educational and cultural context of Ghana, and this process necessitated rigorous study and reflection. At each stage of our discussions we had to ensure that we avoided the legacy of colonialization (Childs & Williams, 1997) that privileged a Western construction of children and childhood in order to understand the phenomenon of interest. Despite our best intentions, we encountered a process riddled with challenges, and developed an appreciation for Teagarden et al.'s (1995) warning that "cross-cultural research is not for the fainthearted" (p. 1262).

Rogoff's (2003) socio-cultural theory provided a relevant lens from which we understood early childhood education as a reflection of the cultures and societies of which it is a part. According to Rogoff, different socio-cultural groups have unique beliefs and values that are expressed and reflected differently in their educational systems. Rogoff (1990) used the term "apprenticeship" to describe individuals' involvement with others in culturally organized activity, which has as part of its purpose the development of mature participation in the activity by the less experienced people.

We hoped our transnational project would allow us to explore concepts of citizenship locally while thinking comparatively (Hantrais, 1999; Mangen, 1999). However, coming together as a group of people with a shared interest and purpose did not mean that we were ready to function effectively within a collaborative partnership. Since this was our first experience collaborating with one another as part of an international research team, we had to learn to work together.

Confronting communication challenges

All research teams face challenges negotiating the day-to-day processes of communication and implementation, but working across geographic distances and time zones exacerbated the difficulties that surfaced as we tried to make meaning of differences in our cultural conceptualizations and reconcile the mechanics of conducting research within two distinct national contexts. It was clear from the inception of our project that this initiative would require additional effort and focused commitment to bring our work to fruition. With these goals in mind, after we received notification of funding for our project we arranged a two-week period when the team would meet at the university in Cape Coast to refine the research protocol and prepare everyone for data collection.

We were all ecstatic that we had been awarded the funds and wanted to express our tremendous gratitude by giving 100 percent effort. The excitement of the team was reflected in our voices as laughter and noisy chatter filled the room. However, once we dove into our early tasks of designing the project methodology, confusion, frustration, and fatigue shifted the mood, and stretches of silence enveloped the team as the core challenge of miscommunication foreshadowed the difficulties in understanding implicit and culturally constituted meanings of citizenship, childhood, and early education.

Our team was passionate about the research project but recognized that we needed to develop a shared knowledge base of each of our cultural contexts and build the capacity of our team of scholars to pursue inquiry in this field of study. These alternative perspectives would contribute new insights and heighten our awareness of cultural differences. However, uncovering our beliefs and divergent perspectives required us to navigate a minefield of cultural norms around how to initiate communication. Our first team meetings in Ghana began with an extended period of greeting, and the communication had a very formal tone. After we established rapport among the team members, those of us from the US thought that the conversation flowed more freely, but we discovered that ideas and messages of disagreement were subtly conveyed or silenced to avoid offending us. In fact, if one of our Ghanaian colleagues felt uncomfortable with the discussion, they typically said nothing as a sign of respect. We found the best way to overcome the formality and deference to authority was to dedicate a lot of time to developing personal relationships among the team members. We got to know the names of children and family members and engaged in extensive discussion about family before launching into conversations about the research project.

Our US-based team members had to overcome a tendency to take over and drive the agenda. Rather than rushing into discussions about the research, we slowed down our interactions, which meant paying attention to the wellbeing of each person in the room. We replaced the goal of efficiency with a focus on building relationships and communicating our concern for each other. Rather than viewing the exchange of pleasantries as interfering with the research process, allocating time for greetings became a crucial part of our collaborative team building. These interactions included learning the local custom of accompanying each greeting with an animated handshake. The Ghanaian handshake begins with the familiar joining of hands but concludes with using the middle finger to snap the middle finger of the person you are greeting. We would frequently have to remind ourselves to leave space for others to speak, even when this practice resulted in long silences. There were occasional missteps in our communication; for example, when Ghanaian team members referred to elder members of the group as "daddy" or "mommy," the US researchers thought that these members must be related, at least until the US scholars were subsequently introduced as "auntie" and "uncle." These terms of endearment reflected titles of respect and the interdependence of the group. The face-to-face interactions were vital to our team-building process, and we gradually became acculturated to the importance of maintaining harmony and respect rather than benefiting our own individual expression.

Inequitable resources

We eventually decided that we needed to begin by conducting reviews of the literature to explore related research in Ghana and the US, hoping to identify key themes for our comparative analysis while also highlighting the particularities of each local context. Disparities became evident when comparing the number of published articles on Ghana's early education system versus the United States'. Academic knowledge production typically resides in US- and UK-based academic journals, reflecting an Anglophone center (Mazenod, 2018) that accentuates the power dynamics between rich and poor societies (Pence & Marfo, 2008). The university library in Cape Coast was underfunded and poorly organized, limiting access to critical scholarship. We hoped that in the Ghanaian context electronic resources would provide invaluable research tools to complement the limited print-based resources available in the traditional library setting (Dadzie, 2005). However, few of the staff working with us on the project had experience searching in the electronic archives. We worried that the dominance of US-based literature would affect our capacity to develop more contextually relevant understandings and would perpetuate an impoverished frame of Ghana.

We also ran into many problems due to outdated computer operating systems. We arranged training for some team members, but slow network connections and electricity outages hindered progress. During the data-gathering process, unreliable internet connectivity often interfered with communication across the geographic divide, isolating teams from support personnel and structures we had created to guide the work. Procedures for data sharing also encountered problems when the large video files could not be uploaded into a shared cloud-based drive. At first, team members laughed that they should "go grab a Snickers" when system messages reported slow upload speeds, but when it transpired that it would take over a week for a single file to upload to the cloud, their humor quickly turned to frustration. After attempts to locate faster servers in the university campus failed to yield positive results, we realized that we would have to courier the data when team members made intermittent visits between Ghana and the US.

Conceptions of place and identity

Collaborative research that spans international settings offers rich opportunities to explore diverse cultural contexts, but also entangles the researchers in complex ethical and methodological dilemmas. In a reflexive manner, we attended to our role as an international research team. However, these efforts to decolonize the assumptions and processes that typically inform our research practices unveiled the challenges of embarking on research involving two countries, and unique regions within those nations.

As qualitative researchers, we often rely on language and communication to understand interactions, yet, as we collected and interpreted data from kindergarten classrooms in Cape Coast and Tampa, Florida, we encountered barriers that threatened our intention to include diverse perspectives on democratic principles, citizenship, and belonging. Our processes exposed differences in our terminology and required conscious exploration of culturally specific meaning, making our thinking visible.

Human interactions are culturally based (Cazden, 2001), and ways of talking about a subject that may seem natural to one group will be experienced as culturally strange to another (p. 67). Discussions to prepare for the research implementation and subsequent analysis of the findings revealed particular values about belonging, identity, ownership, and choice (Rogoff, 2003). For example, during the development of our interview protocol we encountered an unanticipated disruption in our research process. The very first interview question—"Where are you from?"—revealed a culturally loaded item that required hours of discussion and debate. Interpreted by some of the Ghanaian researchers as code for "To which group do you belong?"—or even "Are you one of us?"—we realized that this question needed rephrasing in a way that allowed individuals to honor both ethnotribal loyalties and definitions of self in the context of the community where they currently live. While cross-national research generally allows for some dissimilarity between countries in interview design and implementation, the methodology also privileges some standardization of questionnaire content. Nonetheless, we changed the question from "Where are you from?" to "Where are you a local?"

The discussion about how to frame interview questions that asked about an individual's identity raised issues concerning the culturally distinct ways in which individuals conceive of themselves. Understanding the unique identity of Ghanaians meant we had to take into consideration the concept of modern-day identity and transhistorical and transcultural influences. The national identity of being Ghanaian masks the reality of a multi-ethnic identity. Since independence, the emerging Ghana has worked to promote unity, but as a nation with over 50 ethnic groups whose common language, values, and institutions define their collective national heritage, identity in Ghana may be dichotomized between the Western perception of an identity that defines oneself in the context of the present and an ethnotribal identity that honors rich traditions. Use of language reflects these tensions. In Ghana the official language is English, but over 60 percent of Ghanaians communicate almost exclusively in their ethno-tribal language, with little or no English. The remaining 40 percent, who are able to communicate fluently in English, do so only in official environments. Individuals' perceptions of their identities reflected a multi-local people, who maintained connections to the region where they were born, the city where they currently lived, and perhaps other areas where they had deeply rooted ties to their ancestral past.

Finding equivalence or consistency of meaning poses a significant challenge in cross-national research (see, e.g., Fitzgerald & Jowell, 2010). During our first discussions we allotted time in our morning session to establish common ground, only to realize how disparate our understandings were about our research topic, our operational definitions of terms and concepts, our beliefs about children, and how all of these elements framed our research questions, our methodological approach, and eventually our interpretation of the data. We found the best way to address this problem was to dedicate a lot of time to the discussion and negotiation of terminology. Timelines were revised again, and we made the decision to extend our planning period as well as schedule more frequent team meetings (biweekly rather than monthly) to ensure an ongoing process of consensus building at each stage. This additional time devoted to building and sustaining trust among the team members allowed us to identify divergent interpretations quickly and negotiate terminology and processes in a way that aligned with the localized context. The team maintained a respectful dialogue while also offering honest critiques as we delayed our data collection in order to dedicate additional meetings for rewriting the interview questions.

Yet, these delays in the design process revealed culturally specific perceptions of time. The Ghanaian concept of time has a more relaxed and flexible connotation, whereas the US scholars perceived time as a scarce commodity. The polychronic culture of Ghana values relationships over tasks, necessitating fluidity in plans and extended time for leisurely meals, unexpected phone calls, and changeable agendas. Subsequently, interruptions were frequent, and progress was slow. Ghanaian belief systems have their roots in a culture based on reciprocity and the redistribution of knowledge and resources, so each decision involved the engagement and participation of large groups of participants.

With these different perceptions of time, working to meet deadlines created tension among team members early in the process. The US researchers communicated strict timelines for completion of each phase of the study in order to meet the expectations of the funder. Fulfilling these requirements required long days and rescheduling of other commitments. The investment of time for planning and implementation often exceeded initial allocated estimates, and the team members encountered periods of mental and physical fatigue as everyone worked to complete the tasks. We had to build in opportunities for rest and rejuvenation so that the team could sustain the effort of designing the research project and engaging in data collection over several months.

While we pushed through the exhaustion and frustration, translation of the interview items into the Mfantse and Ewe languages that were used in the participating schools created ongoing challenges, since terminology designed for the US context lacked a Ghanaian language equivalent. The research team continually had to reorient our positionality to avoid elevating vocabulary and perspectives that framed modes of speaking and thinking about early childhood education in US classrooms. Throughout data analysis we continued to seek alternative ways of understanding locally and culturally derived values and knowledge. For example, when the whole research team watched a video of a kindergarten classroom in Tampa, Florida, we observed a teacher admonishing the children to sit "criss-cross applesauce." We spent hours interpreting not only the use of this phrase to direct children to sit on the rug with legs crossed, but also the focus on regulating children's bodies by limiting their movement. Foucault (1977) argued that this institutional practice in schools produces "docile bodies" (p. 136). While the children often challenged this regulation, they also participated in its enforcement by monitoring their peers' behavior as well as their own. The regimented routines of the US classroom reinforced the controlled environment. When working with the whole class, the teacher instilled in the children a sense of the importance of developing this control for themselves. This was often very subtle—a look, a gesture, or a gentle touch to bring an errant child back into line. If the actions persisted, the child was moved or verbally reprimanded. Conversely, we observed the children in Ghana singing and dancing with great expression. They communicated their feelings and showed their affection for others as they moved their bodies to the rhythm of songs.

We found that the subtleties of language in the classroom were not always easily translatable. Explanations needed to be constantly rephrased, words explained, and dictionaries referenced. We pored over the data together, and patience and understanding from all team members were critical. The research timelines had to be extended on many occasions to accommodate this process. During our collaborative dialogue we often encountered additional sticking points where our viewpoints were different because of our diverse backgrounds, the ways in which we view democracy, and the different selves that influence who we are when we engage in the viewing process. The Ghanaian researchers often viewed children's enactment of democracy through the performance of duties that aligned with a curriculum framework focused on teaching children how to live well together and develop a sense of belonging and obligation to their community. Conversely, the US researchers interpreted actions through curricular standards that focused on individual achievement and watched for evidence of children asserting their voice and agency as they actualized their individual rights.

As we confronted these intellectual challenges, we had to devote time to develop understanding and then offer another way of looking. This negotiated process of fostering inclusivity continued throughout our research implementation and analysis as we worked to overcome social injustices in the research enterprise that typically marginalize epistemologies among people of the Global South.

Cultivating agency among children in research

Our research team members were driven by a shared epistemological stance that privileged local knowledge and children's perspectives. Therefore, we aligned the methodology with Ghanaian approaches to civic learning and action that prepared children to contribute to strengthening the community. In order to reflect culturally relevant understanding of citizenship and promote the active engagement of young children in the research, video-cued and multi-vocal methodology gave voice to participants in each community and engaged them in analyzing the institutions of which they are members. Children are typically positioned as unable to participate as actors in the production of research, so their insights and voices are seldom heard in educational spaces. Using a multi-step video elicitation approach, our project team planned to collect verbal and nonverbal data from children.

However, it was clear from the start that engaging in this research process would create challenges. As we transitioned to the data collection phase of the project, anxiety among the team intensified. There were several individuals in our group who had never before conducted a study that involved video recording or interview protocols. They were apprehensive about meeting the expectations of the funding agency. Only one person from our team had ever been to the participating school sites, and our first visit to a school site revealed communication and language difficulties amongst the team members that threatened the success of the project. We had intended to pilot our data collection with a small cross-national team of researchers and then train the remainder on the protocol; however, a large group of 12 researchers arrived at the first school site and tried to squeeze into a small classroom space, disrupting instruction. Some members of the team began to videotape children, take photos, and interview school personnel unsystematically. Many of the children crowded onto the school grounds to greet the visitors from the US, and it was nearly impossible for us to observe them without becoming the center of attention.

We wanted to capture the ordinary life of the classroom, so all of the key members of the team had to become familiar with the use of video recording equipment and the protocol for collecting data in school-based contexts. The research team therefore underwent a period of training in the theory and methodology guiding the project. This included preparation to videotape a day in each participating kindergarten class. Our video recordings focused on whole-group activities as well as small-group learning centers during which we often moved around the room, documenting exchanges among children and program staff. The visual data became a living archive of the interactions that happened in that space. We subsequently showed brief, edited versions of this footage to selected kindergarten children. The video, which served as both a source of data and a cue for discussion, slowed down the act of looking at classroom practices, which enabled us to explore young children's perspectives deeply while simultaneously valuing and validating their views.

Giving child participants a voice in research in Ghana is still at the "teething" stage, even though children have long been conceived as active participants in their traditional communities (Boakye-Boaten, 2010; Pence & Marfo, 2008). Twum-Danso (2009) asserted that the Ghanaian values of "respect, reciprocity and responsibility play a crucial role" (p. 430) in how families and communities mediate expectations for children's interactions with adults. Beginning at age five, Ghanaian children are characterized as having sufficient sense to assume responsibility "not only [to] work for the cohesion of the family, but also to respect parents and elders at all times and to assist them in case of need" (Twum-Danso, 2009, p. 420). Given this cross-cultural diversity, Rogoff (2003) has argued that the context of children's lives "can be understood only in light of the cultural practices and circumstances of their communities" (pp. 3–4).

Nonetheless, we initially struggled to engage the child participants in video-elicited interviews. The children were five to six years old and were selected in consultation with classroom teachers before the visits. The purposeful sample involved children identified by the teacher as socially and verbally confident. Nonetheless, when the first kindergartener entered the room to participate in the video-cued interview, the implied power and authority of the adult researcher muted the child's voice. In stark contrast to the lively and animated interactions among children that the team observed in the classroom, the child became subdued and shy, fixating on the audio-recording device and computer-based note-taking by the research assistant. After a series of failed attempts to elicit the child participant into a more engaged response, the session was halted.

The research team reflected on how the children's Ghanaian identity had important implications for the researcher–child relationship. In Ghana children are simultaneously cherished and expected to demonstrate reverence for their rightful place among adults (Boakye-Boaten, 2010; Kankam, 2016; Twum-Danso, 2009). Much of Ghanaian children's learning in the early years is factored into peer group activities, more so than through adults' interactions (Nsamenang, 2008). Ghanaian ethnotheory views socialization as a generative process by which children's learning occurs in collaboration with peers through their active participation in their cultural communities (Nsamenang, 2008; Rogoff, 2003).

We revised our methodology to use peer partners (where the interviewee was paired with his or her friend) as a technique to access the voices of the Ghanaian children while still allowing the participants to view the video clips easily on laptops. The children's familiarity with each other boosted the confidence of those who needed it, and their interactions in the dyad enhanced the data-gathering process, allowing the researcher to track what the children focused on when the video was played back. After a successful pilot of the revised process, we implemented team video-cued interviews throughout the remainder of the research, involving pairs of kindergarteners, a researcher, and videographer.

Conclusion

As an international research team of Ghanaian and US scholars, we needed to give ourselves sufficient time and space to explore deeply rooted Ghanaian epistemologies that are often overlooked, ignored, or even distorted. These methodological dilemmas of interpretation across cultural chasms elevated Indigenous conceptual schemes and helped our team contest normative meanings of "good students," "good work," and the role of children as apprentice citizens (Rogoff, 2003). However, establishing inclusivity in the production of knowledge was a slow and challenging process that turned mundane research tasks into powerful learning opportunities that led to deeper dimensions of researcher self-awareness.

Discussions among members of the research team revealed that we often defaulted to Western constructions to articulate a "regime of truth" (Foucault, 1980) that perpetuated binary perspectives. As researchers we learned to be cautious about reinforcing stereotypes or overgeneralizing with regard to how we described the classrooms based on their national contexts. For example, not all the participating US classrooms promoted individual identity as a core principle, just as not all of the Ghanaian classrooms emphasized collective participation. To avoid the effect of othering those who were different than ourselves, it was critical to allow sufficient time for reflective dialogue and the recognition of multiple perspectives to inform our understanding.

Through ongoing discourse and negotiation, we discovered a "hybrid space" (Bhabha, 1994) that required us to reconsider our approaches and allow locally and culturally specific values and knowledge to guide the research process. We had to go beyond our good intentions and commit effort to interrupt the tendency to "gaze through imperial eyes" (Smith, 2012).

Achieving our methodological goals across cultural divides necessitated adapting our processes to unveil the larger structural patterns and overcome shortsightedness imposed by our local biases. The inherent differences among the people on our team confronted us with alternative viewpoints, but it was the intentional effort to value these differences and consciously develop a team environment built on a relationship of trust that fostered our subsequent success in completing the research. Without regular communication, it was easy to misconstrue intentions and neglect project tasks. Therefore, we created structures to ensure that research team members dedicated the necessary time and space to the research process, and no one disappeared for too long. The trust we built was critical to our rich and productive collaboration.

Nonetheless, we also recognized that our enthusiasm to initiate the research study diverted us from allotting adequate time to discuss our epistemological positions at the inception of the project. These differences sometimes created misunderstandings, and our initial efforts to resolve tensions yielded compromises that maintained harmony. However, these polite exchanges often steered us away from constructive debates that provided deeper insight. The passage of time eventually allowed us to establish trust and consciously develop a team environment in which members felt comfortable enough to engage in open communication so that we could disagree with respect and compassion.

Our interpretation of the findings questioned stereotypes of Ghanaian education to reveal the diversity of communities. Children are simultaneously cherished and expected to demonstrate reverence for their rightful place among adults. Traditions are interwoven with contemporary realities. Our research contested common depictions of African schools as deprived settings. Global media have routinely perpetuated a discourse of pessimism and a childhood in Ghana defined by existential challenges; however, we discovered opportunities exemplified in the educational experiences that celebrate and provide civic outlets for children's fortitude, resilience, creativity, and sense of agency.

References

Arnot, M., Casely-Hayford, L., Wainaina, P. K., Chege, F., & Dovie, D. A. (2009). *Youth citizenship, national unity and poverty alleviation: East and West African approaches to the education of a new generation* [RECOUP Working Paper 26]. Retrieved July 12, 2011 from: www.dfid.gov.uk/R4D//PDF/Outputs/ImpOutcomes_RPC/WP26-YGC_MA.pdf.

Bhabha, H. K. (1994). *The location of culture*. London: Routledge.

Boakye-Boaten, A. (2010). Changes in the concept of childhood: Implications on children in Ghana. *Journal of International Social Research*, 3(10), 104–115.

Cazden, C. B. (2001). *Classroom discourse: The language of teaching and learning*. Portsmouth, NH: Heinemann.

Childs, P., & Williams, P. (1997). *An introduction to post-colonial theory*. Harlow: Prentice Hall.

Christensen, H. P. (2004). Children's participation in ethnographic research: Issues of power and representation. *Children and Society*, 18(2), 165–176.

Cutter-Mackenzie, A., Edwards, S., & Quinton, H. W. (2015). Child-framed video research methodologies: Issues, possibilities and challenges for researching with children. *Children's Geographies*, 13(3), 343–356.

Dadzie, P. S. (2005). Electronic resources: Access and usage at Ashesi University College. *Campus-wide Information Systems*, 22(5), 290–297.

Dockett, S., Einarsdóttir, J., & Perry, B. (2011). Balancing methodologies and methods in researching with young children. In D. Harcourt, B. Perry, & T. Waller (Eds.) *Researching young children's perspectives* (pp. 68–81). New York: Routledge.

Ebrahim, H. B. (2010). Situated ethics: Possibilities for young children as research participants in the South African context. *Early Child Development and Care*, 180(3), 289–298.

Einarsdóttir, J. (2007). Research with children: Methodological and ethical challenges. *European Early Childhood Education Research Journal*, 15(2), 197–211.

Fitzgerald, R., & Jowell, R. (2010). Measurement equivalence in comparative surveys: The European Social Survey—from design to implementation and beyond. In J. A. Harkness, M. Braun, B. Edwards, T. P. Johnson, L. Lyberg, P. P. Mohler, B.-E. Pennell, & T. W. Smith (Eds.) *Survey methods in multinational, multiregional, and multicultural contexts* (pp. 485–495). New York: John Wiley & Sons.

Fleer, M. (2008). Using digital video observations and computer technologies in a cultural-historical approach. In M. Hedegaard & M. Fleer (Eds.), *Studying children: A cultural-historical approach* (pp. 104–117). Maidenhead: McGraw Hill and Open University Press.

Foucault, M. (1977). *Discipline and punish: The birth of the prison*. London: Penguin.

Foucault, M. (1980). Truth and power. In C. Gordon (Ed.) *Power/knowledge: Selected interviews and other writings 1972–1977* (pp. 63–77). New York: Pantheon Books.

Hantrais, L. (1999). Contextualization in cross-national comparative research. *International Journal of Social Research Methodology*, 2(2), 93–108.

Kankam, B. (2016). Citizenship education in Ghana: A traditional and modern perspective in development. *International Journal of Information Research and Review*, 3(4), 2102–2108.

Mangen, S. (1999). Qualitative research methods in cross-national settings. *International Journal of Social Research Methodology*, 2(2), 109–124.

Marfo, K., Biersteker, L., Sagnia, J., & Kabiru, M. (2008). Early childhood development and the challenge of responding to the needs of the under-three population. In M. Garcia, A. R. Pence, & J. Evans (Eds.) *Africa's future, Africa's challenge: Early childhood care and development in Sub-Saharan Africa* (pp. 201–225). Washington, DC: World Bank.

Mazenod, A. (2018). Lost in translation? Comparative education research and the production of academic knowledge. *Compare: A Journal of Comparative and International Education*, 48(2), 189–205.

Nsamenang, A. B. (2008). (Mis)understanding ECD in Africa: The force of local and global motives. In M. Garcia, A. Pence, & J. L. Evans (Eds.) *Africa's future, Africa's challenge: Early childhood care and development in Sub-Saharan Africa* (pp. 135–150). Washington, DC: World Bank.

Oduro, F. (2009). The quest for inclusion and citizenship in Ghana: Challenges and prospects. *Citizenship Studies*, 13(6), 621–639.

Pence, A., & Marfo, K. (2008). Early childhood development in Africa: Interrogating constraints of prevailing knowledge bases. *International Journal of Psychology*, 43(2), 78–87.

Pence, A., & Shafer, J. (2006). Indigenous knowledge and early childhood development in Africa: The early childhood development virtual university. *Journal for Education in International Development*, 2(3), 1–16.

Prabhu, A. (2007). *Hybridity: Limits, transformations, prospects*. New York: State University of New York Press.

Rogoff, B. (1990). *Apprenticeship in thinking: Cognitive development in social context*. New York: Oxford University Press.

Rogoff, B. (2003). *The cultural nature of human development*. New York: Oxford University Press.

Smith, L. T. (2012). *Decolonizing methodologies: Research and Indigenous people*, 2nd edition. London: Zed Books.

Spivak, G. C. (2000). Translation as culture. *Parallax*, 6(1), 13–24.

Teagarden, M. B., Glinow, M. A. V., Bowen, D. E., Frayne, C. A., Nason, S., Huo, Y. P., Milliman, J., Arias, M. e., Butler, M. C., Geringer, J. M., Kim, N.-H., Scullion, H., Lowe, K. B. , & Kim, N. H. (1995). Toward a theory of comparative management research: An idiographic case study of the best international human resources management project. *Academy of Management Journal*, 38(5), 1261–1287.

Tobin, J., Hsueh, Y., & Karasawa, M. (2009). *Preschool in three cultures revisited: China, Japan, and the United States*. Chicago, IL: University of Chicago Press.

Twum-Danso, A. (2009). Reciprocity, respect and responsibility: The 3Rs underlying parent–child relationships in Ghana and the implications for children's rights. *International Journal of Children's Rights*, 17, 415–432.

Twum-Danso, A. (2010). The construction of childhood and the socialization of children: The implications for the implementation of Article 12 of the Convention on the Rights of the Child in Ghana. In N. Thomas and B. Percy-Smith (Eds.) *The Handbook of Children's Participation* (pp. 133–140). Abingdon: Routledge.

Wilson, A. (1999). A global perspective and Ghanaian social studies teachers. *Mate Masie*, 1, 94–95.

PART 2 DISCUSSION QUESTIONS AND ACTIVITIES

Discussion questions for Chapter 6: The predicaments of "being there": conflict and emotional labor

1. Romeo García explores how his identity as a doctoral researcher helped undercut the "insiderness" he initially felt returning to his hometown. What aspects about your identity have helped position you as either an insider or outsider in the research you have conducted?
2. As García notes, conducting research that involves the documentation of challenges such as facing racial prejudice can be emotionally taxing. And even if you are conducting a study that seems unlikely to expose you to stressful or upsetting information, participants sometimes disclose unexpected information. What are some self-care methods you can use to ensure your mental and physical health when you feel overwhelmed?
3. Sometimes IRB approval is insufficient to gain access to a particular setting, as we see with García's experience with the learning center. Was there anything he might have done differently to gain access to that research site or was it best to abandon it and focus on other parts of his research?

Discussion questions for Chapter 7: Researchers or service providers? A case of renegotiating partnership in a research–practice partnership

1. Victor R. Lee, Mimi Recker, and Aubrey Rogowski discuss how turnover and restructuring affected their study. Whether you plan to work in partnership or not, turnover and restructuring can affect many research projects. In your own research, where might these issues happen and what roles might be affected?

2. What actions could you take to reestablish key relationships that your research depends on?

3. Whether you are working in partnership or not, many researchers have found themselves in situations in which someone involved in the research process does not see their own contributions as valuable or undervalues someone else's contributions. What would you include in a tool to help all partners recognize the value each brings? What forms could that tool take beyond the table presented in the chapter (Table 7.2)?

Discussion questions for Chapter 8: Representation and emotion: researching in the rural US in a politically polarized time

1. Todd Ruecker recounts a time when he witnessed harm being done to the students whose experiences he was studying. Have you witnessed harm being done to participants in one of your studies? How have you responded, if at all? If you have not witnessed harm, how do you think you would respond?

2. Which emotions have you felt in the course of your research? How do you think those emotions have affected the collection, analysis, and/or presentation of your data? Have you shared them when disseminating your findings? If so, what was the reaction?

Discussion questions for Chapter 9: Criss-cross applesauce, "Where are you from?" and other intellectual challenges

1. Ilene R. Berson, Michael J. Berson, Aaron Osafo-Acquah, and Joyce Esi Bronteng reflect on their experience developing a collaborative international research project. International collaborations require ongoing dialogue throughout the project. What are some of the key issues that should be discussed with colleagues in advance of planning and implementation?

2. Considering your own collaborative research, even if it is not international, what are some misunderstandings and differences in norms and meanings that you and your collaborators might have?

3. As this chapter suggests, honoring marginalized perspectives does not just involve good intentions or efforts to educate oneself about the history, culture, and social context of the host country and its people. How might researchers negotiate intercultural boundaries through their choice of theoretical frames and methodological approaches?

Part 2 activity

Point of view workshop

Empathy is deeply linked to qualitative research. Certainly, for those seeking emic understanding through ethnographic, participant observation and other field-based or participatory methods, empathy can aid researchers in bridging experiential gaps and leaving the field graciously and gracefully. Empathy can also help us to be more creative problem solvers.

Here, you are tasked with perspective taking as a means to place yourself into the narratives, occupying multiple vantage points. While it may be easy to critique an author's choices rationally from the distal stance of reader, this can become more difficult when you more consciously place yourself in the positions of various individuals in the narratives: the researchers, participants, and other players.

For this activity, pick one of the narratives in this part of the book and explore it in more depth, using the guidance below.

Decision points

Begin by listing key decision points and critical moments that happen in the narrative. Consider the researcher as well as the participants, both named and implied, in the narrative. Try to avoid drawing inferences about motives as you do so. Instead, stay as close to the narrative as you are able to.

Points of view

What are the concerns of the researcher(s), participants, and other players as the narrative unfolds? Over which decisions did they have real ownership or autonomy? What was outside of their control? Take on the role of each in turn and craft a short first-person account of their experience at a critical moment in the narrative. This could be in a traditional written format, like a diary or journal entry, or as letters to the editor of a newspaper, person-on-the-street videos, blog posts, or even social media posts. Don't actually post these publicly, but do strive to take up each role authentically. This may require significant inference in some cases. Do your best to honor and be honest about each person's point of view.

Choices

Consider alternate endings or ways to resolve the narrative. Much like a choose-your-own-adventure storybook, consider ways the narrative might have changed in the event of the players having either more or less empathy. If you were the researcher in the narrative, what would your next steps be?

PART 3

Interruptions during data collection: making it work

10

THINKING BACKWARD AND FORWARD

Everyday interruptions in school-based research

Maggie Dahn

Introduction

The night before the first day of my dissertation data collection felt a bit like the night before the first day of a new school year. As a kid, I had always remembered this night—usually right after Labor Day—as one of mixed feelings that included nervous anticipation, a bit of fear, and a satisfied sense that I had just grown a little older, somehow overnight. Tomorrow, I am officially a fourth-grader, I would think. Many years later, as a classroom teacher, the familiar jumble of feelings returned. The night before that first day of school I worried if my students would learn in the coming year and how I would build authentic relationships, and I wondered which students would challenge and inspire me the most. Those annual first nights were agonizing and exciting, and I never got much sleep.

And here the feelings were yet again. I had been a full-time graduate student and out of the classroom for nearly four years, so I felt pretty rusty in regard to my teaching skills. Yet, for my dissertation, I decided to return to the classroom to examine my own practice following the tradition of teacher research (Cochran-Smith & Lytle, 1993; Lampert & Ball, 1998; Vossoughi, 2014). While I now understood how to organize and develop a decent literature review, I was no longer confident in my ability to structure an engaging, supportive learning environment. In addition to anxieties about my (in)ability to be the visual arts teacher I once fancied myself to be, my beliefs about what school and learning should look like had changed, and I wasn't quite sure how to implement my new ideas in practice. Adding complexity to the situation, I had agreed to teach middle school art—uncharted territory for me as I had previously only worked with younger students. And I was going to take over the visual arts class for all 127 sixth-grade students across four classes because I felt a personal responsibility to offer this particular arts education experience to every student at the school. And finally, after defending my dissertation proposal, the principal informed me that the school would be relocating; there was no longer a designated classroom space for art. This news fundamentally changed my vision for the study and meant I had to transport materials for the projects I had planned, ranging from abstract paintings to costume pieces using fabric and found objects.

My night-before jitters channeled into action because there was no way I would let the students down. However, while familiar with the unpredictability of class-room life, I quickly learned I had forgotten just how adaptable teachers must be, given the daily experience of what it's like to work in a school. From planning around unexpected fire and lockdown drills to attending to students' academic and emotional needs, teaching is a complex exercise in improvisation because some-times teachers just have to make it up as they go. Indeed, while carefully planning for instruction is critical for effective teaching, teachers must also plan for the inevitability that not everything will go according to plan. Plans are negotiated, interrupted, revised, and, at times, thrown out. And so, armed with my rusty teaching skills, my flexibility was imperative.

In this chapter I offer reflections on the persistent and pervasive *everyday inter-ruptions* I encountered during the school-based research I conducted as part of my dissertation project. I define everyday interruptions as the day-to-day happenings in schools and classrooms, both anticipated and unexpected, that cause a change in course or plan. I tell stories about everyday interruptions as they relate to two specific themes: administrative priorities (e.g., fire drills) and classroom management (e.g., Benjamin telling me he hates art). Through reflection on stories of everyday interruptions I show how I engaged in an improvisational dance between research and practice—stepping to the side when necessary as I discovered ways to syn-chronize the shifting aims of my research and teaching. I discuss specific impacts of interruption stories on research and practice—from cutting lessons short to navi-gating strained student relationships that derailed me from focusing on the core concepts relevant to my study—all the while knowing that I was unable to collect the kind of data I had hoped to gather or sufficiently support the pedagogy or discourse spaces I had written about in my neat and tidy dissertation proposal. In practice, my study was anything but neat and tidy.

Central to my discussion in this chapter is the tension between honoring my responsibilities as a classroom teacher while also trying to fulfill my commitment to do systematic research that is fluid and dynamic. I explain that, while everyday interruptions impacted my lessons, data collection plans, and design conjectures (Sandoval, 2014), they also helped me frame the results and story of my research more realistically and in a way that felt authentic to the often complicated nature of doing research. As a graduate student with little experience doing research entirely on my own, I initially tried to eliminate the interruptions I encountered because I felt obligated to "control for" certain variables so that my line of inquiry was clear. And, as I began analysis, my initial plan was to selectively omit inter-ruptions from my final dissertation text, even though my ethnographic memos were littered with interruption stories. However, through continued engagement with the literature and conversations with mentors, I came to realize that everyday interruptions were a necessary part of doing the kind of research I had hoped to do, given my broader goal of bridging theory and practice. Coming to understand interruptions as an asset to the research improved my work as it pushed me to consider more thoughtfully the complexities of working in schools—institutions that are influenced by cultural, historical, and community contexts, including macro-level relations of power that are often unacknowledged in research on teaching and learning (Esmonde & Booker, 2017). Through my reflections in this chapter I aim to offer emerging scholars insight as to how they might navigate and write about similar tensions in school-based research. I end by reframing everyday interruptions as possibilities for bringing together important issues of theory and practice.

Motivation and planning

My study design required doing the work of teaching while navigating an intense data collection plan, including gathering video recordings from ten GoPro cameras placed on students' desks and typing transcriptions of daily post-lesson ethnographic memos. My days were filled with a blur of watercolors, memory cards, glue guns, fieldnotes, sewing needles, and hard drives as I moved clumsily between classrooms, pulling my materials cart behind me. By necessity, I enlisted students as research assistants. They were tasked with turning on and off cameras and ensuring all work was accounted for in portfolios. My feelings were well represented in one of my memos from the middle of data collection when I wrote, "I can't believe I thought I could do this."

Despite a desire to run and hide from the data collection plan I had optimistically drafted for my dissertation proposal, I remained committed to carrying out the research as planned. As a former teacher and emerging scholar, I like getting tangled up in the intricacies of design and implementation, bringing together emergent theories, novel ideas about learning environments, and the realities of practice in the day-to-day, minute-to-minute details of teaching and learning. This orientation is aligned with Erickson (2006), who draws from the history of ethnographic research to argue that, instead of researchers studying teachers and schools through a top-down lens, researchers and teachers ought to work "side by side" and engage in inquiry together through co-research. I aimed to take up his idea and additionally take on the intellectual, physical, and emotionally charged work of teaching, making my own teaching the experiment, an inseparable part of the research (Wilson, 1995).

Design-based research (DBR) is a type of inquiry that acknowledges the complexity of educational settings and aims to develop theory and practice simultaneously through design (Brown, 1992; Cobb et al., 2003; Collins, 1992). What draws me to the DBR tradition that is characteristic of much work in the learning sciences is its explicit focus on the "progressive refinement of hypotheses, with theory and data interacting throughout the process" (Engle, Conant, & Greeno,

2007, p. 239). I consider DBR a practical, rigorous way of approaching questions I have about teaching and learning: specifically, how particular choices in learning environment design open up possibilities for analysis. In my study, I was interested in designing for structures and discourse spaces in the arts classroom and analyzing how students interacted and talked about the art they made while they were making it. I knew that this type of iterative and exploratory research could be complex, yet I was encouraged when I discovered a community of researchers who have demonstrated interest in untangling the messiness between design and implementation in DBR (Svihla & Reeve, 2016).

Context

Background information is necessary to depict how I experienced and responded to everyday interruptions as they unfolded. After teaching in Chicago for a few years, I moved to Los Angeles to become the visual arts teacher at a charter school called Esperanza Prep Elementary, where I developed an arts program. A full study description is beyond the scope of this chapter (see Dahn, 2019), but it is important to note that I ultimately decided to take on the role of primary researcher and teacher with the aim of studying how sixth-grade students developed their voices as they participated in a visual arts unit focused on making art about social issues that were important to them (e.g., immigration, cyberbullying, and mental health). I was given access to take over sixth-grade art class (127 students in total; 32 for my case study) at Esperanza Prep Middle, the middle school feeder affiliated with the elementary school where I used to teach, so I had known over half of the students previously. Esperanza Prep Middle is situated in a working-class community in Los Angeles County where 97 percent of students identify as Latinx and 92 percent qualify for free or reduced-price lunches. The curriculum consisted of 20 lessons I designed and taught over the course of a semester.

Everyday interruptions in school-based research

The interruptions I encountered included administrative interruptions, which impacted the time I spent with students, and classroom management interruptions, which impacted my relationships with students.

Everyday administrative interruptions

It was the fourth lesson of the study, and I was excited for us to begin making abstract art centered on students' self-selected social issues. Students would talk about the social issues that mattered to them, link those issues to particular emotions, and talk with each other about how to use artistic tools to represent the issues and emotions through art. They would then create abstract watercolor pieces inspired by a social issue and the associated personal experiences and emotions. At least this was what I had envisioned happening when writing my lesson plan. As I prepped class materials at 6.30 a.m. in the teachers' lounge, the school operations coordinator informed me that we would be having a fire drill that day at the time I taught my focus class for the study. A few hours later, as I began the lesson with the focus class, I kept nervously looking at the clock as I realized how little time we had left. As a teacher and researcher, I had to think and act quickly, given the constraints of the fire drill. I felt anxious and disappointed that the research and lesson were not going as planned.

Moments like these, when school-wide administrative priorities took over portions of my lessons, were not infrequent. In fact, I came to expect and anticipate them as part of the research process. On days when I knew an event or drill was coming, I waited for the intercom announcement to interrupt the lesson flow, always hoping for a few more minutes with the students. As a classroom teacher, I had experienced a similar rhythm of administrative interruptions, yet doing research heightened my sensitivity to their frequency and cause. Figure 10.1 presents an abbreviated list of the administrative happenings that interrupted my lessons over the course of 20 data collection days. The main impact of these administrative interruptions was linked to the amount of time I could spend with the students, which required making decisions about how to spend the time we did have. Sometimes this worked out for the best, but sometimes there just wasn't enough time.

Let me offer a rough breakdown of how these interruptions directly impacted class time. I taught four sixth-grade classes, one of which was my focus class.

Administrative interruptions

Impacted all students

- Picture day
- The Great California Shakeout*
- *required state-wide earthquake drill
- A regular earthquake drill
- A fire drill
- Attendance breakfast celebration
- Staff vs. students soccer game
- Parent-teacher conferences

Impacted individuals

- Field trip as incentive for honor roll students
- CELDT (California English Language Development Test) class pull-outs
- Required pull-outs for minutes on Individualized Education Plans

FIGURE 10.1 List of administrative interruptions

According to the official school bell schedule, each lesson should have lasted 80 minutes. If executed perfectly, this would amount to 1,600 minutes (or 26 hours and 40 minutes) of interaction time per class over the course of the semester. In reality, with transitions between classes and cleanup time, each lesson was around 70 minutes long if it were uninterrupted. Additionally, each administrative interruption outlined in Figure 10.1 reduced lessons to anywhere between 60 and 40 minutes (i.e., an average of about 50 minutes). Seven of the 20 lessons with the focus class were interrupted by one of these events, so the overall time I spent with that class was reduced from the notional 26 hours and 40 minutes to about 22 hours and 10 minutes (50 minutes × 7 classes + 70 minutes × 14 classes). Although it might go unnoticed in some contexts, confronting a loss of 4 hours and 30 minutes of instructional time is shocking. This time could have been focused on student learning, art making, and/or discussion—all of which were critical to my study.

My exact calculations are specific to this study, yet time is a valuable resource in all schools because it is finite, so how teachers and students spend time matters. Rogers, Mirra, Seltzer, and Jun (2014) highlight the construct of *available learning time* in a report on California high schools. They refer to *available learning time* as the time left for instruction after minutes and hours are lost due to "absences, delays, disruptions, and interruptions" (p. 4). Using survey results from 800 teachers, they demonstrate significant differences in available learning time between low- and high-poverty schools, and found that high-poverty schools lose about ten more instructional days than low-poverty schools over the course of a 180-day school year. They call out factors that contributed most significantly to lost learning time, including more frequent interruptions due to standardized testing requirements, emergency lockdowns, and teacher absences.

In addition to these inequities in available learning time, it is common for arts classes to be sidelined when administrators must make difficult decisions about which lessons to prioritize. Yet, this trend of devaluing the arts seems antithetical to what education should be, given that participation in the arts has been linked to improving emotional wellbeing (Malchiodi, 2011), cultivating creativity and self-expression (Dewey, 1934), and offering young people a way to try on new identities (Holloway & Krensky, 2001). In the case of my study, it was discouraging, but unsurprising, that picture day activities happened during art time (instead of, say, math class) and that students were often pulled to take other assessments at the very beginning of our visual arts lessons. Several students also had Individualized Education Plans (IEPs), and their required pullout services were most often scheduled during art or physical education.

In light of the fire drill that was scheduled to interrupt the important lesson I describe above, I had reviewed my lesson plan and decided that I could adjust the lesson so that we would dive right into the new content as quickly as possible. Rather than spend time offering background information, I let the students begin talking about social issues right away. Surprisingly, these precious few minutes of data collection that were cut short by the fire drill led to fairly productive student interactions and rich conversations. Even though the drill was looming, the students had in-depth discussions about different social issues as they talked about their personal connections and emotions related to the art they would eventually make. Of course, I had wanted more time with the students that day, but I found a way to make the lesson plan work with the time we did have together. Anticipation of the interruption changed my curriculum as well as the affective quality of my teaching, forming me into a more precise, thoughtful researcher in the moment.

Everyday classroom management interruptions

As a concept, classroom management is complex, rife with tensions and contradictions. While often perceived as a way of controlling student behavior, from a more holistic perspective, classroom management includes the planning, creativity, and monitoring involved in supporting classroom experiences that encourage high levels of learning for a diverse student population (Gay, 2006). In her 2018 AERA Presidential Address, Deborah Loewenberg Ball described interactions between teachers, students, and their environments as *discretionary spaces* in which inequality, racism, and other forms of oppression can be either reproduced or disrupted. She elaborated that routine classroom interactions are informed by how the teacher's experiences in the world and the institutionalized practices of schools translate to classrooms.

At the beginning of my teaching career I followed advice for inexperienced teachers on effective teaching "techniques" emphasizing control that fail to engage students in meaningful learning and critical thinking (Salazar, 2011). I did this because it was an easier way to teach and a central part of the school's culture and professional development. Yet, as I gained experience, developed a better understanding of my students, and reflected on the kind of teacher I hoped to be, including how that identity aligned and conflicted with my classroom management approach (Milner & Tenore, 2010), my practice turned toward more culturally responsive goals for classroom management, like self-regulation, community building, and social decision making (Bondy, Ross, Gallingane, & Hambacher, 2007; Ladson-Billings, 1995; Weinstein, Tomlinson-Clarke, & Curran, 2004).

When I made the decision to return to the classroom for my dissertation, I hadn't considered that my earlier confidence in managing an effective learning environment was due, in part, to the fact that I had been working with known variables for a while. This meant that I not only knew my students and subject matter well but also understood the physical space of my classroom and how the students and I moved within that space. I was also a deeply embedded member of the larger school community; because I was the art teacher, I taught every child in the school, and I knew just about every parent, too. Feeling "in control" had made it easier to deal effectively with the everyday interruptions that are inherent in teaching. When I began teaching for my dissertation, however, I was no longer in control of the variables on which I had come to depend. For one, I was operating in a "no excuses" charter school affiliated with a well-known national network that already had institutional commitments about the kind of school it would be. While the individual schools in this network are all unique, and many have impressive arts programs in addition to focusing on student achievement, this particular school was under pressure to produce excellent test results because the elementary school feeder had some of the highest scores in the network. The middle school was expected to build on the legacy of those scores. Additionally, I had assumed I would pick up teaching again with ease. However, I had not taught students formally for several years, so both my mind and my body had to get used to being a teacher again.

Everyday classroom management interruptions in the specific case of my dissertation study can be illustrated through one student's story. I had known Benjamin for a long time because I had been his art teacher in elementary school. He had loved doodling when he was younger, so I was unsurprised when I noticed the sixth-grade Benjamin doodling in his sketchbook throughout the class. Upon viewing the video footage from the GoPro placed on his desk, I was fascinated by how he managed to engage in the whole-class discussion while still continuing to doodle. He would whisper ideas to himself or call out suggestions, some of which I picked up and highlighted for the class. When we made abstract watercolor paintings, he created a sophisticated piece about his chosen social issue of "the police." His pattern of engaged participation continued for the first ten lessons. However, he wasn't at school for the 11th and 12th lessons, and I commented in my post-lesson memo, "I was bummed because Benjamin was absent. I'll try to make up the project with him." Then, when he returned, things took a turn. The class was beginning group work to create costume pieces, and I asked Benjamin to choose his work partners since he hadn't been there when the other students had formed their groups. He said he didn't want to work with anyone. He had friends in class, and several students asked him to join their group as they knew he was great at drawing. He replied that art was "stupid." While the other students assembled their costumes using materials from the wardrobe I wheeled from class to class, Benjamin walked aimlessly around the classroom. When I encouraged him to help draw the design for a group, he hid in the supply closet. Throughout the next few lessons he often made random screaming noises when I gave directions to the whole class. At one point he took a ball of yarn from the wardrobe and made a web around the classroom space instead of working on his project. When I asked him why, he said, "Because I'm bored." I told him we should talk about it because I knew he liked art. He responded, "Nah, I hate art."

As an experienced teacher, Benjamin's behavior was not unfamiliar to me, but I was baffled by the control his actions had over my emotions and how I felt about myself as an educator and researcher. In one memo I reflected, "I am not a good middle school teacher. Why did I think I could do this? Why on earth did I want to do this?" Teaching can be an emotionally exhausting endeavor, yet research that includes such raw accounts of emotion is often discouraged (see Chapter 8). I knew that taking on such an intimate role in research would affect conditions in ways I would never know or be able to reconcile (Rose, 1995), yet, despite my mental preparation, I found it impossible to separate my sense of failure from the work I was trying to do. As evidenced by my inability to sustain Benjamin's motivation, I thought I had failed in meeting the emotional needs of all the students (Bondy et al., 2007). I wanted so badly for him to participate (granted, in the way I expected him to), yet we were at a standstill.

I was acutely aware of our uneven power relations and my identity as a white teacher contending with issues related to classroom management operating within a discretionary space. However, while discipline in schools ought to be built on tenets of cooperation, collaboration, and reciprocity (Gay, 2010), I was unable to find a way in. I decided to ask the vice principal to speak with Benjamin. This felt like the ultimate failure on top of the failure I had been feeling throughout our struggle. As a teacher, I rarely let disciplinary issues leave my classroom as I quickly learned that once you did, you lost part of your relationship with a student that you could never regain. However, as a researcher with limited time, and finally thinking about the 31 other students I had ignored because I was so focused on Benjamin (several of them had needed my help with sewing techniques and I had twice forgotten to prompt them to engage in critique—a critical component of the study), I decided to outsource the problem.

I admitted that things were unlikely to end well with Benjamin because, unfortunately, given the constraints of my research plan, we didn't have sufficient time to rebuild our relationship. In a memo I wrote, "My struggle with Benjamin reminds me of having to deal with the emotions of teaching and feeling like you're failing over and over again." In the end, he never fully committed to the group work, but we talked about it, and he wrote a powerful artist statement to accompany his individual art piece for our final showcase. It would be nice to say that everything was neatly resolved, but it wasn't. Moreover, I still don't know if I could or should have acted differently. Would it have been advisable to let Benjamin work on his own? Should I have let him draw throughout his time in art class rather than participate in the project? I'm not sure either of these options would have been any better than the approach I chose.

My relationship with Benjamin was unique in the tension it created, but it was not the only classroom management issue that impacted data collection. For example, one student admitted to giving another a pretty serious burn with a glue gun, which derailed the entire second half of a lesson. On another occasion, I had to mediate a conflict between two groups that were accusing each other of "stealing" costume materials. Such incidents are snapshots of the reality of life in schools and classrooms, details that are routinely forgotten when researchers write up studies for publication. I took Benjamin's actions personally, and my internal identity crisis left me questioning my entire study. I had wanted to highlight classroom conversations about art making, yet there were so many things getting in the way of my vision. I was tired, unsure of how to proceed, and, at times, completely discouraged.

Despite having a well-articulated plan as a researcher, as a teacher I could barely remember to prompt students to share with partners when I was preoccupied with management interruptions, let alone make sure they were having rich conversations about their artwork. Throughout the study my post-lesson memos helped me process the interruptions caused by the management issues I was facing. These memos were audio recorded on my drive home from data collection each day. I reflected on theory (i.e., if the designed discourse spaces I had included as mediating processes in my conjecture map were doing the theoretical work I had predicted they would) and practice (i.e., whether a teacher could plan for and support particular discourse spaces in real moments of instruction).

Reframing interruptions as possibilities

In this chapter I shared two specific cases of everyday interruptions I encountered during a particular data collection process and have offered reflections on how I dealt with challenges as the primary teacher and researcher. While adjusting lesson plans and reflecting on practice through ethnographic memos helped me, I am reluctant to offer explicit recommendations for how to handle such interruptions in all school settings because I recognize that each context is unique. However, I hope that this chapter provides some insights and guidance for how to anticipate, navigate, and even (re)frame the everyday interruptions—specifically administrative and when dealing with classroom management—inherent in research in schools.

At first I considered administrative interruptions a burden, but ultimately they made me operate with more intentionality as a researcher and teacher. Navigating unexpected happenings necessitated adjustments in my plans that gave me a new perspective on how to support the kinds of constructs I had included in my research design. For example, knowing that the fire drill would soon interrupt our whole-group discussion, I facilitated the lesson with a greater sense of urgency to get students to engage quickly with and tell stories about social issues. In channeling this urgency, I was also able to gain a better sense of how the student interactions and conversations I envisioned might take shape in other real classroom contexts. The teacher moves I made to push the lesson forward resulted in short bursts of focused conversation, creating a unique sense of rhythm in our classroom talk.

Everyday interruptions also widened my perspective on how learning was happening. For example, experiences like working around the fire drill required widening my unit of analysis for learning from students interacting in a class to students and myself interacting in a class within the context of a larger school institution. Going into the study, my initial focus was squarely on students, but administrative interruptions highlighted the fact that I was also an actor within research that took place in a school. Fire drills, picture day, and classroom celebrations were everyday aspects of "doing school" that required flexibility and improvisation in my approach. These events became part of what it meant to do research in this context.

Expanding on this idea of widening the unit of analysis, classroom management interruptions pushed me to consider interactional work from a broader perspective than the teacher–student level. Interactions between teachers and students matter, but students also interact with one another and materials, and all of these interactions occur within nested layers, including the school, community, and larger sociopolitical context. The study happened at school, an institution that traditionally constrains and enables particular kinds of learning and participation. Schools are not static, and there were shifts within this particular institution that impacted the study. For example, following repeated staff absences during data collection, the lead teacher of my focus class, another sixth-grade teacher, and even the principal quit and left the school after winter break. Although, in retrospect, these events were not entirely unexpected, mid-year departures can have detrimental impacts on student learning and the continuity of student experience (Henry & Redding, 2018). Viewed through an even wider lens, the broader sociopolitical context moves in and out of learning environments, impacting individuals and communities. For example, the parent of one of my students was deported during data collection; consequently, the student had to leave the school community of which he had been a member since kindergarten.

Classrooms are not isolated environments, so context on different levels cannot be ignored. Teachers and researchers must keep this in mind when designing lessons and studies. Benjamin moved through spaces over the course of his day, bringing with him diverse repertoires of practice particular to the communities of which he was part (Nasir, Rosebery, Warren, & Lee, 2006). These practices ought to be made relevant not only in what is taught in and across the school setting but also in how teachers and researchers think about issues of power in the organization of learning, including social relations in learning environments, how tools mediate student thinking, and how student thought develops (Vossoughi & Gutiérrez, 2017). Considering overlapping contexts reorients the necessary consideration of classroom management from a singular relationship to a more distributed network of influence. Widening this scope of analysis on interactions in schools can help teachers and researchers think more broadly about how to design environments that better support students' academic, social, and emotional needs as they move across learning spaces.

Interruptions as part of the work

In schools, we deal with moving parts that influence one another. Interruptions embedded in macro-, meso-, and micro-level contexts overlap and impact the learning in classrooms. As research in the learning sciences attempts to find ways to engage more effectively with macro-level issues of power in learning contexts (Esmonde & Booker, 2017), it is important for researchers invested in designing for more equitable learning environments to reflect on their blind spots and grapple with challenging questions about how these different scales interact. Additionally, reframing everyday interruptions as possibilities for seeing the broader picture honors the everyday work of students and teachers and can help scholars using DBR meet their ultimate aim of having an impact on both theory and practice.

Good teachers often transcend the systems in which they operate; research that both attends to details of teaching and learning and considers context on multiple levels might help teachers think about creative and grounded ways to do so.

If we consider interruptions to be part of the work, our theories about and practices for designing learning environments can include ways to anticipate and navigate everyday interruptions in school-based research. Embedding interruptions in design work might also help researchers foreground the idea that teachers and researchers have complementary goals. Indeed, an excerpt from one of my memos on how teachers think about planning echoes how qualitative researchers think about iterative design:

> Teaching is just about thinking back and forward simultaneously. You know, going through a quick reflective cycle of what happened and trying hard to improve and then going forward trying to implement those improvements and then make better decisions in the moment. It is impossible to do everything 100% perfectly like you imagined it in your mind, but it is also something you are striving toward.

Understanding this work of "thinking back and forward simultaneously" necessitates feeling comfortable with ambiguity in planning around everyday interruptions. In fact, our work can improve because of the ambiguities we face. This uncertainty can push us, as researchers, to design with students, teachers, and schools always at the forefront of our minds.

References

Ball, D. (2018). Just dreams and imperatives: The power of teaching in the struggle for public education. Presidential Address to the American Educational Research Association Annual Meeting, New York, April 19.

Bondy, E., Ross, D. D., Gallingane, C., & Hambacher, E. (2007). Creating environments of success and resilience: Culturally responsive classroom management and more. *Urban Education*, 42(4), 326–348.

Brown, A. L. (1992). Design experiments: Theoretical and methodological challenges in creating complex interventions in classroom settings. *Journal of the Learning Sciences*, 2(2), 141–178.

Cobb, P., Confrey, J., diSessa, A., Lehrer, R., & Schauble, L. (2003). Design experiments in educational research. *Educational Researcher*, 32(1), 9–13.

Cochran-Smith, M., & Lytle, S. L. (1993). *Inside/outside: Teacher research and knowledge*. New York: Teachers College Press.

Collins, A. (1992). Toward a design science of education. In E. Scanlon & T. O'Shea (Eds.) *New directions in educational technology* (pp. 15–22). Berlin: Springer-Verlag.

Dahn, M. (2019). The weaving of artistic and political voice in art making about social issues. Unpublished doctoral dissertation, University of California, Los Angeles.

Dewey, J. (1934). *Art as experience*. New York: Minton, Balch, & Company.

Engle, R. A., Conant, F. R., & Greeno, J. G. (2007). Progressive refinement of hypotheses in video-supported research. In R. Goldman, R. Pea, B. Barron, & S. J. Derry (Eds.) *Video research in the learning sciences* (pp. 239–254). Mahwah, NJ: Erlbaum.

Erickson, F. (2006). Definitions and analysis of data from videotape: Some research procedures and their rationales. In J. Green, G. Camilli, & P. Elmore (Eds.) *Handbook of complementary methods in educational research*, 3rd edition (pp. 177–191). Washington, DC: American Educational Research Association.

Esmonde, I., & Booker, A. N. (2017). *Power and privilege in the learning sciences: Critical and sociocultural theories of learning*. New York: Routledge.

Gay, G. (2006). Connections between classroom management and culturally responsive teaching. In C. Evertson, & C. Weinstein (Eds.) *Handbook of classroom management: Research, practice, and contemporary issues* (pp. 343–370). New York: Routledge.

Gay, G. (2010). *Culturally responsive teaching: Theory, research, and practice*. New York: Teachers College Press.

Henry, G. T., & Redding, C. (2018). The consequences of leaving school early: The effects of within-year and end-of-year teacher turnover. *Education Finance and Policy*, September, 1–52.

Holloway, D. L., & Krensky, B. (2001). Introduction: The arts, urban education, and social change. *Education and Urban Society*, 33(4), 354–365.

Ladson-Billings, G. (1995). Toward a theory of culturally relevant pedagogy. *American Educational Research Journal*, 32(3), 465–491.

Lampert, M., & Ball, D. L. (1998). *Teaching, multimedia, and mathematics: Investigations of real practice*. New York: Teachers College Press.

Malchiodi, C. A. (Ed.). (2011). *Handbook of art therapy*. New York: Guilford Press.

Milner, H. R., & Tenore, F. B. (2010). Classroom management in diverse classrooms. *Urban Education*, 45(5), 560–603.

Nasir, N., Rosebery, A. S., Warren, B., & Lee, C. D. (2006). Learning as a cultural process: Achieving equity through diversity. In K. Sawyer (Ed.), *Handbook of the learning sciences* (pp. 489–504). Cambridge: Cambridge University Press.

Rogers, J., Mirra, N., Seltzer, M., & Jun, J. (2014). *It's about time: Learning time and educational opportunity in California high schools*. Los Angeles: UCLA IDEA.

Rose, M. (1995). *Possible lives: The promise of public education in America*. New York: Houghton Mifflin.

Salazar, R. (2011). This school year, don't teach like a champion. Blog post, September 5. Retrieved December 14, 2018 from: www.chicagonow.com/white-rhino/2011/09/this-school-year-dont-teach-like-a-champion/.

Sandoval, W. (2014). Conjecture mapping: An approach to systematic educational design research. *Journal of the Learning Sciences*, 23(1), 18–36.

Svihla, V., & Reeve, R. (Eds.). (2016). *Design as scholarship: Case studies from the learning sciences*. New York: Routledge.

Vossoughi, S. (2014). Social analytic artifacts made concrete: A study of learning and political education. *Mind, Culture, and Activity*, 21(4), 353–373.

Vossoughi, S., & Gutiérrez, K. (2017). Critical pedagogy and sociocultural theory. In I. Esmonde & A. Booker (Eds.) *Power and privilege in the learning sciences: Critical and sociocultural theories of learning* (pp. 139–158). New York: Routledge.

Weinstein, C. S., Tomlinson-Clarke, S., & Curran, M. (2004). Toward a conception of culturally responsive classroom management. *Journal of Teacher Education*, 55(1), 25–38.

Wilson, S. M. (1995). Not tension but intention: A response to Wong's analysis of the researcher/teacher. *Educational Researcher*, 24(8), 19–22.

11

TWO STEPS FORWARD, ONE STEP BACK

Obstacles and progress in conducting research in elementary classrooms

Sharon L. Smith, Loren Jones and Luciana C. de Oliveira

Introduction

Planning and implementing research is like any new endeavor. While exciting, it is often intimidating and, at times, completely overwhelming. The obstacles that arise in educational research are often unavoidable, independent of years of experience, established relationships, or familiarity with the research process. Graduate students, novice researchers, and veteran scholars alike grapple with the unanticipated dilemmas and challenges of teacher research (e.g., Strauss, 1995). As a research group of three embarking on our first classroom-based study together, we faced numerous frustrating situations. Although we were eventually able to overcome these issues, our research journey over the last couple of years has been a rollercoaster of emotions.

When our research endeavors began in July 2016, we were first- and second-year doctoral students (Sharon and Loren) working under the mentorship of an experienced researcher (Luciana). Based on our individual teaching experiences and shared research interests, we elected to center our work on instruction for diverse learners with an emphasis on effective scaffolding strategies. Eager to begin our research, we jumped into the process of gaining Institutional Review Board (IRB) approval, recruiting participants, and developing data collection processes. Luckily, we did not encounter any complications in the early phases of the project, such as the ones discussed in Part 1 of this volume, and we quickly began collaborating with and observing a teacher at a local elementary school in Miami.

We had already formed a relationship with this focal teacher as a result of her work with student teachers from our university. On numerous occasions, we had observed her teaching and knew that she was passionate and dedicated to education. Through continued conversations, it also became clear that she was always searching for ways to improve her own practice. Therefore, she was an ideal participant, one with whom we knew we could develop a mutually-beneficial research partnership. We were able to build literacy units in collaboration with this teacher, observing and recording their implementation in her first-grade classroom. This was the first exposure to the complete process of a classroom-based study for two of us (Sharon and Loren). Often due to space requirements, articles tend not to provide in-depth information about the intricate, complicated processes involved in studies. We recall naively thinking that research projects were pretty straightforward and simple, based on what we had read in coursework: you secure approval, find a class, and collect your data. However, after five successful months of data collection, our simplified view of research was abruptly shattered.

This chapter tells our story of interrupted research in an attempt to provide an honest counternarrative to the simplified, linear view of research that is often presented in textbooks. We present a narrative that highlights the reality of conducting classroom-based research. First, we provide examples of the many disruptions that transpired during our data collection processes. Second, we demonstrate how we were able to navigate and overcome these obstacles. Third, we describe the lessons that we learned from these experiences. In order to illuminate the diverse types of interruptions we encountered, we organize our narrative by presenting five general themes that emerged when we examined our experiences with interruptions. Finally, we conclude by synthesizing some of the lessons we learned.

Research restraints, responses, and resiliency

The interruptions we experienced were related to (a) individuals' personal lives; (b) educational institutions' realities; (c) acts of nature; (d) human error; and (e) bureaucracy. We discuss each of these themes as they arose chronologically in our research and then highlight additional, ongoing interruptions that cut across multiple themes.

Individuals' personal lives interrupt research

Life is full of unexpected surprises, and such events have the power to bring a research project to a standstill. Five months into our "perfect" research project, we experienced the reality of research interruptions when our focal teacher announced that she had to start her upcoming maternity leave several weeks earlier than expected. This caused a sudden halt in data collection mid-unit, and our study was put on hold until the teacher returned towards the end of the school year. As 77 percent of US teachers are female, and 71 percent are of childbearing age (Taie & Goldring, 2018), the probability of this specific situation occurring is relatively high. However, while we had planned to pause our research, we had not anticipated doing so several weeks ahead of schedule.

Loren had just started collecting data in this classroom for her dissertation, and this unexpected hiccup in the data collection process came as quite a shock. Unsure if the teacher would return in time for Loren to finish collecting data, she was extremely anxious and feared that this would not only delay her timeline for completing the study, but also jeopardize her tentative graduation date.

This first interruption made us realize that there are many barriers and disruptions over which researchers have no control. With so many individuals involved in each classroom research project (e.g., researchers, teacher participants, student participants, principals, and IRB members at the university and district levels), the likelihood of someone experiencing a personal emergency or illness is quite high. Educational researchers in every institution face interruptions, even if they are not openly documented in their published work or discussed at length in research classes. Recognizing that the "messiness" of research is common even for veteran scholars (e.g., Cravens et al., 2014) can help emerging researchers maintain motivation and patience when things do not go as expected. Luciana shared her previous experiences when she encountered interruptions due to IRB approval and educational realities at other academic institutions and elementary schools, which helped Sharon and Loren realize that this life event and the resulting extended gap in data collection were not uncommon in research. Since it was beyond our control, we had to be flexible, patient, and simply accept it. Fortunately, the teacher did return at the end of the school year, we were able to resume data collection, and Loren was able to gather the data needed to complete her dissertation.

Educational institutions' realities interrupt research

We finished data collection for the 2016–2017 school year after our focal teacher returned from maternity leave and began planning data collection for the following year. We had IRB approval for a two-year study, so we were looking forward to the 2017–2018 academic year, excited about the prospect of a full year of uninterrupted data collection. However, a few weeks before school started, our focal teacher notified us that she was moving from first grade to fifth grade. This sudden change caught us all by surprise. We quickly realized that our IRB approval did not extend to this new grade-level setting, resulting in another obstacle. In addition, we realized that high-stakes testing, which is prevalent in this grade, could affect our data collection.

This interruption was due to the reality and nature of educational institutions. Every year, as the student population changes, the composition of educational institutions is different. At public schools, elementary teachers have to be flexible about what grades they teach, as they are often moved to other grade levels immediately before the new school year begins, or sometimes even after the school year has commenced (Atteberry, Loeb, & Wyckoff, 2017; Riordan, 2013). During her first year as an elementary teacher, Sharon herself was asked to move grade levels two weeks after the school year had started, due to student numbers. Since student numbers vary from year to year and principals often restructure grade-level teams, educational researchers might encounter challenges when teachers move to a different grade. A study may no longer be applicable, or modifications to IRBs may have to be made.

Educators also have to face the demands of high-stakes testing (Au, 2011). With so much dependent on whether students pass these district, state, and national standardized tests, principals and teachers are often hesitant to let researchers into the classroom (Wellington, 2015). Even when researchers do gain access to a classroom or school, their observations or experiments are often delayed during testing periods. With our particular study, our focal teacher moved to fifth grade, one of the grades in which a great deal of time is devoted to testing. After talking with our teacher participant, we realized that it would be better to collect data in the fall, due to state testing and preparation for the tests. The advent of the age of accountability following the No Child Left Behind Act of 2001 ushered in the current era of federally mandated high-stakes testing (Au, 2007; 2011), with an average of nine mandated tests taken in fifth grade, with approximately 23.2 hours dedicated to the tests alone (Hart et al., 2015). With grade promotion and teachers' salaries linked to student achievement, teachers feel significant pressure to "teach to the test," resulting in the narrowing of curriculum and pedagogy, with the weeks leading up to the tests often dedicated to test prep and review (Au, 2007; 2011; Crocco & Costigan, 2007).

We found ourselves rushing to submit a new study protocol to the IRB at our university, cognizant that even after gaining the university's approval, we would still need approval from the school district. However, we were all optimistic that we would be able to resume data collection within a matter of weeks, as only minor changes to the study protocol were needed. As we worked on these changes, we maintained contact with our focal teacher, giving her updates on our projected timeline.

Natural and national disasters interrupt research

We never dreamed that the old adage "You can't control the weather," would apply to our research, but Hurricane Irma proved us wrong. In the midst of drafting our new study protocol, this natural disaster resulted in mandatory evacuations for many of Miami's residents, including our research team. Breaking records as the strongest Atlantic basin hurricane outside the Gulf of Mexico and the Caribbean Sea, over six million people were ordered to leave their homes before Irma made landfall in the continental United States (Miller, 2017). This catastrophic Category 4+ hurricane caused 69 deaths (CBS Interactive Inc., 2017) and approximately 50 billion dollars' worth of damage (National Hurricane Center, 2018), while almost seven million people lost power (CBS Interactive Inc., 2017). The force of Irma led to the university's closure for almost three weeks, delaying our IRB approval and pushing back the start of our 2017–2018 data collection yet again.

This delay made us realize that, just as many events that affect individuals' personal lives are unexpected, it is often impossible to predict acts of nature. Natural disasters (e.g., earthquakes, tornadoes, flooding, and hurricanes) have the power completely to disrupt lives and research. With the changing climate, extreme weather events and natural disasters have increased in frequency and severity (US Global Change Research Program, 2014), and therefore have a higher potential to impact projects. At the same time, large-scale local or national disasters also have the ability to affect studies. In wake of many recent school shootings across the nation, we have noticed an increase in security at schools across our district. There are new sign-in procedures that our research team is required to follow in order to enter schools, and the school where we collect data has had to redistribute funds in its budget to provide additional security personnel to patrol the campus. While these tragedies have not had a noticeable effect on our research, they have shown us how events across the nation can have local impacts.

Although large-scale disasters do not occur on a frequent basis, when they do take place, they can have prolonged, devastating effects. Similar to navigating individuals' personal life events, we learned that we had to be flexible and adapt when faced with a natural disaster.

Human error interrupts research

Upon returning to Miami after Irma, we waited to hear back from the university's IRB, assuming that the delay in approval had been caused by the hurricane. Although we were concerned about how this would affect our study, all of Miami was dealing with the consequences of the storm, and we had multiple other issues vying for our attention at the time. However, after two months with no word from the IRB, Luciana, the principal investigator on this study, followed up to ascertain what was causing such a prolonged delay. We discovered that the new study protocol had never been submitted through the IRB website. After the university's IRB changed its website, Luciana did not realize that an additional button had to be clicked in order for the protocol to be submitted. At this point, we were extremely frustrated with ourselves for overlooking that final click. Admittedly, we also felt a bit defeated, having encountered so many other setbacks.

Although human error is sometimes avoidable, it is also extremely prevalent; one has but to open a newspaper to read headline after headline concerning human error (Woods et al., 2010). It came as no surprise, therefore, that this particular delay was due to human error. Moreover, while the numerous documents and protocols required during the IRB process make this stage of the research cycle especially prone to human error, other research phases (e.g., data collection and data analysis) are similarly susceptible. For example, a researcher could easily forget to start the recording of a lesson, inturrupting data collection. Along the same lines, a lack of knowledge about a subject could lead to complications (e.g., Adamson & Walker, 2011). Technology, procedures, and requirements are constantly changing and developing in the twenty-first century, and, as a result, there are many opportunities for educational researchers to make a mistake or overlook something important. As researchers are not robots, some degree of human error is to be expected in any research project. When we encountered it, we quickly looked for ways to resolve the issue and prevent it from happening again.

Bureaucracy interrupts research

Luciana immediately remedied the situation, and we received feedback from the university's IRB the following month. However, we then faced another obstacle—the reviewers requested changes to documents that had previously been approved (e.g., revision of the language used on our consent forms). This unexpected hurdle was disheartening. To make matters worse, it came right before the holiday break and the end of the Fall 2017 semester, and we anticipated an extended delay before we could continue with the IRB process at the district level. Educational research presents a unique challenge because, in addition to university IRB approval, school district IRB approval is often required. Even once the university has approved a study, the district may require further changes. Previous experience indicated that this step could take several months.

Even if we were able to secure IRB approval at both the university and district levels at the beginning of the Spring 2018 semester, we knew that we would face numerous other challenges, including:

- mid-semester recruitment issues due to our IRB protocol, which required us to speak to the elementary students' parents to gain consent before obtaining student assent;
- heavy testing during the spring semester in fifth grade; and
- our team members' hectic schedules at the end of the Spring 2018 semester.

Discouraged and disillusioned with the study approval and recruitment processes, we decided to revise and resubmit the IRB documents immediately, but then to wait and recommence recruitment and data collection in the Fall 2018 semester when we would be able to recruit and secure parents' consent at the school's open-house event, giving us ample time to collect data with the class before testing began.

The bureaucratic delays, such as the requested IRB changes and the months of waiting for the study protocol to be approved, resulted in the longest interruptions we experienced with this project. The bureaucracy we faced was related to IRB processes and requirements, but we recognize that there can be many other bureaucratic delays in educational research. For instance, even though we were not reliant on a grant for this project, other researchers have discussed the difficulties they have encountered with the bureaucratic grants culture, such as having to change a study to fit the interests of those who are providing the funding (e.g., Daza, 2012; Graham & Buckley, 2014). With our project, even though IRB approval for the new study protocol for a different grade was initially delayed because of human error, this delay did not seem out of the ordinary, based on previous experience with the university's IRB. Our university's IRB process has multiple steps, and at any moment it can be delayed due to the lack of someone's signature, which we experienced with the departmental reviewer. We navigated these challenges with both university and district IRBs through a combination of patience, waiting, and proactively investigating what was holding up the process.

Another significant bureaucratic challenge we faced was due to IRB requirements for parental consent (for more about parental recruitment issues, see Chapter 3). We recognize that elementary children are a vulnerable population (US National Commission for the Protection of Human Subjects of Biomedical and Behavioral Research, 1979) and that parental consent is a necessary step; however, this is often hard to obtain in the middle of a semester. The parental consent forms that are approved by the IRB are often several pages long and can be difficult to understand. When the researchers do not have an opportunity to explain the study face-to-face to parents, our experience is that parents are less likely to consent to their children participating. While we acknowledge that IRBs are put in place to ensure students' well-being—which is also our ultimate goal—the process and the protocol can be quite frustrating. This challenge resulted in us deciding to postpone our consent process until the following semester, which allowed us to speak directly to the parents.

Ongoing interruptions

When we began the resubmission process, we encountered some additional minor delays related to a number of the aforementioned themes. In order to facilitate IRB approval, we needed a new letter of invitation from the focal teacher's principal specifying which grade we would be studying. There was talk about moving the focal teacher to yet another grade for the 2018–2019 school year, so we needed to wait until quite late in the spring 2018 semester, when the principal finally confirmed that the focal teacher would indeed be teaching fifth grade in the fall. This uncertainty was unsettling, and even meeting with the principal herself was a challenge, as she had to reschedule the meeting multiple times.

However, this challenge taught us that a strong relationship with the school in which we were carrying out our project was an important factor to move our study forward. When we were able to meet with the principal and explain that we needed to know the grade in which the focal teacher would be placed, she worked with us because of our past partnerships, even though she had not yet decided upon grade placements for the upcoming year. Working proactively to develop relationships with elementary schools and different individuals at the university level can prove very beneficial when interruptions are encountered.

We were finally able to collect all the necessary paperwork and submitted the study protocol through the IRB website, this time double-checking that we had not missed anything. However, before the protocol could be submitted to the university's IRB, it needed to be reviewed, approved, and signed by the department's reviewer. After a month, we were still waiting for this signature. Without it, the IRB process could not move forward. While recognizing that the end of the semester is a busy time for everyone, we decided that it was necessary to contact the reviewer directly. When Luciana did so, we discovered that the reviewer had never received an approval request from the IRB website. When she realized that we had been waiting for weeks for her signature, she immediately reviewed our study protocol and signed off on it. However, we then encountered another slight delay when it moved on to the university IRB. We were asked to revise the student assent forms to make the language less challenging for fifth-grade students, even though the same forms had been used in our previous first-grade study.

After all the previous setbacks, even these smaller issues seemed quite daunting, and we struggled to maintain optimism and motivation to continue with the project. However, at the time of writing this chapter (July 2018), we had just secured university IRB approval and were only awaiting district IRB approval.

Implications and conclusion

The five themes that emerged from our experiences with research interruptions illustrate one common overarching theme: Some interruptions are within the educational researcher's control (e.g., controlling for human error), whereas others are entirely outside of the researcher's control (e.g., natural disasters). This central theme is reminiscent of Niebuhr's well-known Serenity Prayer: "Grant me the serenity to accept the things I cannot change, courage to change the things I can, and wisdom to know the difference." While this may appear platitudinous, it embodies three strategies we have found useful when navigating research interruptions. In this section, we discuss these strategies:

- accepting interruptions;
- proactively working to move research forward; and
- seeking wisdom through mentorship.

Accepting the multitude of interruptions one might face in the field of educational research can be disheartening, while the numerous bureaucratic issues can be disillusioning. Emerging researchers tend to enter the field with high ideals and creative concepts for the "perfect" research project; however, most are required to modify their ideas when they encounter the reality of educational institutions, bureaucracy, and required protocols. From our personal experiences, we have found that it is important to keep an end goal in mind, while still embracing the messiness and the unexpected (Carter, 2010). This held true for us throughout our project—from anticipating the focal teacher's return from maternity leave to waiting on IRB approval. When our project did not go entirely as planned, and interruptions continued to throw it off track, we accepted that we could not always avoid temporary disruptions or challenges while simultaneously continuing to make a concerted effort to maintain our focus and motivation.

In educational research, inquiry needs to allow for flexibility and must accommodate the unexpected (Bryman, 2004; Chan, 2017). The literature acknowledges that alterations to research designs have to be made in response to unpredictable events (e.g., Chan, 2017). While accepting that some interruptions were beyond our control, we took proactive steps to avoid *prolonged* interruptions. For example, after resubmitting the study protocol with the grade-level change and awaiting IRB approval during the 2017–2018 school year, we proactively approached the principal to discuss grade placements for the 2018–2019 school year. We learned that it is important to start as early as possible with this process, as it can be very time consuming. We also found that it was helpful to work together on the IRB study protocol and submit it as a team, as multiple perspectives can help avoid human error. During each stage of the process, it became important to keep track of what was happening. If it appeared that it had stalled at some point (e.g., when we had to wait for the department reviewer's signature), we learned that being proactive and reaching out to others could help speed up the process.

Since the first time that many graduate students become aware of the interruptions that often occur during research is when they themselves start working on a research project, mentorship is crucial. Without a mentor's advice and encouragement, novice researchers may face disillusionment, self-doubt, and isolation (Strauss, 1995). We all encountered discouraging situations, but Luciana's accounts of her previous experiences were reassuring. Mentors need to be open about the "messiness" of research. The prescribed and institutionalized protocols for academic writing often "de-messify" the research process, presenting it as a simple, linear practice (Chan, 2017). The word-count requirements usually result in concise methodology sections, with the complications that happen during data collection left undocumented. Sharon and Loren felt like there was a disconnect between what they were experiencing and what they were expected to produce, as none of the articles they had encountered discussed any of the aforementioned complications. However, by providing them with previous examples of interrupted research, Luciana was able to help them see that disruptions are to be expected. She was also able to help them navigate the different types of interruptions, discussing those that needed to be accepted and in what areas the team could be more proactive. Veteran researchers such as Luciana can also often leverage their experience and relationships to help facilitate the process, such as when she contacted the department's reviewer directly to ask her to sign off on the study protocol.

Our research project's numerous complications consumed much more time and energy than anticipated, and they resulted in the investigation stalling on various occasions for extended periods. While the study had its own unique challenges, scholars have to make compromises and confront obstacles in the majority of research endeavors (Dornyei, 2007). For instance, many will be faced with complications related to the IRB process, methodology, data collection, and recruitment of participants (Law, 2004; Lunsford & Lunsford, 2008). Obstacles in educational research are unavoidable due to the complex and multifaceted nature of classroom-based studies (Mackey & Gass, 2005). However, we have learned a great deal over the past two years with this project. We hope that this honest account of the multiple interruptions that even a veteran researcher may face, coupled with some practical strategies based on our newfound knowledge and situated in previous research, will help other educational researchers. In addition, we hope that our narrative and the other stories of interrupted research in this volume will challenge and possibly begin to transform some institutionalized research practices that continue to present educational research as a neat and tidy process (Chan, 2017; Jackson & Mazzei, 2012).

References

Adamson, B., & Walker, E. (2011). Messy collaboration: Learning from a learning study. *Teaching and Teacher Education*, 27, 29–36.

Atteberry, A., Loeb, S., & Wyckoff, J. (2017). Teacher churning: Reassignment rates and implications for student achievement. *Educational Evaluation and Policy Analysis*, 39(1), 3–30.

Au, W. (2007). High-stakes testing and curricular control: A qualitative metasynthesis. *Educational Researcher*, 36(5), 258–267.

Au, W. (2011). Teaching under the new Taylorism: High-stakes testing and the standardization of the 21st century curriculum. *Journal of Curriculum Studies*, 43(1), 25–45.

Bryman, A. (2004). *Social research methods*, 2nd edition. New York: Oxford University Press.

Carter, M. R. (2010). The teacher monologues. *Creative Approaches to Research*, 3(1), 42–66.

CBS Interactive Inc. (2017). Hurricane Irma death toll at 69: Florida power outage at 6.8 million people. *CBS News*, September 14. Retrieved March 14, 2019 from: www.cbsnews.com/news/huricane-irma-death-toll-florida-power-outage/.

Chan, A. (2017). Reflection, reflexivity, reconceptualization: Life story inquiry and the complex positionings of a researcher. *Reconceptualizing Educational Research Methodology*, 8 (1), 27–39. Retrieved March 14, 2019 from: http://journals.hioa.no/index.php/rerm.

Cravens, A. E., Ulibarri, N., Cornelius, M., Royalty, A., & Nabergoj, A. S. (2014). Reflecting, iterating, and tolerating ambiguity: Highlighting the creative process of scientific and scholarly research for doctoral education. *International Journal of Doctoral Studies*, 9, 229–247.

Crocco, M. S., & Costigan, A. T. (2007). The narrowing of curriculum and pedagogy in the age of accountability: Urban educators speak out. *Urban Education*, 42(6), 512–535.

Daza, S. L. (2012). Complicity as infiltration: The (im)possibilities of research with/in NSF engineering grants in the age of neoliberal scientism. *Qualitative Inquiry*, 18(9), 773–786.

Dornyei, Z. (2007). *Research methods in applied linguistics*. New York: Oxford University Press.

Graham, B. A., & Buckley, L. (2014). Ghost hunting with lollies, chess and Lego: Appreciating the "messy" complexity (and costs) of doing difficult research in education. *Australian Association for Research in Education*, 41, 327–347.

Hart, R., Casserly, M., Uzzell, R., Palacios, M., Corcoran, A., & Spurgeon, L. (2015). *Student testing in America's great city schools: An inventory and preliminary analysis*. Washington, DC: Council of the Great City Schools. Retrieved March 14, 2019 from: www.cgcs.org/cms/lib/DC00001581/Centricity/Domain/87/Testing%20Report.pdf.

Jackson, A. Y., & Mazzei, L. A. (2012). *Thinking with theory in qualitative research: Viewing data across multiple perspectives*. Abingdon: Routledge.

Law, J. (2004). *After method: Mess in social science research*. New York: Routledge.

Lunsford, A. A., & Lunsford, K. J. (2008). "Mistakes are a fact of life": A national comparative study. *College Composition and Communication*, 59(4), 781–806.

Mackey, A., & Gass, S. M. (2005). *Second language research: Methodology and design*. New York: Routledge.

Miller, B. (2017). All the records Irma has already broken—and other jaw-dropping stats. *CNN*, September 10. Retrieved March 14, 2019 from: www.cnn.com/2017/09/10/us/irma-facts-record-numbers-trnd/index.html.

National Hurricane Center. (2018). *Costliest US tropical cyclones tables updated*. Miami, FL: US Department of Commerce, National Oceanic and Atmospheric Administration. Retrieved March 14, 2019 from: www.nhc.noaa.gov/news/UpdatedCostliest.pdf.

Riordan, K. E. (2013). Involuntary teacher transfer: An underexamined practice. *Intervention in School and Clinic*, 49(3), 181–186.

Strauss, P. (1995). No easy answers: The dilemmas and challenges of teacher research. *Educational Action Research*, 3(1), 29–40.

Taie, S., & Goldring, R. (2018). *Characteristics of public elementary and secondary school teachers in the United States: Results from the 2015–16 national teacher and principal survey* [NCES 2017–072rev]. US Department of Education. Washington, DC: National Center for Education Statistics. Retrieved March 14, 2019 from: https://nces.ed.gov/pubs2017/2017072rev.pdf.

US Global Change Research Program. (2014). *National climate assessment: Full report.* Retrieved March 14, 2019 from: https://nca2014.globalchange.gov/report.

US National Commission for the Protection of Human Subjects of Biomedical and Behavioral Research. (1979). *The Belmont report: Ethical principles and guidelines for the protection of human subjects of research.* Retrieved March 14, 2019 from: www.hhs.gov/ohrp/regulations-and-policy/belmont-report/read-the-belmont-report/index.html.

Wellington, J. (2015). *Educational research: Contemporary issues and practical approaches*, 2nd edition. New York: Bloomsbury.

Woods, D., Dekker, S., Cook, R., Johannesen, L., & Sarter, N. (2010). *Behind human error.* London: CRC Press.

12

ON PURSUING QUIXOTIC GOALS

What are worthwhile interruptions to research?

Michael Tan

Introduction

If interruptions are inevitable in the process of doing research, and such interruptions are often accompanied by significant stress, it might be useful to consider which kinds of goals are worth suffering the stress for. Writing about the nature of educational research, well-placed observers have noticed its complexity and difficulty in contrast to the traditional "hard" natural sciences (Berliner, 2002; Phillips, 2014). Education research, they posit, labors under conditions that most natural scientists would find intolerable: contexts with inseparable confounding variables, continually shifting theoretical lenses, and widespread misunderstanding of the goals of science in one's field. In contrast to other disciplines where the cooperation of human subjects is often unnecessary for the successful conduct of one's research (e.g., in the natural sciences), the agentic cooperation required for education research (Labaree, 2004) sets up conditions that are especially prone to disruption.

In this chapter, I relate the interruptions that occurred during the course of two years of research into makerspaces as sites for particular forms of learning. While I set out with different goals, I would eventually figure out makerspaces—modified engineering workshops for youth—as sites for developing students' creative intentions. Traditional instruction in the science, technology, engineering, and mathematics (STEM) disciplines tends towards the communication of canonical knowledge and less on nurturing the development of student design intentions. I propose that being open to unplanned interruptions in one's research can be helpful in the development of a research trajectory. More significantly, despite the risks, researchers should continue to pursue lines of inquiry that may lead to interruption, because they are likely to reveal more productive problems.

My story of interruption begins with the award of a research grant in Singapore. I set out to research makerspaces, which I had sensed at the outset required a form of pedagogical expertise that was likely unusual in my local context. I had believed that makerspaces would be most powerful when they supported a student-led instruction specifically in non-canonical practical investigations into technologies. This occurs in activities such as the improvisational tinkering required to repurpose items for novel ends. However, from my prior experience as a local teacher, I had sensed that the funding agency was more keen to fund research that would provide technical responses to the problems of schooling. Specifically, I believed that the funders were more likely to support projects intending to show how and why educational interventions were beneficial to the educational "bottom line" of student test scores. In response, I wrote a proposal that I felt represented a compromise I could accept. I proposed to study the nature of embodied interactions that were occurring in a school makerspace, so as to characterize the kinds of learning that were being carried out and how each type could be said to contribute to learning within makerspaces. At the time, makerspaces were still largely experimental spaces that were organized for out-of-school activities. While they did attract the attention of more forward-thinking teachers and school leaders, most teachers were unfamiliar with the activities that typically made a makerspace worthy of the name, let alone the instructional designs that could maximize the learning in these places.

I must acknowledge that this was my first time leading research that was interventionist in nature. Straight out of graduate training, I had until that time been involved only in observational studies; I had not tried to influence the curriculum or pedagogy of mainstream school settings. With a mixture of anticipation and bravado stemming from inexperience, I thought I could finally make some real changes in a school context. As I will detail below, this view was overly optimistic, to say the least.

The first problem I encountered was to find a makerspace to study. Given the variability of such spaces, I also had to decide what qualified as a makerspace for my research purposes. Did they have to be, as much of the popular media portrayed them, rooms full of digital fabrication devices, such as 3D printers, laser cutters, electronic paraphernalia, power tools, and an excess of prototyping material? What were the possible learning goals for activity in makerspaces—STEM, or its cousin, with arts infused, STEAM? How formal were makerspaces supposed to be? As the interdisciplinary STEM movement in Singapore was still non-existent, few, if any, teachers understood, let alone appreciated, the notion of construction as a means to learn science. As the learning goals tended towards preparing students for high-stakes examinations, teachers tended to view classroom activities instrumentally, valuing them according to how much they seemed to align with assessment goals (Hogan et al., 2013). Since there was no formal assessment of making in science, I decided to turn to another discipline that did include assessment of making—design and technology (D&T). This also allowed me to build on an existing relationship.

Through a previous development grant on which I had assisted, I had been in contact with a school that had started to equip and furnish a space for making activities. I had been in contact with a teacher named Alice (a pseudonym), who had been teaching D&T for about ten years and was now head of department. When I discussed my intention to study learning in a makerspace with her, she was enthusiastic and seemed highly committed to fostering student engagement in her subject. In subsequent meetings to discuss setting up a makerspace, however, she expressed some reservations. She ruled out working with programmable electronic components (such as the Arduino) as she thought her students were "not good enough" or "not academically inclined," and needed more accessible activities to develop their skills and interests. She also insisted that the organizational structure of the makerspace needed to be clarified from the outset, in part because of the potential bureaucratic complications she foresaw. Finally, she rejected the notion of running the makerspace as a formal club, as this would require approval from the school administration and the development of formal goals, such as participation in inter-school contests and the deployment of sufficient leadership roles for student participants.

As Alice continued to consider the complexity of setting up makerspace activities in a form that met her expectations, my research grant had already been approved. As with grant funding all over the world, the disbursement of funds was time limited. In this instance, the funds paid the salary of a full-time research assistant for six months while Alice delayed the establishment of a group of students with whom I could work. Sensing her unease over leading the learning in a makerspace, at one point I suggested that I could work with the students myself, heading the club and directing their activity. Her response was one of bemused surprise. I never asked her why she reacted in this way, but my suspicion is that she didn't believe I could manage her students. I probably did myself no favors by openly acknowledging that I had been a physics teacher, that I had not trained in D&T, and that I had never taught such a class. Needless to say, I was never trusted with leading the club.

Our meetings started to become less frequent. At first, we met about once every two weeks, and I'd receive frequent updates about how materials were being bought and the space was being developed. I'd discuss possible projects that could be launched and the techniques of instruction in such a space. However, after about four such meetings, Alice told tell me that the end-of-term exams were just around the corner, and school activity was to shift towards test preparation; therefore, she did not want to be disturbed by research activity. I'd attempt to resume contact as soon as such blackout periods were over, but I would always be given an appointment later than I suggested. It became clear that my project was not a priority for Alice, and the makerspace remained always just around the corner. As I write this, I realize I did my project no favors by not acknowledging this particular teacher's anxiety over a new instructional context, which was heightened by the fact that it would not be within the sanctioned school program. I recall my own time as a teacher, and the seemingly endless amounts of work that had to be done, and now realize that I could have done more to make Alice's job less stressful.

However, grant money was steadily being used, with nothing to show for it. I felt terrible that my research assistant had so little to do. To say that I was worried would be an understatement. I did have a co-principal investigator (co-PI), who had more experience than me, but he had little to offer. As is somewhat common practice, he joined the project to provide some guidance on navigating the grant proposal process, but he had no experience with makerspaces. I therefore knew that I would be working on the project myself. As this was my first attempt at leading an educational intervention project, and though I was not completely naive about how teachers could resist change, I had failed to prepare alternative research activities that would have made more productive use of the time. As the research grant designated only a small amount of money for equipment and tools (it was mostly intended to pay for human resource labor), it was impossible for me to consider setting up a makerspace from scratch and then attracting my own students for research. I simply had to accept that six months of effort generated no productive data whatsoever.

A second attempt

After half a year of unproductive engagement with Alice, I happened to attend the local Maker Fair, where an acquaintance introduced me to Charlie, the art teacher in a local public school. As research activities go, this was an event that could not have been foreseen. I had not sent out invitations to participate among the network of makers; I had not planned to meet anybody during the fair; and I had never expected to work with an art teacher. As a person who did not grow up in the local community, Charlie did not know the norms of schooling in Singapore.[1] That apparently served his purposes well. He felt uncomfortable with the culture of schooling in Singapore, which expected him, minimally, to comply closely with departmental plans for curriculum sequencing and pacing. For instance, as an art teacher, he was expected to introduce to his grade-eight students to different media of expression. Conventionally, teachers would interpret this curriculum requirement by getting students to use paint, charcoal, or perhaps a digital medium. Charlie, convinced that his students were not sufficiently "hands-on," thought otherwise, and had his students work on craft projects using recycled materials and electronics components as interactive art objects. He turned his ignorance of the local norms to his advantage by occasionally ignoring tacit rules that governed the department and choosing to work autonomously. When called out, he would simply highlight his status as an expatriate and often escape with an explanation of what he should have been doing instead. In fact, it would be fair to say that Charlie firmly espoused the principle of asking for forgiveness, not permission. Here, I thought, was an ideal teacher and context for my study. Charlie was an expatriate working in a school of motivated, relatively high-achieving students, so he was not implicitly bound by local cultural norms that dictated what schooling, teaching, and learning ought to look like. Moreover, he was already cognizant of the general principles of making.

When all the relevant permissions had been granted by the school administration and I was finally able to observe Charlie's class—nine months into my grant period—it was already close to the end of a school term. His lessons were decidedly different from the local norms of schooling. In contrast to local teachers, who tended to charge unsympathetically into the lesson's learning objectives right from the outset, Charlie took time to get to know his students, developed coherent cultural norms of what was to constitute creative practice in his class, and did not place strict boundaries on what constituted learning activities. He tolerated students' explorations with materials that did not seem to be particularly goal directed and clarified that he welcomed exploratory behavior, as it was necessary for idea generation. He also got his students to make use of electronic components, such as LEDs, sensors, and motors. These devices were part of the aesthetic design of their projects, so the students did not need to understand their working principles.

In observing Charlie's class, one particular experience took me by surprise. I was watching a student working on a project, and to my "untrained" eyes he seemed to be off-task. He was attaching and removing parts of his artifact in a rather undirected manner, as if he were pretending to be busy while waiting for the lesson to be over. When I asked Charlie about the student's behavior, he calmly responded that I needed to change my interpretive filters. The student was not clock watching, Charlie explained; he was *experimenting*, and schools should give all students the time and space to do so. While I fundamentally do not disagree with this assertion, I still have doubts about whether Charlie, as one who was not from the Singaporean culture, interpreted the student's behavior accurately. On the other hand, I cannot deny the possibility that my interpretation was wrong. In any case, the generosity of Charlie's interpretation stayed with me; it taught me an important lesson about not hurrying the processes of creativity.

This became an important outcome that changed the direction of my research. I had previously internalized a vision of science learning whereby knowledge of particular principles determined one's ability to understand what was happening in a practical scenario. I had not considered partial knowledge and the process of moving from ignorance to knowledge (e.g., Abrahamson, 2012), let alone the process of creating new knowledge. I had proposed the research based on the notion that certain actions were useful in students' cognitive learning of specific scientific principles, and had therefore planned to document the relationship between those actions and learning. Yet, here I was, in a visual arts classroom because I could not obtain access to science classrooms that were making use of makerspaces for learning. I felt ill-equipped to understand the arts concepts that were at work here. I was unclear what students were supposed to be learning. If Charlie was right, and students were experimenting and incubating ideas while apparently engaged in behavior that seemed unproductive, how much access could I get to cognitive processes, if all of these were internal? I had planned to make a wide-angle video record of the students' actions in the room, but when I examined the video, the angle was far too wide, and there was insufficient resolution for me to code what the students were doing accurately. In any case, even if the students' gestures were visible, their intentions were not. For instance, with regard to the student who repeatedly attached and removed parts, was he on- or off-task? In light of the absence of logistical means to carry out a video-stimulated recall protocol and ongoing uncertainty about my research purpose, I froze into inaction. Which students should I choose? Why select them? What was theoretically interesting? While my previous research had included observational approaches, here I was trying to make decisions that aligned with my grant project.

This was compounded because I was unfamiliar with the learning goals of an art class, and although the students were making use of technological devices such as electronic components to create light, sound, and motion, these were used in a highly instrumental manner. The components had some basic degree of programmability through fundamental electric and electronic circuit principles; however, as it was an art class, no attempt was made to explain the functioning principle of, say, a light emitting diode. Also, the electronic components were foolproof, magnetically connectable items that did not allow the students to create non-working circuits, which deprived them of opportunities to detect errors in their mental models. Charlie had a different opinion about this issue and proudly explained that students in a previous cohort had played with his components and were now being introduced to the science; some had even thanked him for giving them a head start in understanding the scientific concepts. Whatever the case, it was clear that my attempts to see science learning in Charlie's classes were not going to be straightforward.

Learning to see learning in Charlie's art class took time. While my classroom observations continued, I struggled to understand the import of particular actions and gestures on the diverse possible processes that were going on in the classroom. Shuttling between classroom observations, reading, and discussion sessions to understand the theoretical significance of the observations helped change the direction of the research project. I moved away from framing learning as the acquisition of scientific concepts and their technological application in engineering problem solving and toward a more general creative problem-solving frame. This was nerve racking. As a new scholar struggling to establish a professional identity as an expert in a particular field of study, it was not at all helpful to feel like a complete neophyte whose peers were churning out publication after publication while my metaphorical wheels continued to spin in the mud.

An unexpected change in instruction

As I began to see this creative problem-solving frame, I thought that this interruption was ending, but the worst was yet to come. Towards the end of the school year (which coincides with the end of the calendar year in Singapore), I introduced Charlie to the laser cutter as a tool that might increase the technological sophistication of his art class. I had imagined that having students create two-dimensional designs on computer software would lead them to deal with some basic mathematical concepts as they worked to create three-dimensional artifacts by connecting plane objects together. However, I did not discuss specific learning activities with Charlie, as he had always come across as someone who did not appreciate prescriptions as to how his class should function. I understood that trying to change his lessons was futile, so settled in for whatever he decided to do with the laser cutter. In any case, by this time I had shifted gear to thinking about makerspaces as sites for creative problem solving, and I was happy merely to study his class as a site where I could learn about students' reactions to what they perceived as unconventional pedagogy.

When he returned from his year-end vacation, Charlie appeared ready to go deep into serious work with the laser cutter. On visiting his class, I learned that he had planned a scaffolding activity of cutting and assembling a paper sculpture from a printed template. However, the art class proper had changed in tone from the previous year. Instead of the open-ended, student-led investigations that had resulted in a dozen or so distinct projects, all of the students were now busily working on a single paper template. Charlie had changed the character of the class such that the students were now engaged in what was essentially a painting-by-numbers exercise—the sculpture would be completed by students following a series of predetermined steps. He explained this was a warm-up activity before the students' projects in the second phase. He made them perform the steps in a linear, stepwise manner, waiting for every last person to finish the current step before proceeding on to the next.

If seeing this approach in Charlie's class took me by surprise, the fact that it took the students five weeks to assemble a rather uncomplicated sculpture became a mini-crisis for my research. Not only could I not observe any learning of scientific principles, but Charlie's previous, innovative facilitation strategy for enhancing students' creative problem-solving processes had also evaporated. In its place there seemed to be a regressive, uninteresting, theoretically barren context—or so I thought at the time. Later, a colleague told me that a senior professor he knew had boasted that he could write a journal article from any five-minute observation of a classroom interaction sequence. I supposed that person could enter Charlie's class and write a book from those five weeks of step-by-step sculpting. However, for me, at that time, fixated on specific research goals, it was impossible to see how I could make metaphorical hay from the mushrooms that had sprouted. Of course, mushroom soup would have been delicious, but at the time I was only interested in bales of hay, and I could see no potential in my observations of Charlie's class.

When I asked Charlie about the changes in pedagogy, he explained that he fully expected changes to result in failure, especially when those changes were radical, such as the ones I had been proposing. The laser cutter, although promising, was not located in his school; instead, it was at my university campus, approximately 30 minutes away by taxi. Charlie had to learn to make use of vector drawing programs to create designs that could be laser cut. Through it all, he had complained rather bitterly about how the school administration's policy of prohibiting the teachers from leaving the premises during school hours was inflexible and disrespected the professional autonomy of the staff. He had wanted to visit my campus to use the laser cutter, but could do so only after school hours, which intruded into his personal time. He already sacrificed a lot for his students. He would come into school an hour early to ensure that all of his students received sufficient feedback. He would take the time to move students' works in progress from storage onto their desks before each lesson. And he would even purchase electronic components for the students' art projects with his own money, spending upwards of $2,000. However, he complained that the three or four additional hours of preparation to use the laser cutter were simply too much, even for him. I did not understand the significance of this, but accepted his explanation that the extensive preparation meant he had to slow down the progress of the class.

I have wondered about my own role in this interruption. If I had not introduced the laser cutter, and instead had simply studied another iteration of Charlie's facil-itation of creative problem solving, would I have made better observations with regard to accomplishing my research goals? With the benefit of hindsight, I feel that my laser cutter suggestion was rather naive. I had attended a conference where a keynote speaker had argued that researchers should carefully consider the items they use in a makerspace. While the emblematic device was a 3D printer, its low speed and relative imprecision compared to a laser cutter made recommending it rather difficult. When I returned from the conference and learned that a laser cutter was available, I excitedly suggested it to Charlie. Being something of a technophile, he also recognized the exciting potential of such a device, but we both failed to consider the logistical and instructional implications of using it. In the first semester, Charlie persisted with trying to deploy the laser cutter in his class, but because of the logistical constraints of having to supply the materials personally, spend time cutting at the university, and then return with the prepared materials, the scale of the students' projects was severely restricted. I offered to cut out and deliver his designs to the school as part of my commitment as a researcher, but he preferred to make the trip to the university and work with the laser cutter himself. I had thought the students would use the laser cutter to generate their own personalized designs, but it eventually became a mass-production device to produce cardboard templates that could then be manipulated into predetermined forms. So, what was intended to be a means for expanding individual agency became a tool that crimped everyone's creative outcomes to one of five preselected designs.

This became another six-month phase in which I could not obtain data that fit my preconceived notions of what I was supposed to be looking for. At numerous debriefing sessions, I would ask Charlie what had led to this state of affairs, while arrogantly assuming that I bore little responsibility for what had happened. Our relationship improved as we spent more time exploring each other's motivations and teaching philosophies. We would get into productive discussions, which helped us understand each other's assumptions about teaching and learning. Over time, we became more comfortable with each other and started discussing private matters that were unrelated to my research. Charlie confided that his contract with the school had not been renewed, so the current academic year would be his last. He was exploring other options, including leaving the country to find work elsewhere. I cannot be sure, but I suspect that the stress of finding a new job, coupled with the low-level resentment he felt toward the school and its management strategies, contributed to Charlie not doing his best work for the students. He often maintained that the quality of his students was terrible that year, pointing out that they lacked even basic skills, such as knowing how to handle a pair of scissors to cut paper. Whatever the truth of that matter, it was clear that my data collection work with Charlie was at an end.

Concluding thoughts

This chapter has been concerned with whether it is worth suffering the stress of interruptions in order to achieve certain education research goals. As the title suggests, quixotic, idealistic goals tend to lead one down the path of more frequent interruptions, especially when teachers' agentic participation is an expected component for the success of the research, as it was in my project. The nature of education research, and the exemplar model for the conduct of such research, merits consideration here. It should be clear that the natural science model of reductionist experimentation with passive materials is inapplicable; even the medical or psychological model may be inappropriate when we consider that the phenomenon of interest in education is learning of the sort that involves multiple complex interactions that cannot be anything but confounded. Attempting to characterize learning in a makerspace, especially when I was interested in liberatory end results, always meant that my research was going to be especially prone to interruption. If I were to remain true to the spirit of liberation, it would have been hypocritical of me, as a researcher, to prescribe to Charlie precisely how liberation should be carried out in his classroom. This was especially the case given the specific relationship I had with Charlie; as an experienced teacher, he did not care that I possessed a theoretical sophistication that could explain why certain goals were more desirable.

The theoretical recommendations of this case lie in the acceptance of the complexity and risk of the educational context and the seemingly proportional relationship between such *risk* and the *value* of the educational project being undertaken. In this case, it would be fairly easy, with the benefit of hindsight, to identify the various control procedures, missed opportunities, more efficient processes, and more tightly delimited scope in order to minimize the risk of research interruptions. However, it may not be in the researcher's best interests to minimize risk, as Biesta suggests:

> We do educate because we want results and because we want our students to learn and achieve. But that does not mean that [...] a situation in which there is a perfect match between "input" and "output" is either possible or desirable.
> *(Biesta, 2016, p. 1)*

For Biesta, human agency and autonomy are important qualities that need to be respected and nurtured. For there to be an educational interaction worthy of its name, even constructivist instruction can be suspect if the intention is to construct curriculum-committee-approved conceptual structures mechanistically within students' heads. We may seek the emancipation of our students through their education, but that emancipation should not be sought on their behalf in a manner of colonial imposition; we cannot perform acts of liberation for (or upon) them. We can, however, recognize our complicity in their oppression and act in a manner that unites us in an effort to challenge the status quo.

To be sure, increased risk, especially in education research settings, may not necessarily connote increased value, as inadequate planning can result in unnecessary risk. All things considered, however, Biesta's argument regarding the educational setting also applies to education research. This correlation of risk and value arises because education research that reduces the variability and exposure to chance likely also minimizes its ecological validity. In the cases of both Alice and Charlie, the raw, messy conditions presented risks that were far greater than I could have foreseen, and with which I was ill-equipped to cope. However, at the same time, they presented research contexts that were completely genuine and could have resulted in authentic changes in instruction for teachers and students alike.

Mistakes were certainly made in the conduct of my research. This chapter has been the most difficult piece of writing I have done, in no small part due to the challenge of acknowledging my errors in public. At the same time, it needs to be recognized that these mistakes resulted in much learning that informed my subsequent research direction. Makerspaces have been predominantly conceived as sites for engaging students with new technologies. For instance, Blikstein (2013) and Bevan et al. (2015) acknowledge the value of attracting students with interesting phenomena and technologies that make its aspects of high value learning clear. However, both of these authors caution against merely leaving students at the level of engagement and not investing enough in the subsequent difficult learning. Taken to a more extreme end of the critique, it may even be possible to describe some of the more overblown claims of technology in education as "bullshit" (Selwyn, 2016). As educators, we may be particularly prone to the fetishization of new technologies because of the occupational hazard of dealing with humans undergoing continual change (Burbules, 2016). Through the interruptions in my research, and attempting to understand how to proceed, I eventually came to the conclusion that much of the work that needs to be done in schools is not the apparently complicated and glamorous work of using technologies as means to initiate change, but, as Biesta (2013) suggests, the simple yet hard work of using our uniquely human qualities of judgement and integrity. We also need to overturn the taken-for-granted notions of the ideal teaching–learning interaction *before* attempting to amplify changed cultural norms with technology (Toyama, 2015).

Attempting to change technologies of instruction without changing the content of the learning, the purposes of such instruction, and the relationships between teacher and learner (Biesta, 2013) likely resulted in the interruptions I faced during my research. Alice believed she had an optimized instructional sequence for D&T and did not want to expand the content and purpose of her routine, even though she enjoyed the support of her administration. Her successive delays were, in hindsight, inevitable. Charlie's dramatic deviations from school-based norms of what constituted art education likely did not help his case when the school underwent a staff reduction. Indirectly, the school management disciplined the staff into particular norms of behavior that excluded Charlie's archetype. My introduction of the laser cutter created interruptions because there was no significant correlation between its use and the goals of learning for Charlie's class. To conclude with a stereotypical happy ending, Charlie seemed to land on his feet as he found a job at another school. When I visited him, he was back to his usual effective, ambitious, and effervescent self. Moreover, there appeared to be greater alignment between content, purpose, relationship, and tools of instruction.

I shifted my research focus slightly to characterize the cultural basis of successful makerspaces in an educational system that was somewhat ambivalent to the ambitious goals of education in makerspaces, and am glad to have had the opportunity to recount this episode and its lessons for me. It may be trite to claim that readers should learn from my mistakes; *I* should learn from my mistakes, and readers should make their own and learn from them. I am glad to have made mine, and now appreciate the interruptions for what they were: opportunities to learn and grow as a researcher, and to conduct education research of significant value. With sincerity, I hope every reader will have similar opportunities.

Note

1 Charlie was an expatriate teacher on a short-term contract, and because of the small size of the community, I am deliberately obfuscating personal details due to the risk of identification.

References

Abrahamson, D. (2012). Rethinking intensive quantities via guided mediated abduction. *Journal of the Learning Sciences*, 21(4), 626–649.

Berliner, D. C. (2002). Comment: Educational research: the hardest science of all. *Educational Researcher*, 31(8), 18–20.

Bevan, B., Gutwill, J. P., Petrich, M., & Wilkinson, K. (2015). Learning through STEM-rich tinkering: Findings from a jointly negotiated research project taken up in practice. *Science Education*, 99(1), 98–120.

Biesta, G. (2013). Interrupting the politics of learning. *Power and Education*, 5(1), 4–15.

Biesta, G. (2016). *The beautiful risk of education*. Abingdon: Routledge.

Blikstein, P. (2013). Digital fabrication and "making" in education: The democratization of invention. In J. Walter-Herrmann & C. Büching (Eds.) *Fablabs: Of machines, makers and inventors* (pp. 1–21). Bielefeld: Transcript.

Burbules, N. C. (2016). Technology, education, and the fetishization of the "new". In P. Smeyers & M. Depaepe (Eds.) *Educational research: Discourses of change and changes of discourse* (pp. 9–16). Cham: Springer.

Crespo, M., & Dridi, H. (2007). Intensification of university–industry relationships and its impact on academic research. *Higher Education*, 54(1), 61–84.

Hogan, D., Chan, M., Rahim, R., Kwek, D., Maung Aye, K., Loo, S. C., Sheng, Y. Z., & Luo, W. (2013). Assessment and the logic of instructional practice in secondary 3 English and mathematics classrooms in Singapore. *Review of Education*, 1(1), 57–106.

Labaree, D. F. (2004). *The trouble with Ed schools*. New Haven, CT: Yale University Press.

Phillips, D. C. (2014). Research in the hard sciences, and in very hard "softer" domains. *Educational Researcher*, 43(1), 9–11.

Selwyn, N. (2016). Minding our language: Why education and technology is full of bullshit … and what might be done about it. *Learning, Media and Technology*, 41(3), 437–443.

Toyama, K. (2015). *Geek heresy: Rescuing social change from the cult of technology*. New York: Public Affairs.

PART 3 DISCUSSION QUESTIONS AND ACTIVITIES

Discussion questions for Chapter 10: Thinking backward and forward: everyday interruptions in school-based research

1. Maggie Dahn reflected through memos and iteratively adjusted her lesson plans to respond to the everyday interruptions she encountered during the research process. Considering your own research, what are some everyday interruptions you might encounter?
2. How might you adapt to expected and unexpected interruptions in your research?
3. Dahn suggests that everyday interruptions widened the perspective that informed her research. In what other ways might interruptions be beneficial to a research process?

Discussion questions for Chapter 11: Two steps forward, one step back: obstacles and progress in conducting research in elementary classrooms

1. Sharon L. Smith, Loren Jones, and Luciana C. de Oliveira discuss that, while sometimes you have to accept interruptions, there are also things you can do to move the research forward proactively. After reading this chapter and the others in this volume, what are some of the things that you think are most important to keep in mind in order to be proactive?
2. Smith, Jones, and de Oliveira discuss how their relationship with the local school helped facilitate their research, despite interruptions. What are some relationships you have or can develop that could serve you in this way? In what ways can you foster these relationships?

Discussion questions for Chapter 12: On pursuing quixotic goals: what are worthwhile interruptions to research?

1. Michael Tan discusses how it might be useful to consider which goals are worth suffering the stress that comes with inevitable interruptions. How would you prioritize your research goals?

2. Your priorities might not align with those of your co-authors or your research team, or they might not align with the goals of the educational settings where you are conducting your research. How can you reconcile these differences?

Part 3 activities

Interruption planning

While we cannot anticipate every potential interruption that might occur during the data collection process, planning for likely interruptions can make even a novice researcher seem expertly improvisational. In this activity, map out likely interruptions during data collection and plan your responses. Consider the impact each interruption could have on your research process. Share your map with others and work through solutions together.

Learning from others

Seeking wisdom through mentorship can help novice researchers gain a more realistic view of the complexities of educational research. In addition, it can help expose them to interruptions and solutions or strategies that they might encounter in the future. For this activity, you should interview a veteran researcher in your field about the interruptions they have faced during data collection and the different ways they dealt with those interruptions. Take notes during the interview. Discuss your notes with peers, comparing and contrasting your findings.

PART 4

The disruptive forces of scholarly peer review

13

EXCESSIVE PEER REVIEW AND THE DEATH OF AN ACADEMIC ARTICLE

Grant Eckstein

Introduction

In order to become a professional English language teacher, I decided many years ago to enroll in a rigorous graduate program at a large research institution. It wasn't long before I understood that the program and the faculty strongly and overtly stressed the need to publish primary research in order to secure meaningful employment and remain current in their field of second language learning and teaching theories.

Swimming in these currents, I pursued a master's degree research project that combined second language acquisition with speaking and listening pedagogies. The study involved over 100 language learners completing a 26-item strategy use questionnaire and comparing their results to their actual language use. I didn't think it was earth-shattering work, but I did want to publish it because of the programmatic message that I should do so. Though I encountered trials, setbacks, and frustrations while designing the study, recruiting participants, and working with the data, the complications I describe in this chapter began only after I had completed the study, written the results in an unwieldy monograph format, and finally started the process of reducing my 26,000-word thesis to a submission-worthy 8,000-word manuscript.

Deciding on a venue

Selecting a publication venue, according to the received wisdom of the graduate program, seemed easy: start with the most prestigious journal in the field and move to the next most prestigious if the article is rejected. The strategy of having multiple journals in mind at the start has been proposed by publication scholars elsewhere (Belcher, 2009; Gray, 2015), but more common advice is for new scholars to target mid-tier journals, since they usually have higher acceptance rates and more supportive peer review processes (Johnson & Mullen, 2007).

In consulting with my three advisors, I chose a top-tier journal in applied linguistics that carried immediate recognition among fellow students, inspired respect among the faculty, and played to my ego instead of my better judgement. I knew that getting into my journal of choice was a long shot as this was my first formal attempt at an empirical investigation, my understanding of my statistics was no better than marginal, and I was a novice at academic writing. But, as a graduate student, deciding on a venue can be a bit of a political decision between appeasing an advisor who wants publication in a prestigious journal and sending a manuscript where it might be more readily accepted.

Sending out the article

In my nebulous plan to publish, I figured I would be on my own when reworking the manuscript's format and length, so I was pleasantly surprised when one of my advisors offered to take my defended manuscript, cut it down, and burnish it for submission. Initially, I was most concerned about the logistics. Was it my job to mediate or coordinate the revisions? How would we decide authorship? Would everyone who helped with the article be cited as co-authors or would a simple acknowledgement of their assistance suffice? I didn't have the answers to these questions, nor even know how to ask them. Now that I serve on graduate committees, I try to prevent confusion by engaging students with similar questions from the outset. We discuss their goals and map out how we will work with the manuscript beyond the drafting stages. At the time, however, I was just relieved when, after several months, the advisor returned the fully revised and much more coherent manuscript, with my name as first author, followed by the names of the three advisors as co-authors.

Alongside my program's pressure to publish was an eagerness to celebrate a manuscript submission. So, after drafting a new title, a fresh abstract, and short biographies for the perfectly formatted cover page, the mood among the co-authors was jubilant. "Great news! It looks absolutely fantastic! You are all amazing:)," wrote one author. Another agreed: "This is so exciting! … I look forward to seeing what the editors tell us."

Throughout the revision process and especially now, amid all of this enthusiasm, I remained convinced that my chosen journal was the perfect venue. So, tying up the last few loose ends, I printed out the required three paper copies, placed them in the mail, and then waited … for four months and 18 days.

The first response

On January 20, I received a letter in the mail: the article had been rejected on the basis of 18 comments from two reviewers. One cited "insufficient relation to practical application" and voiced concerns about the literature review, while the other felt the connection to application was sufficient but agreed that the literature review was weak and felt that the manuscript was poorly defended overall.

It was a painful blow and felt like a personal attack, even though the manifest purpose of peer review in academic publishing is to "ensure that only quality work is brought before the scholarly community" (Shatz, 2004, p. 15). Eventually, I realized that the reviewers were actually protecting me from myself. After all, in a report from the Publishing Research Consortium, 90 percent of more than 3,000 respondents agreed that peer review improves the quality of published papers (Ware, 2008). Upon further reflection, I was grateful that the decision was accompanied by feedback, since editors and reviewers don't always provide helpful guidance (Gould, 2013).

With this painful turn of events, I understood why nearly 30 percent of writers who experience rejection abandon not only the article in question but the whole associated line of research (Garvey, Lin, & Tomita, 1972). I was committed not to fall into this category, especially since more recent research by Rotton, Foos, & Van Meek (1995) reported that approximately 85 percent of academic authors send their rejected articles to other journals. I was confident that the next journal would bite (in which case there would have been no need for the present chapter, as my research would have continued uninterrupted). But that's not how this story goes.

As my co-authors looked over the comments from the editors and reviewers, they noticed some inconsistencies. While the editor had declined to accept the article, the letter itself appeared to invite resubmission. Sometimes the wording of such a letter like can be rather opaque, since journal editors are free to compose decisions any way they choose (Page, Campbell, & Meadows, 1997) and do not always use standardized terminology to classify their decisions. In fact, ambiguity in decision letters, I have learned, is sometimes intentional: editors might disagree with reviewers; reviewers might provide harsher reviews; or authors might be viewed as only marginally capable of adequate revision. There are other reasons, I'm sure, but the point is that an ambiguous decision allows for negotiation, and negotiation, as Hyland (2015) explains, is nearly always an option in academic publishing. My co-authors seized on the opportunity to resubmit.

Of course, this decision contradicted my plan, but telling my friends that I had received a revise-and-resubmit offer from the prestigious journal sounded so much grander than admitting to an outright rejection. This time, I took the role of lead reviser to control the revision process. Almost nine months later, with the help of other researchers and a writing group fashioned after Tara Gray's (2015) *Publish and flourish* model, I had addressed the 18 reviewers' comments and submitted a fully revised draft to the new editors via the new online submission platform. I was proud of the manuscript and the improvements I had made.

The second response

Although editors enjoy broad executive freedom regarding the fate of a manuscript, most of them base their decisions on recommendations from two or three peer reviewers for papers that are not desk rejected. In an ideal world, these reviewers would all make the same recommendation for the paper: accept, reject, or revise.

The reality, however, is that, despite an overwhelming recognition of the importance of peer review (Ware, 2008), scholars have lamented shortcomings of the process for many years (Gould, 2013; Hyland, 2015; Shatz, 2004). For instance, reviewer agreement is notoriously low in the social sciences: Marsh & Ball (1989) reported a mean correlation of just .27 across 15 studies of reviewer judgements in a meta-analysis of peer review research. As an experiment, Peters & Ceci (2004) resubmitted 12 articles to psychology journals that had already accepted and published the self-same articles, only to receive recommendations for rejection from nearly 90 percent of referees. Moreover, specific elements of the peer review process can vary substantially: reviewers can be capricious or biased; high-quality studies can be rejected for no good reason; and weak studies (or even completely fallacious ones) can be accepted (Bohannon, 2013; Gould, 2013; Page et al., 1997).

Such a necessary yet flawed process has led to countless anecdotes about unhelpful, unkind, and outright hostile reviewer comments. One of my colleagues, for example, received a series of withering notes from a well-known sociolinguistics researcher (in an open review) such as "the task of a rewrite for a journal is to FOLLOW the DIRECTIONS!" amid several pages of unprofessional and insulting language that ended with a rejection from the journal.

Fortunately, this was not the fate of my manuscript. On New Year's Eve— almost 17 months after initial submission—the new editor of the journal recorded a decision: "Reviewers … are advising that you revise your manuscript. If you are prepared to undertake the work required, I would be pleased to send your revision out for further review." Unlike the first rejection, this was a clear invitation to revise-and-resubmit. I was thrilled, since research indicates that as many as 75 percent of submitted papers in education research are accepted subsequent to revise-and-resubmit requests (Henson, 1999). My foot was in the door!

The letter stated that one reviewer had registered "substantial doubts about this paper," how the participants were incentivized, and how the statistics worked, while the second had complimented the structure, theoretical explanations, and data analysis. Given these conflicting reports, the editor had asked a third reviewer for their opinion. Unfortunately, they had vacillated between revise-and-resubmit and rejection:

> It is first of all incredibly good in some ways, so on target, so interesting and perceptive in what it attempts … In other ways, however, the paper is mediocre … If the mediocre can be addressed so that the good parts of the study are evenly matched, the paper will be worth publishing. If it can't, the paper should be rejected for publication.

A helpful editor will tell an author which comments to address, and this editor attempted to do just that: "Pay particular attention to the third reviewer's comments," she wrote, but then added, "though all of the other comments are worthy of consideration as well, of course." As a new researcher, I was unsure how to interpret this seemingly contradictory advice. Looking back on it now that I have more experience in academic publishing, I can easily read between the lines. The editor would judge my revisions primarily on the basis of the third reviewer's comments. Any comments by the first two reviewers that failed to align with those of the third could probably be safely rebutted. I didn't revise in this way, though. Instead, I focused on the second reviewer, because their comments had been so positive. Then I moved on to the first reviewer, because they had provided only six notes, all of which seemed easy to address. Finally, with what energy and drive remained, I took a stab at the third reviewer's comments. I realize now that this strategy was doomed by its ordering. Fatigued, unsure, but still optimistic, I submitted the revisions within four weeks, as requested.

The third response

Forty-nine days later, I received the journal's response, and the reviews were bad. The first and second reviewers seemed to have flipped their opinions (although I had no way of knowing if they were even the same reviewers). The first labeled the paper "reader-friendly" whereas the second expressed "utter frustration" with the "sloppy scholarship"—a comment I found wholly demoralizing. There was no third reviewer this time. The editor invited me to revise again, but also hinted that it might be advisable to submit to a different journal. I was unsatisfied with this decision, especially since the reviewers were still split. Page, Campbell, & Meadows (1997) note that "it is kinder to reject immediately than to encourage the author to put more work into something of doubtful value" (p. 52). I agreed. I felt like the editor was stringing me along when a lesser journal would probably be enthusiastic about the piece. I emailed this thinking to my co-authors, who responded, "Let me think about this before making a recommendation" and "Let's talk it over. I personally think that we can satisfy the objections of the second reviewer."

We did talk it over three weeks later. I still wanted to go to a different journal but I was outvoted. One of my co-authors insisted, "We've come so far and we just have to make a few changes to satisfy the reviewers." It was sound advice, and the kind I would hear myself giving to graduate students later in life. However, at the time, I was demoralized with revision fatigue, ambiguity, and reaching beyond my ability. To my co-authors, the revisions were a bothersome gnat; to me, they were a biblical plague.

I needed what most young researchers need: an apprenticeship experience (Wegener & Tanggaard, 2013). Collins, Brown, & Newman (1987) explained that cognitive apprenticeship models allow for "the externalization of processes that are usually carried out internally" (p. 4), such as writing and reading. Apprenticeship stands in contrast to pragmatic approaches, which emphasize learning through following explicit steps but without direct intervention from experienced masters (Breuer & Schreier, 2007). An apprenticeship model encourages modeling, coaching, and scaffolding so that specialized knowledge and experience are transferred in a natural way from master to apprentice while promoting lifelong problem-solving skills (Collins et al., 1987).

Numerous researchers have emphasized the value of apprenticeship for academic co-authoring (Kamler, 2008; Kamler & Thomson, 2006; Wegener & Tanggaard, 2013). Kamler (2008), in particular, argues that graduate student publication flourishes under "skilled support from knowledgeable supervisors" (p. 284). Lee & Kamler (2008) describe this support as student–supervisor interactions relying on interpreting reviewer comments together, negotiating revision strategies, and explicating the internal problem solving associated with such decision making. These are practices, Nettles & Millett (2006) argue, to which few developing scholars are exposed, despite increased pressure to publish while still in school (Paré, 2010).

I realize now that my senior co-authors were giving me an apprenticeship, but I didn't view it that way at the time or understand how to capitalize on it. They took time to meet with me and respond to my emails. They offered encouragement and made revisions when I requested them. Perhaps, then, it was me who needed to be a better communicator of my needs. Now, as a graduate advisor, I appreciate students who are forthright about their concerns, self-aware about their strengths and weaknesses, and able to engage in conversations when they don't understand my comments or those of external reviewers. I'm also more acutely aware of how stretched for time advisors can be, with multiple projects to balance against classes and basic grading requirements. Thus, it is important for a student to be a self-advocate in order to be an effective apprentice—something about which I was not wholly aware at the time. So, I struggled with most of the revisions alone. I worked for two days short of two months, then resubmitted.

The fourth response

When the email arrived two months later, I barely had the emotional strength to open it as even the sound of a new message in my inbox gave me micro-terrors.

The editor's comments read: "The reviewers are essentially quite pleased with your paper but are still advising some minor changes. Upon resubmission, further external review will not be needed." Most of the "minor changes" involved switching a word for a synonym or removing an overstated claim. Easy!

I experienced exhilarating joy at this decision. I revised and resubmitted the paper in just six days and confidently announced to my peers that I would be published in the journal. My feelings of self-doubt and ambiguity disappeared. If the article I had toiled to revise over 713 days (two weeks shy of two years) was finally accepted for publication in a top-tier journal, and some graduate-school research formed the basis of that article, then did it matter how difficult and bumpy the road had been?

Paranoia

The euphoria lasted for a week before the paranoia began. I was suddenly and inexplicably racked with self-doubt. Was my research flawed? Would readers accuse me of presenting lies as fact? Would additional research prove my results to be fallacious? Would hundreds of ESL students be given listening-and-speaking interventions on the basis of incorrect research?

Today, these fears seem wholly idiotic. As a reader, you probably rolled your eyes during that last paragraph. But paranoia is not the product of a rational brain, and my psyche was ripe for cognitive distortion after years of poring over the same research to address criticism after criticism in an academic endeavor that was both new and puzzling. It is tempting to say that my negative self-talk was a product of my inexperience with publication, but Boice (1985; 1993) has argued that nearly all authors, irrespective of experience, have discouraging voices that belittle their creativity and inhibit their productive accomplishments.

My inner critic came alive at a strange time in the writing process. Instead of hindering the drafting or revision stages, my writing demon sought to destroy a well-formed article that others had approved. I barely resisted the urge to write to the journal and withdraw my paper completely just as it seemed to be on the verge of full acceptance, something that Forman (1988) calls "scuttl[ing] the project" (p. 182). He suggests that this is a common but usually fleeting response, as it was for me. Surely, I eventually reasoned, numerous academics had reviewed the details of my research and would have stopped its progression if the science had been truly flawed.

I probably could have applied additional strategies to deal with my anxiety. For instance, I might have told myself that my research was part of a larger conversation where the point is to propose hypotheses for scrutiny, replication, and revision, rather than present absolute truth. I might also have grappled more thoughtfully with the notion of "truth" and been more discerning about whether the scientific method can even produce something so definitive, or whether it simply leads to observations that appear true within a certain context. In addition, I have learned to calm my inner voice by seeking feedback earlier in the drafting and revision processes from trusted, rigorous, yet kind colleagues. I have also developed expertise in my particular academic niche. Knowledge, it turns out, is a powerful antidote to self-doubt. I often find that I criticize myself most for those things that I don't understand, but when I take the time to understand those things, my inner voice is forced to find a different area of weakness.

In any event, I quieted my writing critic and waited anxiously for the journal to slate my paper for publication.

The fifth response

Two weeks later, I was wounded and returned to a state of self-doubt, imposterism, and ambiguity. Actually, that description fails to capture the depth of my horror.

Instead of issuing an acceptance, the editor remarked, "I asked a reviewer to look specifically at your statistical analysis … s/he raises several questions. I hope you will address these in your next resubmission." She also elucidated an additional concern about the framing of the article that the previous reviewers had overlooked. I was given another month to fix the problems.

The notes from the new reviewer pushed my spirits to a new low. "I cannot agree with their interpretation about the numbers," the reviewer stated in reference to our goodness-of-fit statistic. My confusion became a tsunami of self-doubt and criticism. I was indeed an imposter, and this reviewer had exposed me.

In hindsight, I should have simply explained that we reported several goodness-of-fit statistics, and the one the reviewer highlighted was both the easiest to interpret and the least precise, with different statisticians recommending a number of variations and cut-off points. I could then have removed the offending statistic and replaced it with a more precise and favorable one, while adding some caution in the interpretation. However, it took me two additional statistics classes and three years of distance from the review to develop the acumen to address this reviewer's comment. This resonates with Kamler's (2008) observation that student writers must take an authoritative stance within a field of experts before they can feel authoritative. At the time, I did not feel authoritative in my statistical knowledge, so I was fearful of taking an authoritative stance.

Over the next month, I read (but did not understand) multiple statistical explanations of goodness-of-fit measures, consulted with three statisticians, recalculated our figures, and wrote several new versions of the paragraph the reviewer had found problematic. None of this overcame the words that were still ringing in my ears: "I cannot agree with their interpretation." This comment interrupted my sleeping, eating, teaching, thinking, and sometimes even breathing.

Ultimately, one of my co-authors consulted a statistician and revised the paragraph by stating that our model fit closely enough, given so-and-so's cut-off criteria. However, his professional and appropriate response did not match my naive expectation for a more precise statistic or a stronger rebuttal. Moreover, it did not feel truthful. I succumbed to the fallacy that editorial and reviewers' comments are "truth" rather than merely "text" (Lee & Kamler, 2008). I did not like the idea of submitting my co-author's paragraph, but the alternatives seemed even worse: withdraw the paper entirely and stuff it in a drawer; submit it to a different journal and wade through another multi-year review process; or submit my own version of the paragraph with new, unauthoritative statistics. None of these options seemed right.

I finally included my co-author's paragraph and sent off the article, only to lose a night of sleep worrying about the statistic and my integrity as a researcher. I asked another co-author whether we should recall the paper. He suggested waiting to see what the editors said. I did not like that answer. I was so overwhelmed by thoughts, feelings, and the excruciating review process that I could not see reason.

Research interrupted

In horror movies, the choices are obvious: for instance, don't take a screwdriver to a chainsaw fight. I should have understood that recalling the paper was a screwdriver choice. To this day I shudder that, just two days after submitting the revised manuscript, I requested more time from the editor to address the statistics. Reflecting on it now, it is clear that this was the decision that brought my research to a halt. The editor and reviewers were not the problem; I was.

My inexperienced thinking even misinterpreted the editor's speedy and kind reply to "take the time you need." Was she insinuating that my research was so flawed that I definitely needed extra time? Was she happy to get my paper off of her desk? Had she looked over the revised paragraph and decided that anything would be better than that?

While kicking myself for recalling the paper, I met with a different statistician who agreed with the reviewer. Over eight laborious, complicated months, a complete course on structural equation modeling, biweekly meetings, and rigorous revisions to the entire results and discussion sections, we recalculated and re-reported the data using more advanced statistics to illustrate a stronger model fit.

I finally resubmitted almost three years after my first submission. The process had taken so long that I was now dealing with a third editor.

Nothing

After three months and twelve days of silence, I emailed the new editor, who admitted that nothing had happened with my article. It was summer, when reviewers tend to be less responsive, and he had struggled to find any who could understand the paper's dense statistics. I responded by suggesting a couple of applied linguists who had published similar statistics to those I was using. He replied, "Thanks."

The end

I heard nothing more as the weeks, months, and eventually a whole year went by. I was too miserable to reconnect with the editor and ask where things stood. Every once in a while, I would contemplate that I might have been published in the journal if only I had kept my cool, but this thought filled me with despair, so I pushed it out of my mind. Meanwhile, I was finding success elsewhere, with a published book review (a much better place for a neophyte researcher to cut his teeth) and a research article in a mid-tier journal. I was also collecting data for my master's degree that would result in more articles, and I had been admitted to a doctoral program.

Eventually, I did hear from the journal, but it was merely a request to serve as a reviewer. At the time, it did not occur to me to invoke a quid pro quo: I'll do the review if you tell me where my article sits in the review process. (More recently, I have used that tactic to usher articles along at other journals.)

Several more years passed, and when going up for my third-year review in a tenure-track position, I realized that the article was still listed on my CV as "in review" at the journal. It certainly was not in review anymore. Besides, the statute of limitations for that journal was something like five years. Because of inaction on the manuscript, it had officially dropped out of the system.

Ultimately, then, my paper was neither accepted nor formally rejected. It simply languished in round after round of review. I learned that outright rejection is not the only way to kill an article; death can also come slowly, through unending and unnerving rounds of peer review.

Is it possible that such a prolonged and unsatisfying revision process is ever helpful? Certainly, the allocation of reviewer time alone can be a spectacular waste of resources. Ultimately, I realized that the stagnation of research during the review process is still research interrupted, even though the research aspect has been concluded.

Lessons learned

My experience with demoralizing peer reviews is, unfortunately, far from unique. It seems that every academic can recount a similar revision horror story. Moreover, this process does not only happen when pursuing publication. Researchers and graduate students often change topics, abandon projects, or fail to make requested revisions because of souring peer reviews or other constraints (Aitchison, 2010). Thus, my experience will likely resonate with a wide range of students and researchers, especially those at the early stages of their research.

However, my interrupted experience is counterbalanced by the benefits I gained from so many rounds of critical reviews. As a learning opportunity, I carefully read through a total of 30 pages of reviewers' and editorial comments multiple times, including in preparation for this chapter. Obviously, the first few passes were painful, but over the course of weeks, months, and finally years, I came to appreciate well-crafted criticism. Authentic, detailed, audience-specific comments on my work illuminated additional avenues for improvement and built on the scaffolding already provided by my graduate advisors. In a sense, then, I came to see the journal's editors and their reviewers as a second supervisory team. Additionally, as I made improvements to the manuscript in response to their notes, I could apply similar principles to new projects, which were much more easily published. I have also learned—and now teach my students—the importance of communicating with editors early on to gauge their interest in a manuscript (something I failed to do with the article that is the subject of this chapter).

Moreover, the emotions evoked through interpreting, misinterpreting, analyzing, and responding to the reviewers' comments helped shape who I am as a researcher and a mentor. I have pursued the study of response to writing, as it is a powerful tool to build or destroy an author's confidence. I strive to employ my own painful experience as a tool to mentor budding academics through the research process. I have found simple empathy to be a profound mentoring tactic. This agonizing ordeal was part of my process of developing both a "thick skin" and compassionate mentoring.

Perhaps the biggest lesson, however, was learning how to think like a reviewer and an editor, as their purpose for interacting with texts differs from those of advisors at the graduate level. Graduate faculty may evaluate a text through the lens of program evaluations or standardized grading rubrics. Reviewers, on the other hand, read manuscripts as a form of intellectual activity (Edgington, 2016). In my case, they questioned my text, argued with me, and worked to make sense of my prose both for their own purposes and in a gatekeeping role for a wider readership. Because of this attitude, when reviewers saw a flaw in my manuscript, they provided suggestions on how to address it or appease their concerns. All of this made a tremendous difference when I began reviewing manuscripts myself. In a sense, I received an academic reviewer apprenticeship as a consequence of my doomed publication attempt in a form of legitimate peripheral participation (Lave & Wenger, 1991).

As I became more successful in my publication efforts, I also came to appreciate the numerous letters I received from journal's editors. They were tactful communications that ranged from implicit rejection to conditional acceptance, with numerous varieties of revise-and-resubmit requests throughout. Therefore, through the submission of a single paper, I had the good fortune to see many aspects of the editorial process in a relatively short period of time. This was especially helpful when I later helped establish a new academic journal for writing response research and ultimately became its co-editor. My arrested research project eventually came full circle, illustrating one way in which failed research can result in unforeseen academic achievement.

My tale is not meant to be a guide to dealing with crippling peer review, as obviously I did not deal with it well in this experience. Nor is it meant to be a probe into the relationship between graduate students and advisors, or even a cautionary tale of how to conform to academic pressure to publish. Instead, I hope my agonizing ordeal of failing to publish an article after numerous rounds of peer review provides a single experience upon which other writers and supervisors can reflect when making decisions about when, how, and with whom to publish academic papers. It might also provide some solace for early career researchers who are suffering their own painful experiences with publication. Certainly, the path to effective research is labyrinthine and messy, full of miscues, accidents, miscommunications, and sometimes failures. However, understanding the intricacies of a process that often continues right up to publication will hopefully help researchers to prepare for and react wisely to the frustrating research interruptions that they will inevitably face.

References

Aitchison, C. (2010). *Publishing pedagogies for the doctorate and beyond*. New York: Routledge.
Belcher, W. L. (2009). *Writing your journal article in 12 weeks: A guide to academic publishing success*. Thousand Oaks, CA: Sage Publications.
Bohannon, J. (2013). Who's afraid of peer review? *Science*, 342(6154), 60–65.
Boice, R. (1985). Cognitive components of blocking. *Written Communication*, 2(1), 91–104.
Boice, R. (1993). Writing blocks and tacit knowledge. *Journal of Higher Education*, 64(1), 19–54,

Breuer, F., & Schreier, M. (2007). Issues in learning about and teaching qualitative research and methodology in the social sciences. *Forum Qualitative Sozialforschung/Forum: Qualitative Social Research*, 8(1). Retrieved March 6, 2019 from: www.qualitative-research.net/index.php/fqs/article/view/216/477.

Collins, A., Brown, J. S., & Newman, S. E. (1987). *Cognitive apprenticeship: Teaching the craft of reading, writing, and mathematics* [Centre for the Study of Reading Technical Report No. 403]. Champaign, IL: University of Illinois at Urbana-Champaign.

Edgington, A. E. (2016). Split personalities: Understanding the responder identity in college composition. *Journal of Response to Writing*, 2(1), 75–91.

Forman, B. D. (1988). The process of journal article publishing. *Counselor Education and Supervision*, 28(2), 181–185.

Garvey, W. D., Lin, N., & Tomita, K. (1972). Research studies in patterns of scientific communications II: The role of the national meeting in scientific and technical communication. *Information Storage and Retrieval*, 8, 159–196.

Gould, T. H. P. (2013). *Do we still need peer review?: An argument for change*. Lanham, MD: The Scarecrow Press.

Gray, T. (2015). *Publish and flourish: Become a prolific scholar*, 2nd edition. La Cruces: Teaching Academy, New Mexico State University.

Henson, K. (1999). *Writing for professional publication: Keys to academic and business success*. Boston, MA: Allyn & Bacon.

Hyland, K. (2015). *Academic publishing: Issues and challenges in the construction of knowledge*. Oxford: Oxford University Press.

Johnson, B., & Mullen, C. (2007). *Write to the top: How to become a prolific academic*. New York: Palgrave Macmillan.

Kamler, B. (2008). Rethinking doctoral publication practices: Writing from and beyond the thesis. *Studies in Higher Education*, 33(3), 283–294.

Kamler, B., & Thomson, P. (2006). *Helping doctoral students write: Pedagogies for supervision*. London: Routledge.

Lave, J. & Wenger, E. (1991). *Situated learning: Legitimate peripheral participation*. Cambridge: Cambridge University Press.

Lee, A., & Kamler, B. (2008). Bringing pedagogy to doctoral publishing. *Teaching in Higher Education*, 13(5), 511–523.

Marsh, H. W., & Ball, S. (1989). The peer review process used to evaluate manuscripts submitted to academic journals: Interjudgmental reliability. *Journal of Experimental Education*, 57(2), 151–169.

Nettles, M. T., & Millett, C. M. (2006). *Three magic letters: Getting to PhD*. Baltimore, MD: Johns Hopkins University Press.

Page, G., Campbell, R., & Meadows, J. (1997). *Journal publishing*. New York: Cambridge University Press.

Paré, A. (2010). Slow the presses: Concerns about premature publication. In C. Aitchison, B. Kamler, & A. Lee (Eds.) *Publishing pedagogies for the doctorate and beyond* (pp. 30–46). New York: Routledge.

Peters, D. P., & Ceci, S. J. (2004). Peer review practices of psychological journals: The fate of published articles, submitted again. In D. Shatz (Ed.) *Peer review: A critical inquiry* (pp 191–214). Lahnam, MD: Rowman & Littlefield.

Rotton, J. P., Foos, L., & Van Meek. (1995). Publication practices and the file drawer problem: A survey of published authors. *Journal of Social Behavior and Personality*, 10(1), 1–13.

Shatz, D. (2004). *Peer review: A critical inquiry*. Lanham, MD: Rowman & Littlefield.

Ware, M. (2008). Peer review: Benefits, perceptions and alternatives. *PRC Summary Papers*, 4, 4–20.

Wegener, C., & Tanggaard, L. (2013). Supervisor and student co-writing: An apprenticeship perspective. *Forum Qualitative Sozialforschung/Forum: Qualitative Social Research*, 14(3). Retrieved March 6, 2019 from: www.qualitative-research.net/index.php/fqs/article/view/2030/3586.

14

FROM BROADER IMPACTS TO INTELLECTUAL MERIT

An interruption in interdisciplinary publishing

Vanessa Svihla

Given the journal, you should assume that the bulk of your audience is comprised of librarians, not necessarily professionals with backgrounds in instructional design, instructional technology, educational psychology, or psychology. So you should probably offer a bit more of a definition of "affordance" early in the paper. You might even provide an illustrative example of how the term tends to be used in the field of design, which I inferred was the way you were using the term. I had a colleague look at a few pages from the first half of the paper, and she somewhat irritably asked why you kept using the word "affordances" instead of "benefits." Your paper introduces a concept and term that may be unfamiliar to a sizable percentage of your readers, and they have a concept and term that they may believe is just as good. I would recommend explaining your concept and term as you would to a layperson.

(Reviewer #3)

In this excerpt from a recent review I received on a collaborative, interdisciplinary project, the reviewer rightfully asked for clarification on an unfamiliar term: "affordances." As a learning scientist who commonly collaborates across disciplines, I am usually pretty successful at avoiding jargon and defining key technical terms, such as this one. As it turned out, I had done so with my collaborators—so well that they saw no need to define the term either—and they quickly agreed with me that "affordance" and "benefit" were not synonymous. In this case, I was grateful to the reviewer for calling the matter to our attention, because it helped us communicate a specific idea more clearly.

In this chapter, I first describe some of the successes and typical considerations I've had with interdisciplinary publishing, because I do not want to give the impression that the interruption I experienced was due to either naivety or some perceived impossibility in interdisciplinary publishing. Rather, I wish to highlight how the review process shaped and reshaped a particular manuscript. I gradually reshaped something that might have had what the National Science Foundation refers to as *broader impacts*—"the potential to benefit society and contribute to the achievement of specific, desired societal outcomes"—into something that may possess what it terms *intellectual merit*—"the potential to advance knowledge" (ch. 3, A.2). This may seem like a positive outcome, as surely intellectual merit is what academic publishing is all about? However, I see this shift as unfortunate. To explain why, I'll revisit some of my early data collection to illustrate how the setting shaped my original research goals. I'll recount how I shaped the manuscript for three different venues, hoping to get the implications in front of science faculty who could implement them. And, finally, I'll discuss why I abandoned that approach and refocused my manuscript as a more typical study for my own discipline.

On being interdisciplinary

Perhaps it is because of the circuitous path I took to becoming a learning scientist that I value interdisciplinarity so much. Or perhaps it is due to the opportunities I had during my doctoral studies to collaborate across disciplines on large projects. I have published and presented in several fields and many sub-disciplines, but this has not always gone smoothly. I have collaborated with engineers, architects, computer scientists, museum personnel, nutritionists, genetic counselors, teacher educators, teachers, mathematics education researchers, art education faculty, linguists, and others. For instance, I worked on a project funded by the US Department of Agriculture to develop instructional technology that allowed undergraduate students to role-play as dieticians. By working closely with faculty in nutrition and architecture, we were able to overcome a number of jargon issues within our research team. All fields have insider language—jargon, technical terms—and some also have words that appear understandable to an outsider, but actually have very specific meanings. While we certainly used technical language, we were selective and specific, and we made sure everyone on the team, including the graduate and undergraduate students, understood the terms we were using. These included nutrition terms like *lifecycle, metabolic syndrome*, and *problem, etiology, and signs & symptoms (PES) statement*; terms from education research, like *guided interactivity, instrumentality*, and *formative feedback*; and instructional technology terms, like *branching*. When we submitted our mixed-methods manuscript to a journal aimed at nutrition faculty, we tried to be very transparent in our use of technical language. Because we had built a lab lexicon as a tool for onboarding newcomers, we were very successful in our terminological clarity.

But, of course, specific terms are not the only disciplinary convention boundary-crossers might trip over. I have encountered easily remedied requests from reviewers that generally improved my manuscript, such as making structural changes by adding or removing subheadings, despite having followed the instructions in the journal's author guidelines. I have commonly faced concerns from both natural sciences reviewers and collaborators that my tone is not objective enough. This issue is central to interdisciplinary work as disciplines convey their epistemological stances through writing (Hyland, 2011). As a former geoscientist myself, I was trained to write in this manner (Svihla, 2004):

> The Big Maria Mountains of southeastern California, one of the largest ranges of the Maria Fold and Thrust Belt (MFTB), record progressive noncoaxial, contractional Mesozoic deformation in an intracratonal setting. Detailed structural mapping and kinematic analysis in a portion of the overturned limb of the regional recumbent syncline, which is in contact with a Jurassic pluton, led to the identification of refolded folds and sheath folds and the refinement of existing models.

This writing style, with abundant use of passive voice, reveals the positivist stance I held at the time, aligning to the idea that writing can "communicate truths which emerge from our direct access to the external world" (Hyland, 2011, p. 194). Having transitioned from natural to social sciences, I understand the reluctance of admitting ownership, and therefore potential fallibility, by using first-person active voice. But, having spent four months in the Mojave, living in a tent, traversing, measuring, observing, I know I made many choices about what data to collect, and this set bounds on what conclusions I could draw. First-person pronoun usage is becoming more common, even in the natural sciences (Hyland & Jiang, 2017), reflecting a slow shift to admit that researchers' decisions, like those I made, are not deterministic. Some other researcher, doing research in my same field site, might not have spent days puzzling over the overturned beds (meaning the rocks were upside down from how they had been deposited). This effort provided me with a dataset that was highly influenced by my decisions. And based on my analysis, which was again full of my decisions, I drew inferences about the structure of the rocks that were covered with debris—something I viewed as a truth that could be literally uncovered, if only I had a backhoe and permit to do so.

My own journey from positivist natural scientist to interpretivist was fraught and effortful. I felt like a traitor as I began to see the value in interpretivism, in part because I struggled to reconcile my sense that, where the rocks at my field site were concerned, there was a factual truth that could be uncovered. And, like many natural scientists, it took time for me to value qualitative research. When I did, I realized that the interactions between people I was observing were very similar to the data I viewed when looking at thin slices of rock under a polarizing microscope: neither revealed much that was interesting if the sole approach was quantification; yet rich insights could be gleaned from both through careful comparative analysis.

Having made this progress, it seems ironic that the trickiest type of reviewer request for me to address is tied to epistemological differences as revealed by methods and methodologies. Notably, the uptake of qualitative and mixed methods has varied across fields since the *paradigm wars* (Alise & Teddlie, 2010; Gage, 1989), so it is not surprising that these would pose a cross-disciplinary tripping hazard. We saw hints of this in the requests from one positivist reviewer of the nutrition paper. They asked us to foreground quantitative data, find "a way to consolidate" the qualitative data in a table, and suggested we should rename our participants with more familiar pseudonyms, such as "Jennifer, Ashley, Jessica, and Meghan." We responded in a measured fashion, citing a few sources as a means to educate the reviewer on why our qualitative data were valuable and why we had chosen Latina pseudonyms for our interviewees. After all, the purpose of our project was undergirded by our desire to develop culturally-relevant instructional tools. We successfully responded to the reviewer's concerns without changing much of our paper.

But what stood out to me most in that instance—more than the reviewer's concerns—was their appreciation of what we had done. They explained that the potential impact and relevance of our instructional design was "the greatest strength of the manuscript." Once published, we knew our paper would reach the audience that was most able to act on our implications. I believe this kind of work is well worth the (usually minor) skirmishes with reviewers across disciplinary boundaries.

I collaborate across many disciplines in part because learning is ubiquitous, happening across space and time, and this creates many opportunities to collaborate. That said, collaborating across disciplines can be risky in ways that collaborating within a single discipline is not. For instance, interdisciplinary collaborators may leave the institution—which may or may not have a significant impact on a project—or even leave academia altogether. This can be hard to predict because of differing workplace pressures and norms. I have lost three computer science collaborators to industry—something that rarely happens within my discipline. Likewise, navigating disciplinary hierarchies is not for the thin skinned. I have worked with some wonderful, respectful collaborators who genuinely value my contributions, but I have also encountered would-be "collaborators" who wanted to list someone—typically a social, behavioral, or learning scientist—on a grant proposal but didn't believe that any such scientist had expertise worth contributing.

Yet, when they work, interdisciplinary projects can be spectacularly interesting and rewarding. They provide countless opportunities for collaborators to learn from one another. For instance, as a direct result of collaborations, I have learned about white-nose syndrome, innovations in healing large wounds, measuring limb spasticity, uses of evaporative cooling, the prevention of gestational diabetes, supporting those with sickle-cell anemia, protein folding, and many more topics in greater depth than I would have managed on my own. Learning with and from experts in their respective fields is a thrilling journey.

My own interdisciplinary encounters led me to become curious about how interdisciplinary teams function and frame research problems together. In preparation for a grant proposal, I surveyed 11 research labs as potential data collection sites. All professed to be interdisciplinary through their websites, but most were recently formed sub-disciplines—interesting in their own right, but not actively drawing on external points of view. Three labs were clearly interdisciplinary, but it was Denise's (a pseudonym) that particularly drew my attention and became the focus of extended participant observation over the course of several years.

Origins of a desire for broader impacts

In the summer of 2012, I introduced myself to Denise by email, explaining that I was a former geologist and current learning scientist who was looking to

> study scientists doing the work they do … [I] am particularly interested in finding examples that don't resemble traditional school science. My work in geology didn't have much in common with the idealized, linear scientific method as presented to me in school. I am interested in finding and documenting situations in which scientists engage in more design-like activity of posing questions, revising them, trying to envision ways to answer emergent questions, etc.

Although she did not share any specifics with me, I knew Denise had some reservations about allowing me access. However, her desire to be an effective mentor made her curious about my research. She allowed me tentative access to her lab, with the strict caveat that if any member raised objections, I would not be permitted to return. I made myself useful, sharing early fieldnotes with the lab so the members could see what I had seen and use my notes as records when giving each other feedback.

When I sought lab members' participation, the consent process brought up and resolved a misunderstanding about "data." One member was worried by the phrasing of additional permissions on the consent form: "I agree that my data including my writing may be included in future studies." As beginning researchers, they conceived of data only as the information they were collecting in their own research; they did not recognize the audio recordings, photographs, and fieldnotes I was collecting during their weekly lab meetings as data—an issue I would face repeatedly when trying to publish. This gave me a chance to explain to the lab members that I had no interest in the data they collected, although I was interested in their process of making sense of it. My original research goals focused on the highly iterative and overlapping nature of science practices, particularly related to finding and framing research problems. I was struck by the ways they labeled their work—exploratory and finding the story in the data.

I gradually shifted from observer to participant. In this, my research goals also shifted. While some of this was due to the emergent and exploratory nature of my own research, the biggest shift came about five months into my data collection, in early 2013, when Denise asked me to help her understand what she did that made her lab so strikingly diverse. She had been asked to advise other research labs, but was unsure how to explain her own success. I reviewed my fieldnotes in search of an answer, but felt rather inadequate, given that this was not my research focus. Nevertheless, just as the members of the lab charged into data, trying to find the story, I did so as well, with diversity as my lens. I shared my first-pass analysis with her, then with the lab members, to check my inference that the lab was "a safe space for students to be themselves, yet see that they are scientists." I noted, in particular, that I had observed many instances of students using swear words, and that Denise did not react. I suggested that this signaled to students that she was not trying to change them into people they are not. The students readily agreed with this insight and shared examples where they had cursed in another setting, it had been marked as a transgression, and they had felt obliged to edit or modify their behavior in order to belong. Similarly, they agreed that having undergraduates and sometimes even high school students in the lab made it safer not to know something. With further analysis and literature review, I later connected this situation to near-peer mentoring, but at the time I simply noted that, while Denise provided explicit mentoring on topics such as which conferences to attend, the students also received mentoring "from more proximal sources." I noted the opportunities to engage informally, such as attending parties and celebrating birthdays, helped build trust. Finally, I pointed to occasions when Denise had positioned students as having expertise that she did not possess—a powerful way to help them develop identities as scientists. I later came to see this as an interdisciplinary stance.

As I continued to collect and analyze data, I was influenced by these themes, and, like Denise herself, wanted to share them with other scientists who might implement them in their own research teams.

From desk reject to reshaping and reshaping

In late 2014, a collaborator forwarded a request for submissions to a special issue of a journal that seemed like a great fit for the emerging picture of supports that fostered diversity in Denise's lab. As this was a science—not a science education—journal, the special issue would focus on a broad range of issues, including enhancing diversity in the sciences. In the manuscript abstract, I summarized my findings about these supports as:

> allowing students to come as they are yet be recognized as scientists, near-peer mentoring, positioning students as having relevant expertise and engaging students in framing of research problems. Together, these foster participation from diverse students who might not otherwise have considered careers in science.

I was impressed by the consistency I had observed in the lab, even as members had changed. This extended engagement gave me confidence that my inferences were trustworthy. So, I was dismayed when the editor sent me a desk rejection after only 12 days: "I am returning, without peer review, your manuscript," because it did "not at present reach the standards of scholarship expected ... Although this manuscript makes some interesting claims, it is not quite ready for publication in a research-focused journal." In a helpful gesture, the editor pointed me in the direction of an introductory qualitative analysis textbook and a resource on qualitative analysis in physics education research (even though the journal in question was neither physics- nor physics education-related) and listed a number of specific concerns:

1. Participants (numbers per year, gender, age, major, etc.).
2. Theoretical foundations for the research—particularly, why diversity is important.
3. Research methods, including data collection and analysis.
4. Validity/reliability as appropriate for qualitative research.

It was easy to rebut several of these points. For instance, including detailed information on such a small number of participants would have made them easy to identify, so I had described them across the whole three years of data collection. Following the bricolage approach, I had a clear theoretical framework, and I had treated broadening participation as the *why it matters*, "Diversity is viewed by some as a driver of innovation, and its lack as a threat to competitiveness in STEM fields (Page, 2007; Velasco & Velasco, 2010)." I had also included information about the kinds of data I collected, my analysis process, and a concise explanation of how my research met standards for trustworthy and credible qualitative work.

In looking back critically on what I submitted, I agree that, I ought to have been more explicit in stating my methodology, rather than focusing on my methods. I feared including extensive detail would not play well with an audience that was not steeped in the field's technical language. Had I situated the study as ethnographic, they might have been more open to the lack of a coding scheme. However, I suspect the terms "validity/reliability" even noted "as appropriate for qualitative research" suggest a narrow or singular view of how quality should be assessed. Fearing that my efforts to revise would never fit within this narrow view, I began reshaping the paper for a different journal.

I chose one that seemed like a better fit, as its emphasis was on interdisciplinary education in higher education settings. In addition, it appeared to have a relatively quick turnaround time and though it was not a very well-known journal, it had published a paper that I had quite enjoyed. All of this convinced me that it would be a good home for my article. I reshaped the paper over the next six months, carefully building on articles published in my new intended venue, while also providing more detail about my methods. I added additional citations to explain participant observation and used more direct language about how quality is typically assessed.

I submitted my manuscript to this second journal in late 2015. Eleven months later, after reviewing several articles for the journal in question, I still had not heard anything about my paper. I logged into the journal's review system and was frustrated to see the status: "Declined without review." I wrote to the editor to ask for further feedback. She assured me that it was just a technical error:

> I am deeply sorry for the delay in my response and the mix up with your article submission. For some reason the reviews for your article were not uploaded in a way that you can access them and I had to track back the reviewers to send me a copy of the reviews so I can email them to you. I apologize again for the trouble you had with our website and I would like to

extend an invitation for you to revise your article based on the reviewers [*sic*] feedback and I will fast track it for publication in the spring semester, if you wish.

I was initially delighted by this response, but then I read the reviews, which appeared hastily completed and discouraging. I suspected that the editor had asked the reviewers to redo their reviews. Had I been in their shoes, I think my review might have been similarly hasty and would have reflected frustration that my previous work had been for naught. While both of the reviewers agreed the article was a good fit for the journal, well written, well supported by literature, and well organized, they assessed it as unacceptable in many other regards, using the journal's scoring rubric. Both rated the article as "unoriginal," the title—"Interdisciplinary research as a site for fostering diversity in the sciences"—as not "appropriate, interesting and informative," and the abstract as not reflecting the content of the paper. Given that I had carefully written a concise, structured abstract that reflected the broader problem and the specific purpose of the paper, the methodology, the results, and the inferences, I took this as evidence of a hasty review process.

One of the reviewers suggested rejecting the paper, with the following comments, which I present in full and verbatim:

> The article's thesis can be interesting if it is supported with sound research, which I don't think this is the case here. The article lacks a solid conceptual research. What is the significance of producing hundreds of field notes the author(s) fail to tell us that? The results and conclusion need to provide more evidence to the effects of the lab methodology on students' learning.

The comment that "the article lacks a solid conceptual research" did not align with the score the reviewer had provided on the rubric. In assessing my research methods as unsound and critiquing my detailed account of data collection, I suspected that the reviewer lacked the necessary methodological expertise to evaluate my paper. Moreover, given that my research purpose was to "clarify the types of supports that foster participation by diverse members [and support them] to develop identities and competencies as interdisciplinary scientists," I was perplexed by the accusation that I had failed to provide sufficient evidence of "the effects of the lab methodology on students' learning." Overall, the brevity—a mere 65 words—and lack of care led me to question the quality of the review.

The second reviewer, who wrote 118 words in total, advised me to focus on the near-peer mentoring, which they hailed as "new," even though I had cited literature on the topic from 1998. To me, this suggested that the reviewer lacked the necessary expertise to review the article. Matching reviewers with appropriate expertise to papers is an issue that even editors within disciplinary publishing face, but it is compounded when a paper integrates two or more disciplinary areas of knowledge or introduces methodological norms that are unfamiliar to the editor. I certainly faced this issue with this second reviewer, as another comment suggested both that they assumed I was the lab leader and that my study was unscientific. Again, I quote the review verbatim: "Under results, the author claims that her 'students use of profanity as a resource for learning' without providing any scientific evidence. How does she know that profanity was a contributing factor for their success and not other course factors?" In that section, I had explained that Denise viewed "her students' use of profanity as a resource for learning," yet continued to have concerns about it. This twisting of meaning increased my suspicion that the reviewer simply did not see my research as methodological. They argued for acceptance after major revisions, but fundamentally questioned the potential for contribution: "The premise of the article is that if you create a welcoming and relaxed classroom environment for the students, they will learn better, so what is new?" Having made a somewhat laborious shift from natural to social scientist, from a positivist to an interpretivist (and increasingly critical) stance, I felt overwhelmed by the prospect of trying to communicate all of this to the reviewers. This was compounded by a conviction that their review efforts had been superficial because they had failed to grasp that my study had not taken place in a classroom or course—a fact that should have been obvious. If they had not taken the time to read my paper properly, what chance did I have to convince them that my methods and epistemological stance were legitimate and valuable?

As I reflect now on the suggestion that my research presented nothing "new," I realize that my own epistemology had shifted. As a qualitative researcher, I often approached my work from an interpretive stance. But the notion that my work presented nothing new incubated anger on behalf of the students I had studied. They had all shared stories of leaving other research labs because they had felt obliged to hide aspects of their identities. Several had even considered abandoning science altogether before finding their way to Denise's lab. This suggested I had begun taking up a critical stance, but I was not explicit about it at the time.

The "nothing new" critique and my increasingly critical stance strengthened my resolve to get my paper in front of scientists, so I sought another new venue. I discussed the paper with a mentor, who advised me to submit it to a higher education journal that was commonly read by STEM faculty. I again reshaped and rewrote the manuscript, drawing heavily on papers published in this third journal. I also tackled the concerns raised by reviewers who had failed to view my work as research. For instance, I aimed to educate readers on the idea that participant observation is methodological, and that I had followed the norms and standards outlined by other researchers. I explained my data collection, selection, and analysis decisions in detail and connected these to citations to methodological textbooks and journal articles. In doing so, I felt like I had slipped back in time to writing my dissertation proposal, setting up a defensive line of well-referenced methodological citations and explaining what these looked like in my study.

I also added graphs based on further analysis, driven largely by the fact that I had a much larger data corpus, having continued data collection since the first submission. This re-analysis and reframing felt productive, which led me to create a clearer framework grounded in past research, yet still clearly connected to the normal workings of a research lab. This was important to me, as I wanted others to be able to implement the three interdisciplinary stances I identified. I wanted to disseminate these so other students might yet find themselves remaining in science.

Writing this now, it is clear that my stance was becoming increasingly critical, rather than interpretivist. I had done the various things qualitative researchers typically do to enhance trustworthiness and credibility—engaging in the setting for an extended period, triangulating inferences across sources and over time, conducting external audits with other researchers, and regularly conducting member checking through formal presentations, draft-sharing, and informal interviews. However, because I was so certain that my results could and should be implemented by other scientists to bring about more equitable conditions, I also felt a sense of unease tied to my limited familiarity with critical theory. I suspected that my conviction would seep through and weaken my arguments when read by scientists.

I submitted the paper in late 2017 and received a rejection one month later. One reviewer was enthusiastic, and their comments led me to believe I had achieved my aim, although they suggested a few improvements:

> Please give me more details on the coding process and how I can start looking at my own lab meetings with this lens. The paper will really benefit from a longer discussion on specific activities you used to define behaviors and how this worked with your coding. Is there any future work to develop some kind of "checklist" or survey for labs to start using to evaluate their own meetings in this way?

At long last, I felt that a reviewer understood what I was trying to accomplish.

By contrast, following the tradition noted in popular (academic) culture, reviewer #2 was unproductively critical, complaining (in upper-case letters) about the term "site" in the title, and suggesting that I needed to clarify whether I meant ethnic or cultural diversity in the title. In critiquing the abstract, their stance was clearly positivist: "Then, before writing about the data analysis you should have described briefly your methodology. Who were your subjects/respondents? How many? Are the 3 interdisciplinary stances your variables?" Next, they displayed the now familiar superficial engagement, asking, "In what setting did the research take place? For what science course?" As I read on, I found an increasingly wide divide between my stance and that of the reviewer: "Unfortunately, I still do not have clear [sic] what are you trying to do, neither what your [sic] trying to measure." In critiquing the remainder of my manuscript, the reviewer seemed intent on categorizing what I had done as something other than research:

> Research Design. If you conducted observations there is no need to cite anyone here. The problem I have here is that your description of the research design is NOT a research design to me. What did you observe, For how long?

How did you attempt to reduce your observer's biases while you were making your observations? Also, the description of your subjects (n=16) should have occurred much earlier in the description of your methods section.

Data Collection & Analysis. To what part of your research Design the 50 hrs. of audio refer to [sic]? What was the reason to review repeatedly the field notes? Earlier you wrote about triangulating your data but so far you have collected field notes (from your observations) and audio data. Where is the 3rd data set coming from to do the triangulation?

Results and Discussion. I am really lost here! The reason is due to your flawed methodology.

Nevertheless, they acknowledged that I "dealt with a topic that is original and potentially attractive to science professors who wish to learn how to enhance inclusivity within Lab course and research projects for undergraduate students." Given this, and the fact that the first reviewer had found my study useful, I considered revising and resubmitting, or finding yet another, similar journal. I reached out to the editor for guidance:

I very much appreciate this feedback. I suspect [your journal] is not the right home for this piece, at least based on the second reviewer's comments. Do you have any suggestions for us, as we seek to publish this work? Thanks for any advice.

Admittedly, my request for suggestions was framed from a stance of resignation. Upon reading the feedback, I had, at that point, almost given up on the article altogether. Weeks later, I received a curt and discouraging reply: "I'm afraid I don't have a ready suggestion." Feeling downtrodden, yet still determined, I made the decision to reshape and rewrite the manuscript yet again, but this time for my own field.

Reflections

In reflecting back on this sequence of interruptions in my attempt to publish a qualitative study in journals read by natural scientists, I have gained a sense of closure, even though the article remains unpublished. Writing this chapter has given me a chance to reflect on what I could have done differently. First, I should have been more assertive when communicating with editors, starting with an introductory query. Following such a query after the third rejection, I feel confident that the editor will give it the care and oversight it deserves. I should also have pushed a bit harder with the editors, highlighting the enthusiasm some of the reviewers expressed. I strongly suspect I could have lobbied successfully for the paper to be published in the second venue, despite the discouraging reviews, simply because the editor felt bad that it had been lost in the system; it would have been easy to point out that the reviews seemed rushed. I do not, however, regret my decision to move on from that journal, in part because the third reframing, which included more data, was a much stronger analysis, and this has only been strengthened further by subsequent work.

To appease my desire for broader impacts, I have given talks and workshops to natural scientists based on this line of research, and brought it into my work with science and engineering faculty who are seeking to change their teaching. I am sometimes stunned by how accepting they are of the ideas I present, given the hostility some of their peers expressed about the work in manuscript form. I suspect much of that has to do with the expectations one brings to the task of reviewing a manuscript versus attending a workshop on teaching and learning.

Although my experience was discouraging, I hope that sharing this story will help other scholars with similar commitments find venues that will work with them. I am encouraged, for instance, by the *Journal of Engineering Education* (JEE), which, based on my own and colleagues' accounts of the difficulties we faced when trying to publish qualitative manuscripts, formerly took a positivist stance in review and editorial decisions. JEE has since published papers with guidelines about quality in various approaches to qualitative research (Walther et al., 2017; Walther, Sochacka, & Kellam, 2013) and consequently published more than 20 papers citing these guidelines. Such efforts pave the way for scholars to submit various forms of qualitative research by providing clear guidance and encouragement. There is value, therefore, in pursuing similar efforts in consultation with editors in other fields.

References

Alise, M. A., & Teddlie, C. (2010). A continuation of the paradigm wars? Prevalence rates of methodological approaches across the social/behavioral sciences. *Journal of Mixed Methods Research, 4*(2), 103–126.

Gage, N. L. (1989). The paradigm wars and their aftermath a "historical" sketch of research on teaching since 1989. *Educational Researcher, 18*(7), 4–10.

Hyland, K. (2011). Disciplines and discourses: Social interactions in the construction of knowledge. In D. Starke-Meyerring, A. Paré, N. Artemeva, M. Horne, & L. Yousoubova (Eds.) *Writing in knowledge societies* (pp. 193–214). West Lafayette, IN: Parlor Press and WAC Clearinghouse.

Hyland, K., & Jiang, F. K. (2017). Is academic writing becoming more informal? *English for Specific Purposes, 45,* 40–51.

National Science Foundation. (2018). *Proposal & award policies and procedures guide.* Retrieved March 6, 2019 from: www.nsf.gov/pubs/policydocs/pappg18_1/nsf18_1.pdf.

Page, S. (2007). *Diversity powers innovation.* Retrieved March 6, 2019 from: www.americanp rogress.org/issues/economy/news/2007/01/26/2523/diversity-powers-innovation/.

Svihla, V. (2004). Structural evolution of the east central Big Maria Mountains, Maria fold and thrust belt, southeastern California. Paper presented at Abstracts with Programs, Geological Society of America, Boise, ID, May 4.

Velasco, A. A., & Velasco, E. J. (2010). Striving to diversify the geosciences workforce. *Eos, Transactions American Geophysical Union, 91*(33), 289–290.

Walther, J., Sochacka, N. W., Benson, L. C., Bumbaco, A. E., Kellam, N., Pawley, A. L., & Phillips, C. M. L. (2017). Qualitative research quality: A collaborative inquiry across multiple methodological perspectives. *Journal of Engineering Education*, 106(3), 398–430.

Walther, J., Sochacka, N. W., & Kellam, N. N. (2013). Quality in interpretive engineering education research: Reflections on an example study. *Journal of Engineering Education*, 102 (4), 626–659.

15

"THERE ARE NOTABLE LINGUISTIC PROBLEMS"

Publishing as a non-native speaker of English

Aliya Kuzhabekova

Introduction

Publishing the results of a study is arguably the most important stage of the research process. A study does not exist in the minds of the scholarly community unless it is embodied in a published format to be disseminated for subsequent scholarly discussion. Intriguingly, though, few textbooks I read as a graduate student discussed the nuts and bolts of producing a publishable scholarly manuscript. Budding researchers end up learning the tricks of the publication trade by trial and error, by having multiple versions of a manuscript rejected or revised. The least fortunate ones lose hope, shelve their papers, and never see their theses or dissertations published in academic venues.

For non-native English speakers (NNESs), the process of learning the ropes of academic publishing is complicated by deficits in their knowledge of English—grammatical conventions, the structure of the text, the vocabulary—as well as the stylistic aspects and genres of writing in academic idiom. Many authors (e.g., Canagarajah, 1996; Gibbs, 1995; Wood, 1997) have empirically demonstrated that NNESs are at a disadvantage when it comes to publishing the results of their research as compared to NESs (native English speakers). Some have even reported NNESs' sense of inequality with respect to publication in English (Hanauer & Englander, 2011; Lillis & Curry, 2010).

I was fortunate that my language ability was relatively high for a NNES at the start of my independent scholarly career. Prior to my arrival to an English-speaking country for academic studies, I had been a student in a department of foreign languages, where I had received advanced training in English. I completed a master's degree and then a Ph.D. in Educational Policy and Administration in the United States. Nevertheless, publication has never been easy for me, and lots of my frustrations have been related to the fact that I am not a native speaker. Even now, when I face fewer difficulties as an experienced researcher, I am accustomed to receiving some version of the following comment at the end of the review process: "There are notable linguistic problems throughout the text in terms of grammar and style: you would need to do a professional proofreading of the English. I would recommend that your paper be accepted only after such a linguistic revision" (reviewer for a European education journal).

In this chapter I share some of the experiences I have had as a NNES in bringing my research to publication in scholarly journals. I hope that this narrative—which describes how I interpreted my experiences, how I felt, what I did in response, and what I ultimately achieved—will help other NNESs in the process of learning the ropes of academic publishing.

Pre-publication experience: lessons learned from reviewing another person's paper

My first experience with the process of publication was in the role of a reviewer. In the first year of my Ph.D. studies, I was asked to review a paper on language policy in Kazakhstan by an editor of a European language policy journal. My master's thesis was on the same topic and, at the time, little research on language policy in Kazakhstan had been conducted in English.

I describe this review experience because it clearly demonstrates two challenges that are unique to NNESs and because it prepared me for subsequent publication experiences. First, like many other NNESs, I had very low confidence in my writing ability, which discouraged me from initial submission. Although my advisors recommended submitting my master's thesis for publication, I hesitated. I remembered the countless red corrections on my thesis before I was finally able to satisfy my advisor's expectations. I thought: "What editor would want to waste their time tidying up the imperfections in my English?" Receiving an invitation to review, and thus being recognized as an "expert" by the editor, boosted my confidence to send my thesis for publication.

Second, I struggled to differentiate between scholarly genres. Understanding genre-related differences is important for publication because every journal may distinguish between different types of articles (literature reviews, analytical, theoretical, empirical, methodological), and specific journals, as well as disciplines, may have preferences for particular genres. While all novice researchers have to master the genre conventions, NNESs frequently struggle with differentiation and skillful use of scholarly genres (Al-Khasawneh, 2017).

When I conducted my first review, I was familiar with only one genre—an empirical paper. I had been required to analyze and reproduce such papers in methods courses and found them relatively easy to deconstruct. They systematically used the same approach to organization, with clearly identified and consistently named subsections, and often used formulaic expressions to describe design, methods, and results. As a NNES with limited vocabulary and quite poor understanding of scholarly text organization in English, I quickly noted the standard structure and formulae in empirical papers, and tried to reproduce them in my own work.

Meanwhile, I had more trouble with genres such as literature reviews, methodological notes, and theoretical papers. While I encountered all of these in my studies, they were more difficult to understand, so I often skimmed through them while paying closer attention to monographs and book chapters, where the argument tended to be less condensed and the ideas were more explicitly expressed.

My unfamiliarity with different genres led to a cognitive dissonance during the review process. The paper I was asked to review was analytical, although it did refer to some data collected in prior studies, and I remember having difficulty understanding why the manuscript did not follow the conventional structure of an empirical paper. I ended up arrogantly "teaching" the author that "a properly structured paper should include the following sections: Introduction, Literature Review, Methods, Results, Discussion and Conclusion" and arguing that "it would be advisable for the author to organize their paper in the suggested format." I am not sure my review was beneficial to the author, but I realized I needed to pay more attention to the genres I had been neglecting.

First publication experience: surviving critique and loss of confidence

This experience as a reviewer helped me later in the year, when I received an invitation to contribute a chapter based on my master's thesis. I remember having very contradictory feelings—excitement that someone considered my work worthy of publication but also trepidation due to a suspicion that I might not yet be ready to go solo as an author. However, I understood that publication would be highly beneficial for my future academic career. So I took the risk and decided to make the next step—from being a reviewer to being a contributor.

I contacted the book's editor prior to beginning work on the chapter. I told him that my study had been conducted four years earlier and I had not followed subsequent research on the topic. After carefully reading the editor's reply, I was reassured that he was fine with the old data and felt that he primarily wanted a summary of the main points in my thesis, as well as a brief discussion of new developments.

As I started writing the first draft, I faced three main challenges, two of which will be familiar to all novice researchers, while the third is unique to NNESs. First, I spent lots of time and effort trying to cut my 215-page thesis down to a 25-page chapter. I struggled to distinguish crucial information from less important information, and found it especially difficult to focus the study in such a way that the edited version retained coherence in the argument.

The second challenge was related to my limited understanding of the analytical paper genre, which I ended up employing for the chapter. My essay was a review of existing policy documents, opinion pieces, newspaper articles, and local research on recent developments in language policy in Kazakhstan. The "gold standard" for the structure of an empirical paper that I had recommended in my review of another author's article earlier in the year was clearly inappropriate for my own chapter, so I had to come up with a different structure. I wrote at least three drafts, switching from organization based on sequential presentation of issues, to a historical organization, and, finally, to a combination of both approaches.

Third, I struggled with editing the many grammatical, lexical, and stylistic issues in the paper in the absence of feedback, which I was used to receiving on course papers and my thesis. My master's advisor had retired and I did not feel comfortable asking him for help. It took me at least a week and three rounds of rewriting to edit the language in the final version of the manuscript by myself. By the time I had finished, I hated the paper and felt no desire to look at it ever again.

Here, I would like to digress from the main narrative to discuss some of the issues I had to correct while editing, some of which will be familiar to other NNESs. First and foremost was my tendency to use lengthy and complex syntax, which is characteristic of my native language. Russian sentences are often the length of a paragraph, with up to five levels of subordination, and they frequently include many details and digressions from the main thought. In fact, one paragraph—or even sentence—may express several parallel ideas. This is very uncommon in English, where a single central idea is typically stated at the beginning of a paragraph, and there is one main idea per sentence. To give a sense of the peculiarities of Russian, I quote a sentence from Tolstoy's *Anna Karenina*:

> It is true that Alexei Alexandrovich vaguely sensed the levity and erroneousness of this notion of his faith, and he knew that when, without any thought that his forgiveness was the effect of a higher power, he had given himself to his spontaneous feeling, he had experienced greater happiness than when he thought every minute, as he did now, that Christ lived in his soul, and that by signing papers he was fulfilling His will, but it was necessary for him to think that way, it was so necessary for him in his humiliation to possess at least an invented loftiness from which he, despised by everyone, could despise others, that he clung to his imaginary salvation as if it were salvation indeed.
>
> (Tolstoy, 2002, p. 22)

While my writing does not compare with that of Tolstoy, when I submitted the first draft of my master's thesis, my supervisor asked me to cut every sentence in half. So, I adopted the same approach with the first draft of my book chapter. This was far from easy, because the shorter sentences seemed unnatural and simplistic to me. I thought I did not sound sufficiently intelligent.

Over time, I started to believe that NESs have a smaller comprehension span than Russians due to the nature of English grammar and syntax. There is something about Russian that makes it easier to process lengthier sentences in the language. Meanwhile, NESs might lose their train of thought in any sentence that is longer than two clauses. Given that thoughts tend to be complicated in scholarly writing, I came to the conclusion that it is better to keep sentences short to avoid miscomprehension. Today, I often advise my students to avoid complex sentences and tell them that if there are only two paragraphs on a page, their paragraphs are likely too long and present too many ideas, digressions, and details.

My second major problem with English is overuse of the passive voice, which was first noted by my thesis advisor. Like complex syntax, the passive voice is common in scholarly Russian, but generally discouraged in English. For instance, I recently received the following comment from an otherwise supportive reviewer:

> The authors make a number of unattributed statements and use the Passive Voice frequently, so that they are not naming actors. For example, on p. 2, why was the change in the financing system made? On pages 4–5, the authors use phrases like "are not expected to be" or "are supposed to be" without indicating who set these expectations. Similarly, on p. 11, they write "flagships are believed …" and the inspirational role "is perceived," without stating by whom, and on p. 14 they state "there is a hope." I would suggest that the authors go through the manuscript and eliminate all the uses of the Passive Voice in favor of naming actors. I understand that some of this language use may stem from language structures in Russian, but I think that it is important in scholarly work to name actors.
>
> *(Reviewer for* European Education*)*

I now understand that in scholarly English one needs to specify the agent who performs a particular action. This may stem from the individualistic nature of Anglophone societies, where it is important to claim authorship. However, when I wrote my first book chapter, the use of active voice was still unnatural for me, so I went with the flow of my thoughts in my accustomed Russian style before converting all of the passive structures to active ones during revision.

Of course, NNES writers face countless further issues, such as article use, tense concordance, and word choice, all of which may be experienced in other types of writing. Many of these issues are covered in English classes, but those that are specific to academic writing are typically not addressed during formal courses, so they present a unique challenge to NNES researchers.

To return to the main narrative, all of the time and effort I devoted to the chapter proved to be in vain. Like many other NNESs who attempt to publish in English for the first time, I had failed to read between the lines and grasp what the editor really wanted. Having read my manuscript, he informed me that the chapter should be more of a review and critique of the current language policy in Kazakhstan, rather than an analysis of the prehistory and first few years of that policy (which had been the subject of both my thesis and the first draft).

Looking back at this experience now, as a faculty advisor for many NNES graduate students with little confidence in their language and research skills who tremble at the mere thought of writing a thesis, I think I read only what I wanted to read in the editor's original message—his reassurance that my study was worthy of publication. In doing so, I completely missed his more detailed instructions, which outlined his vision for the book. Obviously, I should have given these much more careful consideration.

I was extremely frustrated with the review because analyzing the literature on recent developments in Kazakhstan seemed to require writing a whole new thesis in the midst of an intensive first year in a doctoral program. However, I had the wisdom to seek advice from my supervisor, who strongly encouraged me to persevere, saying that any publication would be beneficial when I started looking for jobs. In addition, he stressed that revising articles was inevitable in academia and that even experienced researchers sometimes had to make dramatic changes to papers after receiving feedback. Finally, he explained the importance of reading editorial comments carefully, as well as trying to understand any implied meanings that might be hidden between the lines.

In order to avoid making the same mistake, I carefully reread all of the editor's emails to gain a better understanding of the task, then spent many sleepless weeks trying to write a completely new paper. Needless to say, this was followed by another week of proofreading. I did not rush to submit because I did not want to disappoint the editor again, so I sat on the draft right until the revision deadline.

Unfortunately, the editor found the new draft just as unsatisfactory as the first. I received a very harsh and impatient email in which he explained that he was facing a tight deadline and my manuscript still failed to meet expectations. Specifically, it contained many grammatical and stylistic errors. He issued an ultimatum in which he advised me to look quickly through a reviewer's suggestions and agree to the changes. As I read his comments, I realized that this situation could have been avoided if I had submitted the manuscript earlier and given the editor sufficient time to provide constructive feedback, and myself sufficient time to address his concerns.

When I had finished reading the reviewer's suggestions, I felt inept, because they had cut whole paragraphs and reworded many sentences. The edited version was as red as the first draft of my master's thesis. I also felt my voice had been lost. The reviewer was Russian, while I was Kazakh, so we had very different views on the effectiveness of language policy in Kazakhstan, given that Russian had been the colonial language in the republic. Although I wanted to resist their suggestions, I felt pressured by both the deadline and the tone of the editor, as well as the competitive "publish-or-perish" culture in the research-intensive university where I studied. So, I gave in and accepted the reviewer's version of the manuscript. But I had very bad feelings about the whole process and the end product. The last straw was seeing the published version with the following note in the acknowledgements section: "The chapter was significantly edited by ..." This felt like a slap in the face.

This first painful experience with solo publication left me with a sense of incompetence and little confidence to produce any further papers by myself. Without that curt comment at the end of the chapter, I probably would have felt that I had achieved something, despite the traumatic revision process. However, its inclusion meant that I started to doubt my abilities as a researcher. It took several years of co-authoring articles with a very supportive professor for whom I worked as a research assistant to recover. I helped the professor write up sections of manuscripts on prior research, describing the methods we used and the results we obtained, reviewing suggested journals to make recommendations for possible publication venues, and formatting final documents for submission. The professor reviewed and edited my drafts and provided lots of positive and useful feedback, which allowed me not only to improve my publication-related skills and my academic English, but also regain my confidence as an author.

First experience with an article: how to succeed by seeking support from senior scholars

Towards the end of my studies, my dissertation committee members strongly encouraged me to submit at least one first-authored article in my field before I graduated. I felt I was ready to do that about a year before submitting the final version of my dissertation. Recalling the distressing experience with the book chapter, I decided to go cautiously and "protected" myself by inviting two committee members to join me as co-authors. These very distinguished professors graciously agreed, and their help was tremendously useful in five ways:

- they helped me achieve greater coherence and improved the paper's comprehensibility;
- they assisted me with the choice of a potential publication venue;
- they edited my English;
- they helped me interpret decision letters; and
- they pushed me to persevere when I felt frustrated with the process and wanted to abandon the manuscript.

The paper that I prepared for publication was empirical in nature and explored the state of knowledge in the field of international higher education. I was using the same method to explore a different topic in my dissertation, so, as it was familiar to me, I quickly collected the data, implemented the analysis, and drafted the literature review, methods, and results sections. However, drafting the introduction and the discussion section in both the paper and the dissertation proved more problematic. As a research assistant, I had never previously composed introductions or discussions, let alone assembled a complete manuscript in which all of the pieces were connected. Each of my co-authors made significant contributions to these sections and helped me align the literature review, methodology, and results sections, for which I was solely responsible.

While I was aware of some key journals in my field from my coursework, I was not sure which would be most appropriate for this paper. I knew from my research assistantships that I needed to look through the "Aims and Scope" sections of journal websites as well as some of their published articles. So, with due diligence, I pored over the websites of ten journals, but still I could not reach a decision, not least because they all seemed to be so similar. For instance, consider the stated positions of *Research in Higher Education* and *Review of Higher Education*, which are presented below:

> [*Research in Higher Education*] is open to studies using a wide range of methods, but has particular interest in studies that apply advanced quantitative research methods to issues in postsecondary education or address postsecondary education policy issues. Among the topics of interest to the journal are: access and retention; student success; equity; faculty issues; institutional productivity and assessment; postsecondary education governance; curriculum and instruction; state and federal higher education policy; and financing of postsecondary education.
>
> The *Review of Higher Education* provides a forum for discussion of varied issues affecting higher education. The journal advances the study of college- and university-related topics through peer-reviewed articles, essays, reviews and research findings, and by emphasizing systematic inquiry—both quantitative and qualitative—and practical implications.

As far as I can see, the only difference between these two descriptions is that the first provides a bit more detail about topics and methods. In fact, after studying all ten journals, I discerned only one major difference—some were oriented primarily towards scholars, while others were more oriented towards practitioners.

Confused, I approached one of my co-authors, who suggested one of the top journals in the field. He thought this would be the best option because the editor was looking for articles that used unconventional methodological approaches. Seeking guidance from a senior colleague was the best thing I could do in this situation, so I accepted my co-author's advice and submitted the manuscript to the journal's editor. In turn, he sent it to two reviewers.

An intermediate outcome of the decision to send the article to a top journal was an editorial verdict that "the paper cannot be published in its current form and requires major revisions," accompanied by lengthy and highly critical comments from the reviewers. The editor noted that the "reviewers thought that the topic and the manuscript had promise, but both also suggested multiple revisions, and it's likely that a successful manuscript would need to be heavily revised."

In light of this response, I concluded that our paper was a total disaster. To my utter surprise, however, my co-authors interpreted the editor's email completely differently and congratulated me. In their view, the editor considered our contribution worthy of publication and was willing to guide me through the revision process until eventual acceptance. This was a very valuable lesson: especially in the early stages of an academic career, it is always wise to compare one's own understanding of decision letters with those of more experienced colleagues. My co-authors explained that the phrase "the paper cannot be published in its current form" did not mean that it would never be published. Instead, it meant that the editor would consider publishing it if I made the recommended changes. They also directed my attention to the fact that "the reviewers thought that the topic and the manuscript had promise," which also signaled the editor's willingness to consider a revised version. They also clarified a number of seemingly contradictory comments and advised me to pay most attention to the editor's—rather than the reviewers'—recommendations. I could choose which of the reviewers' comments to address, and I was free to disregard others as long as I provided clear justifications for my decisions in an accompanying letter. Finally, they suggested that the accompanying letter should also include a detailed explanation of all the changes I made.

My continuing challenges with language editing as an experienced researcher

At this point, I consider myself an experienced researcher. I have published about 30 articles and book chapters, I have in-depth knowledge of the main journals in my field, and I understand the process of publication and review. I can also make sense of most editors' and reviewers' comments. However, my language ability remains an issue even today. While I have developed a better understanding of how academic text is structured and organized in English, stylistic, vocabulary, and grammatical problems still persist in my manuscripts, and editors continue to urge me to send my final drafts to a NES or even a professional proofreader. For instance, I recently received the following comment from a reviewer who has a progressive attitude towards language difference, but nevertheless feels boxed in by standard language ideologies:

> The chapter is well-written at the sentence level but contains some micro-level features (e.g. article usage, punctuation, etc.) that some readers may find nonstandard. Depending on the needs of the editors and/or publisher, more proofreading may be appropriate.

Such requests have become increasingly difficult to satisfy. I have asked almost all of my NES colleagues to take a second look at one of my papers and I feel I can no longer abuse their kindness. Proofreading is a tedious task, and many members of faculty pursue Ph.D.s specifically to avoid monotonous tasks and do something more creative with their lives, so I do not feel comfortable repeatedly asking colleagues to edit my papers, no matter how accommodating they may be. Some of those colleagues have straightforwardly suggested that I should pay professional editors to check my manuscripts. However, none of the grants I have received have allocated funds for such services, and I could not afford them out of my own pocket. (In Kazakhstan, the cost of editing a single article may amount to a third of a professor's monthly salary.) In addition, I have had trouble finding editors with both sufficient understanding of the subject matter and the requisite English language skills. Whenever an editor does not have a good grasp of the subject matter or does not understand the nature of the research, they either shy away from providing the service or do a substandard job. In the latter case, the edited text often fails to convey the intended meaning and I simply disregard the suggested changes.

My main approach at this point is to team up with NES colleagues or doctoral students with superior knowledge of English. The former do me a favor by checking my manuscripts before submission and correcting any errors they notice. I then return the favor by checking their manuscripts. In the latter case, although I regret perpetuating privilege based on language fluency, I prefer to hire graduate assistants with good English language skills so that I can ask them to review final versions of my manuscripts as part of their responsibilities. Meanwhile, I continue to search for a more sustainable solution to the language editing problem.

My experience compared to those of others

Flowerdew (2000) viewed learning how to write and publish academic papers as a process of socialization into the academic discourse community, defined by Kuhn (1970) as a group of professionals within a scientific specialty who share language, beliefs, and practices. Entrance to this community requires learning a set of norms, rules, processes, and a particular kind of language. Much of this knowledge is tacit and cannot be acquired via formal coursework. Rather, it is learned via initiation by a senior member of the community, who provides an example to follow and assists in interpretation of what is happening (Belcher, 1994; Li, 2007; Prior, 1998). The role of an individual researcher is renegotiated in the process of interaction with the discourse community, whereby a junior researcher gradually moves from a peripheral position to the center (Lave & Wenger, 1991).

My progress in learning the norms and language of the discourse community would have been much more difficult without the assistance of senior colleagues and if I had not sought apprenticeship opportunities in the form of research assistantships, postdoctoral fellowships, and self-initiated collaborations. These people have led me through the initiation process by providing many forms of assistance, ranging from interpreting editorial decisions and reviews, to critiquing methods and proofreading articles, to simply providing encouragement when I lost hope and wanted to abandon all further attempts at publication.

Many of the challenges I have experienced on my journey have been shared by other researchers, with some of them specific to NNESs, as is clear from prior research. One of the main problems for NNESs is inadequate language ability to be able to communicate effectively in scholarly papers (Canagarajah, 1996; Jernudd & Baldauf, 1987; Swales, 1990). Some studies have also noted that trying to address the language issue creates its own complications. Frequently, scholars do not have sufficient funding to cover editing or translation expenses; translators with expertise in both academic English and the researcher's subject matter may be unavailable; an academic form of the researcher's native language may not exist, so they will be unable to write a version of their paper in their first language for subsequent translation; or, if educated abroad, the researcher may not be articulate in the academic form of their native language (Flowerdew, 1999).

Studies have shown that many NNESs use similar strategies when attempting to address language issues (Bazerman, 1988): paying for their articles to be professionally edited; seeking help from NSEs; relying on peer review; trying to understand current discourse by attending conferences; and reviewing other scholars' papers. However, some—if not all—of these strategies may be unavailable. For example, the NNES researcher may have no NES colleagues (Casanave, 1998; Flowerdew, 2007; Swales, 1990); access to recent publications may be severely restricted (Canagarajah, 1996); and funding for translation and editing may not be provided (Flowerdew, 1999).

Finally, there is evidence that NESs and NNESs share some of the same issues at the beginning of their publication experience. Among the difficulties both groups encounter are: developing a sense of academic "self"; overcoming self-doubt; differentiating between various genres of academic papers; choosing the right publication venue; ensuring the paper is a good fit for the chosen venue; understanding the stages and timelines of the publication process, as well as the constraints faced by the editor; interpreting editorial decisions and reviewers' comments correctly; dealing with rejection; and responding to "revise-and-resubmit" decisions (Aitchison, Catterall, Ross, & Burgin, 2012; Badenhorst et al., 2015). However, based on my own experience, and my observations of NNES colleagues and graduate students, NNESs seem to experience greater struggles with these non-language issues. First, a NNES's sense of academic self may be lower initially and subsequently undermined more severely as a result of rejection than that of a NES. Second, as mentioned earlier, NNESs often have greater trouble than NESs distinguishing between different genres of academic texts (Al-Khasawneh, 2017). It takes more advanced language skills to identify subtle stylistic differences and understand deeper levels of discourse. Third, understanding the differences between academic journals may be more challenging since information about their target readerships, types of articles they accept, and topics they cover is not provided in detail on their websites. Finally, people from a variety of cultural and linguistic backgrounds might express support, satisfaction, or dissatisfaction in very different ways, and they may have contrasting norms that regulate communication with authority figures, including those who have the power to determine their fate in publication. A simple "no" or "yes" is communicated differently in written messages in different cultures. These issues are also harder to overcome for both NESs or NNESs who live and work in relative isolation from their discourse community due to geography, being members of smaller institutions, or lack of funding to access full-text databases and international conferences (Gosden, 1992).

Lessons to be learned

Since English for publication purposes is commonly not formally taught in graduate courses (although this is starting to change on some campuses), a NNES needs to learn it independently. One of the best ways to do so is by reading scholarly papers and paying close attention to how arguments are structured, how issues are presented, and the style and vocabulary that are used. Some of the traditional strategies for learning languages are useful here: take notes; memorize new disciplinary terminology; outline an article in order to understand its structure; note some commonly used transitional and introductory phrases; and pay attention to how an argument is presented.

Another strategy is to subject your own writing to critique from peers or senior scholars. The review will help you understand the tacit conventions more clearly. It will reveal parts of your argument that are ineffective, redundant, or require more clarity about your own positionality as a scholar. In addition, reviewing others' papers for journals or simply as a colleague will help, because it brings to consciousness some subtleties that you may overlook when writing your own papers.

Understanding publication conventions in your specific field requires active engagement with your disciplinary community at conferences as well as some sort of apprenticeship with or continuous support and advice from senior scholars. At conferences, you will have many opportunities to hear editors' requirements for publishing in their journals, you can participate in senior scholars' mentorship workshops, and you can put clarifying questions to speakers. An apprenticeship as a research assistant or postdoctoral fellow will allow you to observe an experienced scholar at work and ask questions based on those observations. Having a regular formal or informal mentor either in your department or outside will allow you to seek advice when dealing with the complexities of editorial correspondence and choosing a journal.

Most importantly, remember that no matter how harsh editors' and reviewers' comments may be, and irrespective of your anxiety over writing, submitting, and revising, you must persevere and treat every stage of the process—whether disappointing or promising—as a learning experience, a step forward, not a lost cause. There is always a journal for your paper if you are willing to undertake the necessary revision. Keep in mind that there is no end to the learning process—even the most experienced scholars have trouble with writing and publishing their papers. So, it is essential to learn how to be at peace with this, how to deal with disappointments, and how to continue to find pleasure in your work. I have long noticed that decisions on manuscripts come like black-and-white stripes of life—for every disappointing rejection, there is always a hopeful "revise and resubmit."

References

Aitchison, C., Catterall, J., Ross, P., & Burgin, S. (2012). "Tough love and tears": Learning doctoral writing in the sciences. *Higher Education Research and Development*, 31(4), 435–447.

Al-Khasawneh, F. M. S. (2017). A genre analysis of research article abstracts written by native and non-native speakers of English. *Journal of Applied Linguistics and Language Research*, 4(1), 1–13.

Badenhorst, C., Moloney, C., Rosales, J., Dyer, J., & Ru, L. (2015). Beyond deficit: Graduate student research-writing pedagogies. *Teaching in Higher Education*, 20(1), 1–11.

Bazerman, C. (1988). *Shaping written knowledge*. Madison, WI: University of Madison Press.

Belcher, D. (1994). The apprenticeship approach to advanced academic literacy: Graduate students and their mentors. *English for Specific Purposes*, 13(1), 23–34.

Canagarajah, A. S. (1996). "Nondiscursive" requirements in academic publishing, material resources of periphery scholars, and the politics of knowledge production. *Written Communication*, 13(4), 435–472.

Canagarajah, A. S. (2013). *Critical academic writing and multilingual students*. Ann Arbor: University of Michigan Press.

Casanave, C. P. (1998). Transitions: The balancing act of bilingual academics. *Journal of Second Language Writing*, 7(2), 175–203.

Flowerdew, J. (1999). Writing for scholarly publication in English: The case of Hong Kong. *Journal of Second Language Editing*, 8(2), 123–145.

Flowerdew, J. (2000). Discourse community, legitimate peripheral participation, and the nonnative-English-speaking scholar. *TESOL Quarterly*, 34(1), 127–150.

Flowerdew, J. (2007). The non-Anglophone scholar on the periphery of scholarly publication. *AILA Review*, 20(1), 14–27.

Gibbs, W. W. (1995). Lost science in the Third World. *Scientific American*, 273(2), 92–99.

Gosden, H. (1992). Research writing and NNSs: From the editors. *Journal of Second Language Writing*, 1(2), 123–139.

Hanauer, D. I., & Englander, K. (2011). Quantifying the burden of writing research articles in a second language: Data from Mexican scientists. *Written Communication*, 28(4), 403–416.

Hyland, K. (2016). Academic publishing and the myth of linguistic injustice. *Journal of Second Language Writing*, 31, 58–69.

Jernudd, B.H., & Baldauf, R.B. (1987). Planning science communication for human resource development. In B. K. Das (Ed.) *Communicative language teaching* (pp. 144–189). Singapore: RELC.

Kuhn, T. S. (1970). *The structure of scientific revolution*, 2nd edition. Chicago, IL: University of Chicago Press.

Lave, J., & Wenger, E. (1991). *Situated learning: Legitimate peripheral participation*. Cambridge: Cambridge University Press.

Li, Y. (2007). Apprentice scholarly writing in a community of practice: An intraview of an NNES graduate student writing a research article. *TESOL Quarterly*, 41(1), 55–79.

Lillis, T. M., & Curry, M. J. (2010). *Academic writing in global context*. London: Routledge.

Prior, P. (1998). *Writing/disciplinarity: A sociohistoric account of literate activity in the academy*. Mahwah, NJ: Erlbaum.

Swales, J. M. (1990). *Genre analysis: English in academic and research settings*. Cambridge: Cambridge University Press.

Tolstoy, L. (2002). *Anna Karenina*. Translated by R. Pevear and L. Volokhonsky. London: Penguin Classics.

Wood, A. (1997). International scientific English: Some thoughts on science, language and ownership. *Science Tribune*, 2(4), 1.

PART 4 DISCUSSION QUESTIONS AND ACTIVITIES

Discussion questions for Chapter 13: Excessive peer review and the death of an academic article

1. Grant Eckstein chronicles his self-doubts during the review process of an article. What are some ways researchers can prepare for or combat negative inner voices that criticize their writing or research?
2. Eckstein indicates that the decision to submit his article to a particular journal was made only after the research had been completed. At which stage should a researcher choose a journal for article submission, and how strategic should they be in reaching their decision?
3. It is sometimes appropriate to disagree with reviewers' comments. When and how can an author remain polite and measured while still refuting editors' or reviewers' comments?

Discussion questions for Chapter 14: From broader impacts to intellectual merit: an interruption in interdisciplinary publishing

1. Vanessa Svihla reflects critically on a submission in order to understand why and how it failed to meet editorial and reviewers' expectations. She goes to great lengths to analyze a 65-word reviewer's comment. What benefit did she derive from this analysis? How did this particular reviewer's feedback lead to a better (or at least different) paper? How would you have responded?
2. Whether your work involves interdisciplinary collaboration or not, you are likely to engage with others who take a positivist stance and question the legitimacy of qualitative methods. How would you explain the value of your research?
3. What are the pitfalls and drawbacks of publishing interdisciplinary research? What are the benefits and advantages?

Discussion questions for Chapter 15: "There are notable linguistic problems": publishing as a non-native speaker of English

1. Aliya Kuzhabekova points out that academic writing in English tends to be uncomplicated at the clause level. Whether you are a native speaker of English or not, how might knowing typical structures of academic English improve your ability to self-edit? How might you go about learning these structures, given that they are rarely taught in graduate programs?

2. What value did Kuzhabekova derive from contacting the editor in advance of submitting her article? What surprising complications did that interaction create? Based on your response, do you feel it is a good or a bad idea to contact the editor in advance of a submission?

3. Kuzhabekova describes several ways she learned about academic publishing, including reviewing author guidelines, writing with others, serving as a reviewer, and analyzing published papers. What strategies have you used—or will you use—to inform yourself about the norms in publishing your own work? How can you use this information in preparing your manuscript?

4. Mentors can play an important role in reading between the lines of opaque editorial comments and helping you stay on track as a publishing researcher. Who would you turn to if you received seemingly negative reviews? If you are unsure, describe how you might develop a relationship with a mentor.

Part 4 activity

Journal matchmaking

In this activity, compare and contrast potential publication venues that fit your research interests. The goal of the activity is to develop or refine judgement criteria when deciding which journal(s) to choose for submission.

First, identify five journals that may be appropriate submission venues for a current or future research project. Next, use the seven sections below to gather information about the journals from their websites and your interactions with the editors, managers, and others who are familiar with the venues.

Editors

List the names of the editors. Do you recognize them as leaders in your field or sub-field? What kind of research do they personally pursue? What is their orientation toward the methods you use in your research: do they use the same techniques? It is important to learn about the editors since their research interests/ orientations can influence the direction in which they take the journal. You can also introduce yourself to them at conferences or meetings in order to gauge their opinion of your research project.

Journal scope

List keywords that describe the topics and type of research the journal tends to publish. Often the journal's scope is written as broadly as possible to encourage a variety of submissions; additionally, it is frequently out of date, so don't rely solely on the "aims and scope" section of the website. Briefly review the titles and abstracts of articles published over the last three or four years to get a better sense of preferred subject areas.

Author guidelines

List any information that is pertinent to you as a writer, such as word-count limitations, citation style (e.g., APA or MLA), article type, spelling or typesetting requirements, and unique submission policies or procedures.

Typical publication timeline

Note the frequency with which the journal publishes issues (e.g., four times a year) and the number of articles within each issue. Some journals publish additional timing information, such as the average duration from submission to publication. If this is unavailable, it may be worth contacting the journal manager. It is also helpful to know whether a particular journal accepts submissions by invitation only, if it has a backlog of articles that will delay publication of your submission (if accepted), or if the review process is especially long or short.

Credibility value

Try to establish the journal's impact score. Not all journals calculate or publish such a score, but other information can serve as a proxy, such as the age of the journal (older journals tend to be better established and thus more credible), acceptance rate (lower rates tend to signify greater competition for publication and thus higher credibility), discipline specificity (a journal may be highly prestigious within a narrow sub-discipline but otherwise unrecognized), association with a conference or professional organization (which tends to increase visibility, making the journal more credible), and fee-based pricing (pay-to-publish journals tend to be predatory and thus not credible).

Upcoming special issues or flash themes

Determine whether the journal has any upcoming special issues or flash themes that fit your research. It is often easier to be accepted by a special issue because they tend to garner fewer submissions, yet they still carry the "brand" of the journal. Additionally, they impose a firm deadline and generally screen proposals via abstracts or short proposals, so no time is wasted on reviewing an entire article if it is obviously a poor fit from the start. Special issues and flash themes can lead people to your work because, when they find a relevant paper in a special issue, they tend to look at the others, too.

Miscellaneous

Compile a list of everything that is relevant to you or your research, such as comments you have received from colleagues or advisors about a journal's suitability for your research. You might include potential questions for the editors and the journal's position in your list of five possible publishing venues.

Once you have compiled a chart containing information from each of these seven categories, you can compare the five journals, solicit additional information if necessary, then make an informed decision about which is the best fit for your research.

AFTERWORD

What interruptions can tell us about the nature of qualitative educational research

Amanda K. Kibler

Introduction

> *Es para ver como son.* (It is to see how things are.)

In explaining to a fellow student why I had just placed an audio recorder on his desk, Diego, aged 14, succinctly described the purpose of much classroom-based qualitative social science research. Regardless of whether we, as scholars, are exploring ethnographic understandings of educational experiences or investigating the impact of interventions, we strive to see "how things are" in ways that help us understand the nature of teaching and learning more deeply. The contributors to this volume address the complexities of such an undertaking. Through reflections on their experiences of pursuing ambitious research, they share invaluable insights into the ways that interruptions to their research efforts have helped them understand their research sites and participants, themselves, their fields, and research itself more clearly. In doing so, they show dedication to pursuing meaningful scholarship, developing methodological theory and practice, and providing early-career researchers (and their mentors) with guidance derived from their own experiences.

Interruptions *as* research

As I delved into the narratives of research presented in the preceding chapters, I was struck by the notion that moments of interruption—rather than being aberrations to our work—may serve to redefine what research *is*. In this sense, interruptions reveal several fundamental aspects of qualitative research in educational settings: that it is not fully under researchers' control; that it is inextricable from our own and others' positionalities; that it is inherently a joint undertaking; and that it is necessarily an ecological endeavor.

As several authors recounted, when we enter social settings to study them, we are placed within structures and institutional practices over which we may have little control. For graduate students, there may be limited time for fieldwork because of the dictates and timelines of their academic programs (Chapters 2 and 6); for early career researchers, the ticking of the tenure clock may force a quickened pace for research, too. We must also deal with policy and personnel changes at local, state, and federal levels, which at times may support our work (Chapter 3), but at others may delay it significantly (Chapters 7 and 11). In our own institutions, we must navigate IRB requirements and requests that reflect how various stakeholders may apply principles regarding the ethical conduct of research quite differently from each other (Chapter 5). We also inevitably enter into various histories and hierarchies in our research sites, be they racial/ethnic (Chapter 4), professional (Chapter 10), or otherwise. Further, funding cycles upon which we depend often do not account for changes that are taking place in research settings: financial resources can arrive too early (Chapter 12) or too late (Chapter 7), making it difficult to make the best use of the resources that are available to us. As we seek to share our work with others, experiences with peer review may be complicated by linguistic expectations that require scarce financial resources to address (Chapter 15), or disciplinary expectations that can derail methodologically honest or innovative publications (Chapters 8 and 14).

Yet, the interruptions recounted here suggest that the trajectories of research endeavors also depend on how thoughtfully we are able to navigate our own and others' positionalities. For example, assumptions about being closer to the "insider" end of the continuum in a community or context can cause us to underestimate bureaucratic hurdles as well as the importance of (re)establishing trust or credibility with research participants (Chapters 2, 5, and 6). Yet, it serves us well to remember that what matters is not whether *we* view ourselves as insiders, but rather whether *others* view us in this way. Returning to a community is far from a simple undertaking: as García (Chapter 6) explained, despite having grown up in the place where he conducted his study, he was seen as "a changed man ¿que no?" Further, insider administrative positioning within programs we study can lead to a range of complexities, including participants' various misconceptions about the purpose of our research (Chapter 5). In addition to understanding the implications of our own identities, it is critical to understand participants' positionalities. As Rifenburg (Chapter 4) noted, his initial research design regarding student-athletes conceptualized them partially rather than holistically—as only students, rather than athletes, or as both together—which led to difficulties in gaining access and limited the potential contribution of his study. Racial power imbalances between the participants, who were overwhelmingly students of color, and the researcher, who was white, further complicated such relationships. Forces that normalize monolingual English-speaking positionalities can also influence participants in powerful ways, for example by leading some multilingual participants to believe that research interviews are actually assessments of their English ability (Chapter 5).

The accounts presented in this volume also remind us that qualitative research, especially in educational settings, is inherently a joint undertaking. In a research site, the support of teachers and administrators can facilitate students' participation in a study (Chapter 3 and 4) and help researchers surmount bureaucratic hurdles (Chapter 11); their opposition, on the other hand, has the potential to derail research entirely (Chapter 6). Researcher–practitioner partnerships are often a particularly intense form of collaboration, and those described in this volume attest to the importance of building trust (Chapter 3); recognizing the participants' histories ; and reestablishing focus, delineating roles, and validating partners, especially as new members join the team (Chapter 7). Finally, as Berson and colleagues (Chapter 9) suggest, teams of researchers themselves need to attend carefully to developing and negotiating shared understandings: they found that the success of an international, multicultural, and multilingual research team depended on having consistent and frequent interactions and slowing the pace of the work to give space for thoughtful negotiation of varied beliefs and understandings.

Interruptions also provide insights into the ecological nature of qualitative research. Educational systems, schools, and teachers are in a constant state of flux, and researchers working in such spaces often have to modify their plans as a result. Yet, the changing nature of these settings should not be considered an "inconvenience" to empirical study: rather, they are the moving parts of an ecology, so working with and understanding such dynamic patterns is fundamental to conducting meaningful research. For example, the everyday interruptions inherent in classroom teaching forced one teacher–researcher to improvise during instruction, which benefited her curriculum and students in unexpected ways, and to take an ecological perspective in her analysis, which better accounted for the phenomena she documented (Chapter 10). Tan (Chapter 12) extended these ideas by suggesting that classroom-based research that attempts to prevent changes and variation is likely to be less valuable because it has lost ecological validity. From a slightly different perspective, McGee and colleagues (Chapter 3) warned of the dangers of research that takes a less risky (but ecologically questionable) path in terms of recruitment. Districts, schools, and teachers serving the most underserved and minoritized populations, they noted, may be least likely to participate in studies for a variety of reasons. The proactive ethical approach (Blee & Currier, 2011) they used to recruit participants demanded additional time and effort, but it was vitally important as part of their efforts to include minoritized voices in the development of theory and research. As we conduct research with minoritized populations, we also come to see the structural and interactional processes through which non-dominant communities are marginalized. Such work is critical to understanding ecological settings and requires us, as researchers, to confront a range of ethical and emotional dilemmas in our work (Chapter 6 and 8).

Moving beyond "messy"

I would argue that talking about interruptions provides us with a powerful means of not only defining what qualitative research *is*—explored in the previous section—but also what it is *not*. If we take seriously the imperative to conduct ecologically valid research, then we can no longer be apologists for the "messiness" of data collection. Interruptions reflect the₁ nature of social science research, so simply regarding such endeavors as "messy" can undersell our work and its importance while also preserving a false sense of uniformity and "cleanliness" in other types of research. In this way, I argue that messiness *is* the story: to impose uniformity or evenness—or even to expect it—would distort participants' stories and our roles as researchers within them.

To take an example from my own longitudinal qualitative work on Mexican immigrant-origin youth (Kibler, 2019), the writing experiences that one of my five study participants, Fabiola, had in her first semester at university led her to request feedback from me on many drafts of her writing. I agreed, and as a result played a larger role in her development than I did for the other students. I considered it both an opportunity to understand Fabiola's writing in more detail and an ethical obligation to someone who had already opened up much of her life to me and for whom I was genuinely "rooting" throughout the study (as I was for the other four students). This process left me with an uneven amount of writing samples across the five focal students, but that data reflected both the writing required of Fabiola and her use of a "literacy broker" (Brandt, 2001) who was already familiar with academic writing (i.e., me) to help her complete English writing tasks. Without such experiences, I would not have gained such a deep understanding of the ways in which her engagement in argumentative writing developed or how her disciplinary identities emerged.

The longitudinal nature of that study introduced complexities (in the form of interruptions) that some might dismiss as "messy," but I would argue that they were fundamental to understanding the participants' lives and futures. For example, after high school graduation, all of the participants chose different vocational or educational paths and as a result scattered geographically. These separations obviously made data collection more difficult, but they told important stories in and of themselves. Maria, for example, had to move across the country in order to attend religious training because her local parish was affiliated with an international religious order located in Washington, DC. University scholarships that paid for tuition, room, and board likewise took Fabiola and Diego out of their local community, while a lack of scholarships or funding meant that Jaime and Ana had few alternatives but to remain at home with their families and attend community college and vocational school, respectively. Such trends also reflected larger political issues: Fabiola and Diego were able to take advantage of scholarships because they were US-born, whereas Jaime's and Ana's financial opportunities as students without authorization or documentation were extremely limited. Thus, the fact that some participants, though not all, were geographically distant from the community in which they had grown up told an important story, one that was inextricable from their larger interactional histories with languages, literacies, and institutions.

In this sense, moving away from understanding complexities as "messy" and instead focusing on the insights that such interruptions provide can be a key step in reframing the nature and importance of ecologically valid research.

214 Amanda K. Kibler

Moving toward reflexivity

A final benefit that a focus on interruptions can provide is to foreground the importance of infusing reflexivity into every aspect of our work—from study conceptualization through to publication. Critical introspection is vital to conducting ethically sound, humanizing research and improving the quality of our findings (Berger, 2015; Guillemin & Gillam, 2004). Further, such work, as undertaken by researchers in this volume, provides compelling evidence for the ways in which, for example, emotion and emotional labor should be seen as inherent to the research process (Chapters 6, 8, and 12). In this way, the experiences recounted here can support new and experienced researchers alike in reflecting upon "which kinds of goals are worth suffering the stress for" (Chapter 12) and the ethical dilemmas they may be forced to face (Chapter 8). As the preceding chapters demonstrate, such reflexivity is often hard won by researchers, regardless of their level of experience.

Contributing to the field

This volume makes two key contributions to the field of qualitative educational research. First, it highlights the varied and important roles that mentorship can play for new researchers—from study conceptualization and implementation to manuscript submission and review (Chapters 11 and 13)—as well as the reality that such guidance will never fully "smooth out" this learning process. The experiences recounted here may also serve as sources of mentorship in themselves: they may help new scholars to demystify what qualitative educational research truly is; and they may deepen the understanding of more experienced scholars as we engage in new research and interact with colleagues who are undertaking similar pursuits. Second, the contributions in this volume challenge all of us to take the lessons learned here—to view interruptions *as* research; to move beyond "messy"; and to understand reflexivity as a serious, complicated, and ongoing endeavor—and normalize them as what research *is*. Pursuing ambitious and innovative work, particularly with minoritized populations, requires all of us, as researchers, to embrace the risk that comes with such endeavors, to plan for the interruptions we can anticipate, to adapt to those we cannot, and to be open to the possibility that such changes might well enrich our understanding of what we study and how we do so. Such developments are critical to creating more inclusive and realistic understandings for the conduct and publication of ecologically valid, meaningful research.

References

Berger, R. (2015). Now I see it, now I don't: Researcher's position and reflexivity in qualitative research. *Qualitative Research*, 15(2), 219–234.

Blee, K. M., & Currier, A. (2011). Ethics beyond the IRB: An introductory essay. *Qualitative Sociology*, 34(3), 40.

Brandt, D. (2001). *Literacy in American lives*. Cambridge: Cambridge University Press.

Guillemin, M., & Gillam, L. (2004). Ethics, reflexivity and "ethically important moments" in research. *Qualitative Inquiry*, 10(2), 261–280.

Kibler, A. (2019). *Longitudinal interactional histories: Bilingual and biliterate journeys of Mexican immigrant-origin youth*. Cham: Palgrave Macmillan.

INDEX

ABE *see* Adult Basic Education students
academic authors 3–4, 7, 29, 36, 54, 58–59,
    61, 168–74, 176, 178, 187–88, 193,
    195–97, 199–200, 206–8; *see also* authors
academic papers 177, 202–3
academic publishing 169, 171, 181, 207n3
academic researchers 2, 36, 46, 108; *see also*
    researchers
accreditations 29, 81–82, 98
action researchers 3–4, 7; *see also* researchers
activities xiv, 6, 28, 32, 40, 62–64, 82–92,
    117, 122–24, 132, 152, 154–55, 157,
    163–64, 206–9; accessible 153;
    makerspace 153; out-of-school 152; peer
    group 118; school library 82, 84
administrative 7, 23, 61, 99, 161, 193;
    decisions 22; hierarchies 23; interruptions
    130–32, 136; priorities 128, 131
administrators 3, 16, 35, 52–53, 55, 57,
    59–61, 71, 84, 95–96, 102, 106, 132,
    212; CTE 33; rural 96; school 22, 102
Adult Basic Education students 16
adult education 15–17, 21–22
agency (human) 1, 42, 49, 52, 56, 158–159
agreements 19–20, 24, 33, 37, 58, 85;
    formal 18, 21; written 24
applications 15, 17–21, 45, 67, 168–69;
    approved research 15; systems 21–22;
    technological 156
art classes 130, 135, 156–57
articles 1, 5, 45–46, 95, 102, 112, 141, 148,
    169–70, 175, 186, 188, 194–95,
    198–203, 208; journal 2, 5, 157, 177,

188; newspaper 195; peer-reviewed 200;
    published 112, 178, 199; rejected 169
artificial intelligence 26–27
arts classes 132
arts classrooms 130, 155
assessments 9, 52, 56, 58, 60, 87, 132, 152,
    200, 211; empirical 52; formal 152; goals
    152; online 25; standardized 26; tools 52
Auburn University 39–40, 43–45
audio record 75, 117, 136, 184, 190, 210
authors 3–4, 29, 36, 54, 58–59, 61, 168–74,
    176, 178, 187–88, 193, 195–97,
    199–200, 206–8, 211; academic 169;
    conditioned by an increasingly
    competitive research environment 7;
    discusses the changing process of
    soliciting research approvals 3; guidelines
    181, 207–8; *see also* co-authors

basketball teams 42, 45–46
beliefs 7, 102–3, 110, 112, 114, 127, 202;
    personal 103; student 52, 59; varied 212
benefits 10, 24, 36, 87, 106, 158–59, 178,
    180, 189, 206; of data sharing 34; gained
    from critical reviews 176; of participating
    in qualitative studies 58
biases 2, 7–8, 23–24, 77, 103
Board of Education 16, 21–22, 24
boards 3, 44, 90, 98, 100, 213; *see also*
    institutional review boards
BOE *see* Board of Education
bureaucracy 10, 15–17, 19–23, 24–25, 62,
    68, 141, 145, 147

CAFÉCS *see* Chicago Alliance for Equity in Computer Science
campus 40–41, 45, 71, 113, 144, 157–58
Canagarajah, A. S. 193, 202–3
Career and Technical Education Office 33
certifications 29, 81–82, 98; *see also* accreditations
challenges 1–6, 8–10, 40, 43, 52, 56, 96, 111, 113, 115–16, 140, 142, 145, 147, 201–2; cross-cultural 8–9; ethical 120; logistical 95; recruitment 9
Chicago Alliance for Equity in Computer Science 35–36
Chicago Public Schools 8, 27–37; computer science teachers 28–29; and the Office of Computer Science 34–35; and the School Board 34
children 4, 27, 31–32, 109–12, 114–21, 133, 146; elementary school 146; Ghanaian 117–18; kindergarten 117; separated immigrant 106; and their rights 121; young 116, 120
citizenship 110–11, 113, 116
classes 32–33, 35, 37, 39–44, 46, 60, 97–102, 104, 107, 131–32, 134, 136, 153, 155, 157–58
classroom teachers 80– 82, 85, 117, 127–28, 131, 212
classroom management 128, 133, 135–37, 139; approach to 133; holistic perspective 133; interruptions 130, 136; issues impacting on data selection 135; responsiveness 138–39
classrooms 15–17, 19, 21–22, 28, 30, 57–58, 60–61, 64, 71–73, 100–102, 106–7, 116–19, 127–29, 133–37, 143; and activities viewed instrumentally 152; culture of 28; elementary 140, 163; evaluations 29, 156; first-grade 141; Ghanaian 118; kindergarten 9, 109, 113, 115; practices 117; and research projects 140–42, 148, 212; science 155; US 115, 118
co-authors 164, 168–69, 171–72, 174, 199–200
coaches 44–46, 98
Cobb, P. 80, 129
coercion 43, 48–49, 54; inducing 32; issues of 48–49, 63; perceived 43
collaborators (aiding researchers) 83, 123, 180–81, 183, 185
college football 39–45
Collins, A. 129, 171–72
communication 42–43, 60, 112–13, 116, 151, 203; challenges 111; classes 40; open 119

communities 16, 36, 80, 96–97, 101–3, 106, 114, 116–17, 119, 130, 137, 202, 211, 213; academic 24; African-American 29; collective 110; conservative Christian 105; cultural 118; disciplinary 204; ethnic 79; foreign 96; local 154, 213; marginalized 32; Mexican-American 76; racial 48; rural 95, 103; scholarly 169, 193; small 15–17; traditional 117; working-class 130
Community School for Adults 15
computational thinking 90, 94
computer literacy 40, 108
computer science 27–30, 33–35; benefitting students 36; enrollment 38; as a high school graduation requirement 34
conflicts 67–68, 71, 76–77, 85, 87, 107, 122, 133, 135, 170; bureaucratic 68; and emotional labor 67, 122; of identity 68, 76
consent 18–19, 43, 145–46; forms 30–31; informed 31, 55; parental 146; process 146, 184
conversations 22, 41, 45–46, 51, 55, 68–70, 83–85, 88–90, 103, 106, 108, 112, 133, 136, 172–73; candid 58; critical 77; productive 105
correspondence 57, 85, 204
courses 34, 43, 51–52, 54, 58–59; computer science 28, 33–34; first-year writing 43; methodology 1; university-level English-instructed 54, 59
CPS *see* Chicago Public Schools
CSA *see* Community School for Adults
CTE 2, 32–34, 213; administrators 33; IT program in CPS 28, 32
cultures 49, 67, 78–79, 98, 100–101, 111, 115, 119, 121, 123, 139, 154, 189, 203; dominant 100; police 103; polychronic 115; restrictive 5
curriculum 20, 29, 33, 37, 73, 99, 97, 101, 130, 133, 143, 149, 152, 154, 160, 200, 212

data collection 8, 10, 29–30, 36, 52–53, 56, 59–61, 115–16, 131–32, 136–37, 141–45, 148, 164, 186–88, 213; and analysis 190; identifiable 33; instruments 18, 105; methods 42; plans 128–29; process 10, 136, 140–41, 164
Data Governance Office 18–21, 24
data-sharing agreements 8, 15–17, 19, 21–22, 24, 33–34, 62
DBR *see* design-based research
decision letters 169, 199–200

decisions 22–23, 31, 41–42, 44, 114–15, 124, 133, 138, 169–72, 175, 182, 190–91, 199–201, 204, 206; informed 209; political 168; "revise-and-resubmit" 203
degrees 20–21, 27, 81, 175, 193
Democrat Party 96, 102
demographics (students) 30, 39
Department of Education 8, 15, 17, 20–21, 28
deportations 9–10, 100
design 1, 3, 9, 45, 49, 61, 84–85, 97, 105, 110, 128–30, 134, 138, 152, 157–58; of curricula 67; instructional 152, 180, 183; learning environment 130; personalized 158
design-based research 129–30, 137
development 27, 36, 80, 111, 113, 151, 153, 195, 198, 204, 212–14; economic 110; professional 26, 28–29, 33, 35, 82, 133; program 28–29; *see also* professional development
DGO *see* Data Governance Office
discussion questions and activities 63–64, 123–24, 164, 207–9
dissertations 20, 42, 67, 73, 127, 133, 141–42, 193, 199; and conversations with committee members 77, 199; projects 128; proposals 128–29, 188; studies 134
district restructuring 9, 85
doctoral programs 175, 198
doctorates 64
DOE *see* Department of Education
Dörnyei, Z. 53–54, 56, 148
drafts 104, 196, 198–99, 213; final 201; first 49, 195–98; revised 169

ECS *see* Exploring Computer Science Program
editing 196, 201–3
editorial correspondence 204
editorial decisions 191, 202–3
editorial discussions 7, 174, 206
editors 10, 124, 168–71, 173–76, 185–87, 190–91, 194–95, 197–98, 200–201, 203–5, 207, 209; of journals 4, 169, 176–77, 200; new 169–70, 175; professional 201; and reviewers 169, 175; willing to consider a revised manuscript 201
education 4–5, 7, 15, 24, 70, 99–100, 132, 140, 159–61; civic 9, 109; early childhood xiii, 111, 115; postsecondary 200; practices 31; processes 20; programs 26–27; public 15, 17, 22, 138–39; rural

96, 105; special 30–31; urban 138–39, 149
education research 7, 10, 47–48, 56, 80, 83, 90, 140, 145, 147–48, 151, 159–60, 164, 170, 181; community 92; engineering 192; physics 185; rural 95
educational researchers 7, 83, 142, 144, 148
educators 24, 76, 81, 83, 93, 110, 134, 143, 160, 181
EFL *see* English as a Foreign Language
elections 95–96, 98–101, 104–7
electronic components 153–56, 158
elementary schools 82, 97, 101, 130, 134, 140, 142, 146
ELLs *see* English Language Learners
email invitations (outlining project goals) 51, 57, 60
emotional labor 67–68, 72–74, 122, 214
emotions 75–77, 95–97, 99, 101, 103, 105, 107, 123, 130, 133–35, 140, 176, 214; experiencing private 105; stimulating intense 75
empirical papers 194–96
English 8–10, 15, 51–52, 54–55, 58–60, 74, 97–98, 101, 106–7, 114, 193–94, 196–97, 199, 201–2, 207; and ESL classes 97, 197; placement exams 51–53, 55, 58; proficiency in speaking 9, 51, 53–55, 59–60, 211; for publication purposes 203; and Spanish speakers 96; studies 11, 47; teachers 59, 97–98
English as a Foreign Language 15
English as a Second Language xiv–xv, 15, 52–53, 56–57, 59, 61, 96–100, 103, 105, 107, 173
English Language Learners 15–17, 20–21, 25, 98
EPE *see* English placement exams
ESL *see* English as a Second Language
ethical obligations 213
ethics 8, 27, 35–36, 52, 56, 62–63; managerial 103; proactive 27, 32, 36, 62; research 41, 56
ethnic groups 110, 114
ethnographic dissertation projects 3
ethnographic researchers 6, 105
ethnography 3, 11, 67–68, 78–79, 97, 107–8
everyday interruptions 10, 128–30, 133, 136–38, 163, 212; navigating 138; persistent and pervasive 128; in school-based research 10, 127, 130, 163
evidence 35, 82, 116, 187, 203, 214; based decisions 24; empirical 35–36

Exploring Computer Science Program
27–32, 34–35, 38; classes 33; curriculum
28–29; implementation 30, 34; students
30, 33; teachers 33; workshops 33

faculties 45, 71, 85, 167–68, 181, 201; art
education 181; athletics 45; members and
administrators 71–72
failure rates 35
families 10, 17, 74–76, 100–101, 105–6,
112, 117, 213
Family and Education Right and Privacy Act
18, 24
feedback 3, 19, 21, 64, 87, 96, 104, 106,
169, 173, 184, 186–87, 190, 196, 199;
constructive 198; receiving 145, 198;
requesting 213; reviewer's 206
FERPA see *Family and Education Right and
Privacy Act*
field research 78–79
fieldnotes 68, 71, 73, 85, 129, 184, 187, 190
findings 5, 10, 40, 47–49, 91, 95, 110, 113,
119, 123, 159, 164, 184–85, 188, 190;
controversial 6, 11; published 5–6;
sharing 4
focal teachers 10, 140–43, 146
focus classes 131–32, 137
football see college football
Foucault, M. 115, 118
funding 16, 24, 28, 83, 106, 111, 145,
202–3, 213; agencies 116, 152; cycles 83,
211; federal 16, 22
funds 81, 84, 111, 144, 153, 201

gaining access (concept) 43, 62, 103,
122, 143
gatekeepers 4, 9, 42–49, 63, 68
Gay, G. 133, 135
GED see General Education Development
classroom
gender 6, 28, 33, 76, 186
General Education Development classroom
16–17, 25
genres 193–95, 203
Ghana xiii, 9, 109–10, 112–14, 117,
119–21; children of 117; singing and
dancing 115; and the valuing of
relationships over tasks 115
Ghanaians 109–10, 112, 114, 116, 118, 121;
belief systems 115; culture of 110;
displaying values of "respect, reciprocity
and responsibility" 117; ethnotheory of
118; researchers 9, 114, 116
goals 16, 20, 60, 83, 87–88, 91, 93, 96, 109,
111–12, 147, 151, 159, 161, 164;

idealistic 159; learning 152, 156;
quixotic 151, 153, 155, 157, 159,
161, 164; research 55, 157–59, 164,
181, 184
grades 37, 54, 57–58, 75, 97, 142–43,
145–46; fifth 142–43, 145–46; first 142;
participation 97; placements 146, 148;
switching 10
graduate programs 17, 167, 207
Graduate Record Exam 51, 55
graduate students 2, 8, 15–17, 19, 24,
51–52, 54–59, 61, 67, 140, 168, 171,
176–77, 203–4, 211
graduates 20, 40, 58, 73, 181, 204; see also
graduate students
grants xv, 20–22, 32–33, 37, 49, 84, 145,
147, 201; applications for 25; for projects
83, 156; and the proposal process 85,
154, 183
GRE see Graduate Record Exam
groups 6, 26–27, 62, 80–81, 87–88, 111–13,
116–17, 134–35, 153, 169, 202;
marginalized 27; socio-cultural 111;
university outreach 86–87
guidelines 42, 48, 191; for authors 181,
207–8; federal 42, 48; institutional 48

Harlingen (Texas) 67–68, 73
health 16, 23–24
High School Equivalency Test 16, 25
high schools 28, 34–35, 37, 132, 139; local
64; public 37; students 30–31, 33, 185
higher education xiii, 49, 67, 74, 76, 161,
177–78, 200, 204; institutions 39;
international 199
HiSET see High School Equivalency Test
"Hispanics" 73
home institutions 71–72
humanizing research 7, 11, 214

identities 43, 67–68, 77, 107, 113–14, 118,
122, 133, 135, 185, 187–88, 211;
children's Ghanaian 117; disciplinary 213;
ethnotribal 114; multi-ethnic 114; racial
107; shared 110
identity conflict 68, 76
IEPs see Individualized Education Plans
IES see Institute of Educational Sciences
immigrants 2, 96, 100, 102, 104–7; adult xii;
populations 95; students 9, 64, 96,
98–100, 102, 106
incentives 27, 32, 36, 62
Individualized Education Plans 132
Institute of Educational Sciences 16,
20–22, 25

institutional review boards 3, 64, 71,
142–43, 145, 147; applications 44, 53;
approvals 77, 122, 142, 145–47; office of
the 53–54, 56, 71–72; process 10, 71,
144–46, 148; requirements for parental
consent 146; study protocol 53, 57, 63,
96, 102, 145, 148; website 144, 146
institutions 4, 6, 17, 25, 51–53, 71–73, 83,
86–87, 114, 116, 129, 137, 142, 211,
213; academic 142; educational xiv,
141–42, 147; research 167
instructions 19, 32, 128, 132, 136, 140, 153,
156, 160–61, 181, 197, 200, 212; diverse
and creative approaches to 101; research
application rubric 19
instructors 15, 40–41, 45, 54, 58, 60; GED
17; language arts 22; program's 57
interactions 75, 79, 86, 90, 104, 112–13,
117–18, 133, 137, 182, 202, 207;
children's 117; classroom 133;
educational 159; interpersonal 79
interruptions 2–3, 8, 10, 26, 41, 70, 128–33,
136–38, 141–42, 146–48, 151, 158–61,
163–64, 180, 210–14; administrative
130–32, 136; frequency of 132, 159;
intentional 77; management 133–34, 136;
minimizing research 26–27, 36, 68,
71–72, 75, 77, 141, 147, 159, 177;
multiple 148; prolonged 147;
unplanned 151
interview protocols 9, 113, 116
interview questions 41–42, 47–48, 53, 102,
114–15
interviews 6, 9, 41–43, 45–47, 51, 53–61,
67–70, 72–76, 82, 89–90, 98–99, 104,
164; back-to-back 74; conducting 55,
72–73, 76; informal 189; qualitative 52;
research 211; video-elicited 109, 117–18
IRBs *see* institutional review boards

JEE *see* Journal of Engineering Education
journals 4, 10, 47, 104, 168–76, 180–81,
185–87, 190–91, 194, 199–200, 204,
206–8; academic 178, 203; articles 2, 5,
157, 177, 188; pay-to-publish 208;
prestigious 167–69; research-focused 185;
scholarly 194
Journal of Engineering Education 191

K-12 education system 16–17, 22
Kazakhstan 194–95, 197–98, 201
key informants 9, 42–49, 63; *see also*
gatekeepers
knowledge 41, 44, 89, 92, 97, 109, 115,
118, 155, 173, 181, 187, 193, 199, 202;

canonical 151; creating new 155;
generation 90; privileged local 116;
specialized 172; statistical 174

language 49, 52, 54–55, 60, 68, 86, 96,
100–102, 113–14, 116, 145, 147, 170,
196–97, 202; colonial 198; common 87,
114; ethno-tribal 114; ideologies 201;
learners 15, 25, 100, 167; native 196, 202;
official 114; proficiency 55, 61; sexist
103; technical 181, 186; usage 167, 197
Law, J. 5–7, 11, 105, 108, 148–149
learning 2, 4, 127, 129–30, 133, 136–38,
151–61, 164, 183, 187–88, 191, 193–94,
202, 207, 210; cognitive 155; experiences
204; goals 152, 156; high value 160;
processes 204, 214
learning centers 67, 71–72, 117, 122
learning sciences 3, 129, 137, 155–56, 161
The Learning Partnership xiii, 28–29, 33–35
lessons 10, 16, 37, 128, 130–32, 134–36,
141, 144, 155, 157–58, 161, 176, 194,
200, 203
letters 21, 31, 124, 168, 201; of agreement
20; ambiguity of content 169–70; of
commitment 21; decision 169, 199–200;
inviting resubmissions 169; from the IRB
office 53
librarians 9, 80–92, 94, 180
libraries xiii, 39, 68–69, 74–75, 81–87,
89–92, 94, 98; *see also* public libraries
literacy xii, xiv, 49, 67, 78, 81, 95–96, 102,
107–8, 213, 215; computer 40; functional
103–4; social/contextual 103–4
literature reviews 168–69, 185, 194–95, 199
Lower Rio Grande Valley 67–71, 73, 77
LRGV *see* Lower Rio Grande Valley

maker programs 83, 88, 91–92, 94
makerspaces 151–55, 157–61
management interruptions 133–34
manuscripts 168–70, 175–77, 181, 183,
185–86, 188–91, 193, 195–202, 204,
207; scholarly 193
Maria Fold and Thrust Belt 182
master's program 15, 39
methodological 10, 188, 194; challenges 3,
109, 138; goals 119; processes 3
methodology courses 1
Mexicans 74, 96, 215
Mfantse and Ewe languages 115
MFTB *see* Maria Fold and Thrust Belt
middle schools 84, 130, 134
multi-site studies 110
multilingual research teams 212

National Science Foundation 28, 32–33, 36, 180, 191
natural disasters 10, 143–44, 147
navigating 8–10, 23–24, 128–29, 136, 154; administrators 51–61, 63; bureaucracies 8, 13; research interruptions 147
NNESs *see* non-native English speakers
non-native English speakers 193–97, 202–3
novice researchers 3–4, 16, 23, 140, 148, 164, 194–95; *see also* researchers
NSF *see* National Science Foundation

obligations 76, 87, 116; ethical 213; familial 76
observation 29, 67, 71–72, 82, 84–86, 88, 143, 152, 156–157, 189–190, 203–204 *see also* participant observation
observers 44, 79, 84, 97, 184; insider participant 79; well-placed 151
Office of Computer Science 34–35
Office of Research 33
online assessments 25
online submission platforms 169
organizations 23–24, 80, 83, 194, 196; community-based 16; grassroots 21; historical 196; professional 208; research 80–81; rules 23
Osmo-based apps 90
outcomes (societal) 181
outreach 79, 87, 90; components 86; efforts xii; services 81; work 86

papers 40, 97, 107, 159, 170–76, 180, 183, 186–91, 193–96, 198–204, 206, 209; academic 177, 202–3; empirical 194–96; research 97; and the role of reviewers 187; scholarly 202–3; submitted 170
paperwork 18, 22, 74, 146; additional 71; associated 99
parent permission forms 30
participant observation 76, 123, 183, 186, 188
participant recruitment 1, 52–53, 56–57, 61, 63, 148; and the ESL writing program 56–57; strategies 48–49, 63; and students' perceptions of their English proficiency 53
participants 1–2, 4, 6–9, 41–42, 48–49, 55–56, 59–60, 63–64, 73, 78–79, 115–16, 122–24, 183–84, 186, 210–13; minority 27; multilingual 211; recruiting 2, 8, 13, 27, 69, 140, 167; student-athlete 42; targeting of 53–54, 60
partners 21, 35, 81, 83–85, 92, 105, 123, 135; district-based 93; external 35–36, 85; practitioner 85, 93; trusted 91

partnerships 32, 36, 47, 80–85, 87–92, 122–23, 146; collaborative 24, 111; long-term 32; practitioner 35–36, 212; research-practice 35, 80, 84, 93, 122; teams 92
pedagogy 40, 73, 128, 143, 152, 157
peer reviews 64, 167–79, 185, 203, 206, 211
permissions 10, 43–44, 48–49, 91, 98, 154–55; additional 184; granting of 32; of the lead instructor 41; parental 31, 35, 49
personnel 20, 44, 81, 85; additional security 144; Athletics Department 45; museum 181
pilot testing 20, 26, 84, 90
placement 51–52, 54–56, 58–59, 61; assessment 56, 61; decisions 52; exams 51, 55, 57; practices 59–60; procedures 52–53, 58, 60–61; research 63; techniques 9
planning 8, 85, 109–10, 115, 123, 128–29, 133, 138, 164; guides 86; and implementing research 140; inadequacy of 160
policy xii, 6, 24, 34–36, 64, 72, 139, 197, 211; academic 42, 45; effective public 23; evidence-based 25; federal higher education 200; of poverty eradication 110; of school administration 157; topics 60–61; university's placement 57
political issues 213
political sympathies 7
politics 78, 103, 108, 161, 205
Ponisciak, S. 26
population 15, 30–31, 43, 49, 76, 110; changing immigrant 105; diversifying student 28, 96; marginalized 27, 31; migrant ESL 96–97; minoritized 212, 214; vulnerable 146
positivist 182, 188–89; paradigms 4; stance 182, 191, 206; traditions 3
power 16–17, 24, 103, 129, 137, 141, 143, 203; dynamics 8–9, 48–49, 63, 112; hierarchical 60; imbalances 53, 60, 63, 80–81; implied 117
power relations 53, 59, 61, 63, 109, 135
practitioner partnerships 35–36, 212
prejudices 8, 96, 98, 103, 122
pressure xiii, 81, 134, 143; academic 177; economic 9; financial 40; program's 168; to publish 172; workplace 183
principals 17, 35, 142–43
privilege 76, 85, 87, 102, 114, 139; children 109; evidentiary 108; perpetuating 202; researchers 7; status 85
problems 28, 52, 56, 110, 113–14, 135, 152, 174–75, 181, 189; complex 24;

grammatical 201; language editing 202; linguistic 193–204, 207; of practice 87; research 183–84
professional development xiii, 26, 28–29, 33, 35, 37, 82–84, 86, 88, 133; free 86; model 28, 37; scheduled activities 86
proficiency, in English 9, 51, 53–55, 59–60, 211
programmatic assessment 52, 56, 63
programs 8–9, 16, 20–22, 24, 26–28, 30–31, 36, 39–40, 44, 52–53, 57, 59–61, 83–84, 89, 97; administrators 9, 53, 57, 61; assessment research 53, 56, 59–60; design 83, 88; facilitators of 92; resources 84; workshops 39
projects 7–10, 51–54, 57–58, 60, 64, 82–86, 89–92, 101–6, 109–11, 116–17, 134–35, 145–48, 153–55, 157–59, 183; craft 154; educational 159; funded 84; interdisciplinary 180, 183; team 116; transnational 111
protocol 4, 71, 116–17, 144, 146; institutionalized 148; required 147; video-stimulated recall 156
public health 16, 23–24; see also health
public libraries 68–69, 85; see also libraries
publications 8, 10, 103, 106, 156, 168, 170, 172–73, 176–77, 185, 187, 193–95, 197–203, 208, 214; experiences of 195, 203; premature 178; timeline 208; venue 167, 199, 203
publishing 10, 47, 104, 170, 193, 200, 204, 207; doctoral 178; interdisciplinary research 180, 206; journal articles 2, 5, 112, 157, 177–78, 188, 199

qualitative interviews 52
qualitative researchers 3, 8, 10, 39, 42–43, 49–50, 67–68, 113, 138, 182, 186, 188–89, 191, 210–12
qualitative studies 58, 190
questions and activities 63–64, 123–24, 164, 207–9

race 28–29, 33, 48–49, 92; disparities among students 28; dominant 49; and ethnicity 6–7, 211; and power imbalances 211
racism 27, 79, 133; actions 99; behaviors 9; comments concerning 101, 105
recommendations 32, 36, 169–71, 199, 201; explicit 136; theoretical 159
recruitment 24, 30, 42, 57, 63, 72–73, 212; of participants 2, 8, 13, 27, 69, 140, 167; plans 57; procedures 53–54; strategies 39, 42, 47–49, 51, 63

reflexivity, moving toward 56, 68, 214
reforms 29, 38
regulations 48, 99, 115; bureaucratic 32; chlorofluorocarbon 103; federal 31; institutional 53
rejections 2, 4, 21, 169–70, 176–77, 189–90, 203–4
relationships 6–9, 24, 26, 46–48, 78–79, 81, 83, 87–89, 91, 93, 105–6, 135, 140, 158–61, 163; authentic 127; collaborative 86, 105; developing 27; important 45; industry 161; reestablishing 84; strong 146
religious training 213
Republican Party 96, 98, 102
Request for proposals 20, 83
research 1, 30 43, 47–49, 56, 63, 120, 211; ethics 41, 56; goals 55, 157–59, 164, 181, 184; humanizing 7, 11, 214; interruptions 26–27, 36, 68, 71–72, 75, 77, 141, 147, 159, 177; interviews 211; makerspaces 151; methodology and administrative status 53; papers 97; practitioner partnerships 35, 37, 80, 84, 93, 122; problems 183–85; teams 64, 83–91, 110–11, 115–19, 143–44, 164, 181, 185
researchers 1–10, 23–24, 26–27, 31–33, 47–50, 52–56, 59–61, 79–93, 104–6, 108–10, 112–18, 122–24, 137–38, 142–48, 210–14; academic 2, 36, 46, 108; action 3–4, 7; and teachers 137–38
review process 4, 168, 170, 174–76, 178, 180, 187, 194–95, 206, 208
reviewers 2, 4, 21, 104, 145–46, 168–77, 180–81, 183, 186–90, 194–95, 198, 200–201, 203–4, 206–7; applied linguistics 4; comments 2, 170–72, 190; considers the topic and the manuscript has promise 200–201; departmental 145; and editors 169, 175; external 172; first 171, 190; matching with appropriate expertise to papers 187; natural sciences 181; new 174; and the promising manuscript 200; second 171, 187–88; supportive 197; third 170–71
RFP see Request for Proposals
rhetorical 41–42, 49, 61, 67, 78–79, 108; consequences 50; ethnography 67, 78; opponents 41; research 50, 67
risks 2, 5–6, 8, 31, 33, 39, 75, 79, 106, 151, 159–61, 195, 214; increased 160; professional 8
Rogoff, B. 109, 111, 113, 117–18
RPPs see research-practice partnerships

salaries 143, 153, 201
samples 1, 30, 34, 64, 117, 213; biased 26, 30; of documents 19; sizes of 42, 47
sampling criteria 42
scholars 2, 47, 111, 137, 148, 170, 191, 200, 202–4, 210; critical 102; developing 1, 129, 172; experienced 204, 214; new 156, 167, 214; non-Anglophone 205; nonnative-English-speaking 205; prolific 178; senior 199, 204; veteran 140, 142
scholarships xiv, 48, 113, 139, 171, 185, 210, 213
school districts 21, 29, 31, 36–37, 81, 83, 86, 88, 93, 143; collaborating 81; local 99; partnering 81, 83; semi-rural 80
school teachers see teachers
school year 10, 29–30, 34–36, 83, 127, 132, 139, 141–42, 146–48, 156
schools 9–11, 15–18, 20–22, 29–31, 33–35, 39–40, 70, 74–76, 80–87, 95–107, 127–29, 132–39, 142–46, 154–55, 157–62; administration 22, 102, 153, 155; budgets 82; elementary 82, 97, 101, 130, 134, 140, 142, 146; high 28, 34–35, 37, 132, 139; high-poverty 132; librarians 80–85, 94; libraries 68–69, 82–85, 87, 90, 92, 94, 98; low-poverty 132; private language 15; public 142; rural 95, 102, 107; secondary 100; vocational 213
science 151–52, 156, 173, 185, 187–89, 191; social/behavioral 191; technology, engineering, and mathematics see STEM; traditional school 184
science education xii–xiii, 28, 33, 93, 161, 185
science faculty 27–28, 181
science teachers 28, 86
scientists 10, 183–85, 188–89; computer 27, 181; interdisciplinary 187; natural 151, 182, 190–91; social 188
second language 15, 52, 57, 60; acquisition 25, 167; learning research 15; speakers of English 9; writing 57, 60
self-doubt 4–5, 148, 172–74, 203, 206
semesters 7, 20, 22, 39–40, 56, 59, 64, 73, 130, 132, 145–46
service providers 9, 80–81, 83, 85, 87, 89, 91–93, 122
shared goals 23
skills 9, 153, 159; advanced language 203; English language 201–2; publication-related 199
social science 7, 47, 50, 170, 178, 182

social science research 11, 108, 149, 213; classroom-based qualitative 210; methods book 47
sociologists 5, 103, 107
sociology 37, 103, 215
software 25, 27, 40, 97, 156
speakers 21, 96, 204; guest 21; native English 193; non-native 10, 193, 204, 207; non-native English 193
stakeholders 24, 211
statisticians 174–75
statistics 168, 170, 174–75
STEM xiii, 151–52, 161, 197; connections 90; disciplines 26, 62; fields 186; integration 88; oriented maker programs 84–85
strategies 8, 26, 52, 56, 61, 63, 87–88, 147–48, 164, 167, 171, 202–4; applied additional 173; developing 56; effective scaffolding 140; innovative facilitation 157; negotiating revision 172; potential 56; resulting renegotiation 91; traditional 203
Strauss, P. 4, 140, 148
student-athletes 39–46, 211; experiences of 46; male 48; matriculating 40
students 10, 27, 31, 54, 56, 92, 118; behavior 133; data collection 30; failure rates 35; participants 53, 57, 59–61, 142, 153; populations 31, 56, 60–61, 133
study 3–4, 30–33, 40–43, 51–54, 57–60, 62–64, 103, 110–11, 130–32, 135–37, 141–42, 144–46, 193–95, 199–200, 211–14; approval 3, 145; design 3, 129; groups 39; hours 39–40; protocols 143–48; sites 62, 102
switching grades 10
systems 16, 18, 20, 23–24, 76, 138, 176, 190; bureaucratic 16, 23; community college 80; early education 112; financing 197; online 18; public education 16, 100; of teacher evaluation 29

Taste of Computing 29, 33, 36, 38; courses 33; partnerships 34; projects 28–29, 32–34; research 34; students 31; teachers 30; teams 35
teachers xiii–xiv, 28–30, 32–36, 41, 43, 81–83, 86, 95, 97–102, 105–6, 115, 128–43, 152–54, 159–60, 212; art 133–34, 154; elementary 142; emergency substitute 82; forward-thinking 152; history 97–98; inexperienced 133; interviewing 64; local 152, 155; new 26, 30; research 127, 140; and researchers

137–38; rural school 97; science 28, 86; secondary 150; student 140

teaching xii, xiv, 20, 35, 40, 97, 128–30, 133–35, 138–40, 146, 149, 174, 178, 191, 195; effective 128, 133; and learning 104, 129–30, 138, 158, 191, 210; level of confidence in 29; mathematics 93

team members 85–86, 112–16, 145; Ghanaian 112; research 64, 84–86, 88, 116, 119; US-based 112

technology xiv, 144, 151–52, 160–62; computer 120; educational 138; instructional 180–81; new 160

TESOL certification 98

tests 25, 90, 143; eye 46; high school equivalency 16, 25; low standardized 55; mandated 143

Tolstoy, Leo 196, 205

Trump, Donald J. 95–96, 99–100, 106

undergraduate students 54–55, 58–60, 181, 190

UNG see University of North Georgia

United States 9, 16, 25, 39, 48, 55, 74–75, 95, 99, 108–9, 112–13, 117, 121, 149–50, 193; college composition programs xiv; scholars 112, 115, 118;

teachers 141; and UK-based academic journals 112

university xii–xv, 17, 37, 45, 47–48, 55, 59–61, 71–73, 78–79, 83–89, 93, 142–43, 145, 158, 204–5; administrators 53; assessment practices 9; campus 40–41, 45, 71, 113, 144, 157–58; groups 86–87; libraries 113; research 84, 198; researchers 80–81, 83, 85–87, 106; scholarships 213; student clubs 86; teams 85, 88–92

University of North Georgia 42, 45–46

video record 109, 113, 115–118, 129, 134, 155

visual arts classes 127

visual arts lessons 132

visual arts teachers 127, 130

WIA see *Workforce Investment Act*

WIOA see *Workforce Innovations and Opportunities Act*

Workforce Innovations and Opportunities Act 16, 22

Workforce Investment Act 16

youth 7, 11, 87, 89–90, 92, 110, 151; adolescent 83; of immigrant-origin 215; programs 84